LESSONS FOR
ADDITION AND
SUBTRACTION

GRADES 2-3

THE TEACHING ARITHMETIC SERIES

Teaching
ARITHMETIC

LESSONS FOR
ADDITION AND
SUBTRACTION

▲▲▲▲▲

GRADES 2-3

BONNIE TANK
LYNNE ZOLLI

MATH SOLUTIONS
SAUSALITO, CALIFORNIA, USA

Math Solutions
One Harbor Drive, Suite 101
Sausalito, California, USA   94965
www.mathsolutions.com

Library of Congress Cataloging-in-Publication Data
Tank, Bonnie.
   Lessons for addition and subtraction : grades 2–3 / Bonnie Tank, Lynne Zolli.
        p. cm.
Includes index.
     ISBN 0-941355-32-2 (alk. paper)
   1. Addition—Study and teaching (Primary) 2. Subtraction—Study and teaching (Primary) I. Zolli, Lynne. II. Title.
     QA115 .T36 2001
       372.7'2—dc21

                                                    2001003871

ISBN–13: 978-0-941355-32-2

Editor: Toby Gordon
Production: Melissa L. Inglis
Cover & interior design: Leslie Bauman
Composition: Argosy Publishing

11 12 13 14 15 16 17 18   31   20 19 18 17 16 15 14 13

A Message from Math Solutions

We at Math Solutions believe that teaching math well calls for increasing our understanding of the math we teach, seeking deeper insights into how children learn mathematics, and refining our lessons to best promote students' learning.

Math Solutions shares classroom-tested lessons and teaching expertise from our faculty of professional development consultants as well as from other respected math educators. Our publications are part of the nationwide effort we've made since 1984 that now includes

- more than five hundred face-to-face professional development programs each year for teachers and administrators in districts across the country;
- professional development books that span all math topics taught in kindergarten through high school;
- videos for teachers and for parents that show math lessons taught in actual classrooms;
- on-site visits to schools to help refine teaching strategies and assess student learning; and
- free online support, including grade-level lessons, book reviews, inservice information, and district feedback, all in our *Math Solutions Online Newsletter*.

Also, we have expanded our own efforts and have collaborated with Scholastic Inc. to create a new intervention program titled Do The Math™ that supports at-risk and struggling students. Written with a team of Math Solutions consultants and based on the lessons from our Math Solutions Teaching Arithmetic® series, Do The Math provides teachers with lessons carefully sequenced and paced to meet the needs of students who would benefit from intervention. To learn more about this program, please visit the Do The Math website at *www.scholastic.com/DoTheMath*.

For information about all of the products and services we have available, please visit our website at *www.mathsolutions.com*. You can also contact us to discuss math professional development needs by calling (800) 868-9092 or by sending an email to *info@mathsolutions.com*.

We're always eager for your feedback and interested in learning about your particular needs. We look forward to hearing from you.

FOUNDED BY MARILYN BURNS

SCHOLASTIC

CONTENTS

INTRODUCTION

Addition and subtraction are major topics in the early elementary grades. For many years we have been reflecting upon how best to teach addition and subtraction, upon the mathematics involved, and upon what kinds of activities and tasks help students build their mathematical understanding and skill with these operations. This collection of activities provides students with experiences that go beyond rote memorization of facts and procedures. The lessons engage children in mathematical activities that help them develop computational and problem-solving skills while also building understanding of our number system.

We began working together in 1989, designing and implementing units of work that provided alternatives to the traditional textbook. Over the years we have added, extended, deleted, and fine-tuned lessons. With this collection of lessons, children will experience problem-solving investigations, data collection, and activities connected to literature and real life. The lessons focus on addition and subtraction but include measurement, geometry, probability, statistics, and algebraic thinking. For each lesson, children have opportunities to share their ideas and strategies and communicate their thinking orally or in writing.

Our interest in developing meaningful activities to support children's learning led us into learning more mathematics ourselves and using our new knowledge to understand the mathematics involved in the students' tasks. As a result of this work, we have come to develop a set of beliefs that has changed our teaching practices and guided the writing of this book.

First, we believe that meaning is developed over time. Addition and subtraction should be a part of the math curriculum throughout the year, not addressed only in specific units of work. Too often the rush to memorize basic facts and use rote procedures for multidigit addition and subtraction takes priority over children making sense of numbers. The amount of attention given to numbers less than one hundred is sometimes compromised because of increased curriculum demands. Having regular and ongoing experiences with small numbers throughout the year enables students to build and deepen number relationships.

Knowing basic number facts is essential for efficiency in computation. However, to build understanding of our number system, it is important for children to go beyond rote memorization of facts and see their connections and relationships to our system of tens.

By giving students ongoing opportunities with breaking numbers apart and putting them back together in various ways, we can help students become flexible with numbers both when doing mental arithmetic and when using pencil and paper. We want students to move away from counting by ones, have flexibility in decomposing and recomposing numbers, and apply basic number facts to large numbers as they build their understanding of place value.

We believe that students need to make sense of addition and subtraction in their own ways. Imposed algorithms can interfere with and inhibit this sense making. Rather than moving too soon to abstract ideas and symbolic notation, we hope to offer alternatives that help children gain a broader view of arithmetic. We want students to work and learn together and to share their ideas and strategies. To understand students' thinking and reasoning, we must listen to our students and know the mathematics ourselves in order to ask questions and provide meaningful tasks that support learning.

This book is a collection of addition and subtraction lessons that support our beliefs about curriculum and instruction. Each lesson has been taught many times to many different classes, and each time the lessons changed in some way. The activities in this collection are rich with child-friendly contexts that are fun and engaging, giving students opportunities to gain computational skills while developing their own confidence in and enjoyment of mathematics.

Just as students benefit from working and learning together, we feel fortunate to have been able to work and learn together through these years and to have had the opportunity for ongoing professional dialogue.

The Mathematics of Addition and Subtraction

Three elements are essential for the understanding of addition and subtraction: counting, the decomposition of numbers, and our place value system of tens.

Students need many counting experiences to learn the sequence of counting (1, 2, 3, 4, 5, 6, 7, 8, 9, 10), the repeating patterns of counting (1-2-3, 11-12-13, 21-22-23), and the growing patterns of counting (1-2-3, 10-20-30, 100-200-300). Also, knowing that the last number in a counting sequence represents the quantity is an important understanding.

To understand addition and subtraction, students must be able to recognize that a number can be separated into two or more parts. This is called decomposition. For example, the number 9 can be decomposed into 4 and 5; 1 and 8; or 2, 3, and 4. When a number is decomposed, the quantity it represents is not changed. Knowing how to decompose numbers up to ten lays the foundation for working with larger numbers.

Building a system of tens is vital for understanding the place value structure of our number system and for using this structure when doing arithmetic computations. Children need to be able to decompose two-digit numbers into tens and ones in order to move from counting by ones to more efficient methods of computation. When algorithms are taught without this understanding, numbers often lose their place value meanings and the operations are reduced solely to one-digit computations. For example, when children use the standard algorithm to add 25 and 13 by first combining 5 and 3 and then combining 2 and 1, they typically think of all the digits as ones, thus not focusing on the quantities the numbers represent.

In their simplest form, addition is the combining of quantities, resulting in an increased amount, and subtraction is the taking apart of a quantity, resulting in a decreased amount. Addition and subtraction can become more complex in different contexts or when they involve negative integers.

Understanding the properties and the relationships of addition and subtraction helps students build number sense and mental strategies for computation. For example, knowing that the order of the addends does not affect the sum (commutative property of addition), students can transpose the numbers and make an easier problem. For example, it's generally easier to add 9 + 2 than 2 + 9 when first working with basic facts. Knowing that there is an inverse relationship between addition and subtraction can help students build skill in working with missing addends and deepen understanding of the part-whole relationship.

The complexity of addition and subtraction can be seen when numbers are in contexts. In addition problems, the result may be known or unknown. Consider this example: *There were four birds in a tree. Three more came. How many birds are there now?* This situation can be represented as 4 + 3 =?, and the result is unknown. However, consider the following example: *There were four birds in a tree. When more birds came, there were seven in all. How many birds came?* In this situation, the result (7) is known, and the problem can be represented as 4 + ? = 7. Although the "result known" problem can be solved by using the operation of subtraction, it is actually a combining problem that requires additive thinking.

Subtraction differs from addition in that the initial quantity is decreased. For example: *Jane had nine candies. She gave four candies to Bill. How many candies does she have left?* This subtraction problem can be represented as 9 − 4 = ?, and the result is unknown. This is known as the take-away model for subtraction.

In some take-away cases, however, the result is already known. Consider this example: *Jane had nine candies, but now only five are left. How many were eaten?* In this situation, the result is known but what happened is unknown; the problem can be represented as 9 − ? = 5. In other subtraction problems, the beginning is unknown. For example: *Jane had some candies. She gave four of them away and had five left. How many did she have originally?* This problem can be represented as ? − 4 = 5. Both of these types of "result known" subtraction problems, whether the unknown is the original amount or what happened to it, can be solved using additive thinking. This illustrates the inverse relationship between addition and subtraction.

The comparison model adds further complexity to subtraction. Comparing problems involve finding the difference between two quantities rather than decreasing one of the quantities. For example: *Maria caught ten fish. Jill caught seven fish. How many more fish did Maria catch?* While we typically think of this as a subtraction problem represented as 10 − 7 = 3, its meaning is better expressed by additive thinking, represented as 7 + ? = 10.

Measurement offers many contexts for the comparison model of subtraction, for example, when we ask how much longer, how much colder, or how much heavier. Two separate amounts are involved when we compare measurements. We do not decrease the larger amount or take away anything. Instead, we find the difference between the two amounts. For example, if we compare yesterday's and today's high temperatures, we have two separate measurements, and we find the difference between them. If the high temperature yesterday was sixty degrees and today's high is sixty-eight degrees, there is a difference of eight degrees. The sixty-eight-degree temperature has not been decreased even though the result can be found by using subtraction $(68 - 60 = 8)$. A more meaningful representation is shown using one of these equations: $(60 + ? = 68)$ or $(68 - ? = 60)$.

Because of these varied applications of addition and subtraction, it's important for students to have many opportunities to work with numbers in contextual situations. Word problems provide one way of building understanding of the properties of addition and subtraction in addition to introducing the mathematical language associated with these operations.

The Goals of Addition and Subtraction Instruction

The goals of the lessons in this book about teaching addition and subtraction include giving all students the opportunity to

▲ have varied and ongoing experiences using addition and subtraction throughout the school year;

▲ understand the meanings of addition and subtraction and their inverse relationship;

▲ use multiple strategies for computation;

▲ represent word problems with appropriate equations;

▲ use basic facts to build relationships and connections with other numbers;

▲ build facility in mental computation;

▲ make reasonable estimates to computation problems;

▲ apply addition and subtraction to a variety of problem-solving situations; and

▲ make connections between addition and subtraction and other areas of the mathematics curriculum.

The Structure of the Book

The lessons in this book provide a wide variety of addition and subtraction experiences in contextual situations. None of the lessons has students working with numbers in isolation. Contexts include playing a game; reading a piece of literature; working with personal information such as names, body measurements, pockets, and telephone numbers; interpreting newspaper data; working with money for shopping and making a penny collection; and writing word problems about real and imagined experiences.

The lessons can be used at any time throughout the school year. An activity such as *Pockets* can be repeated many times, while others such as *Letters in Our Names*, *Billy Goes Shopping*, and *Name Values* can be revisited with slight changes or through extensions. *Pennies in the Jar* is a weeklong investigation. *Little Boxes* can be incorporated into a geometry unit. *Telephone Number Totals* and *More* involve basic number facts and are very suitable for early in the school year. *Estimate and Measure* is a nonstandard measurement activity that would naturally precede the standardized measurement lessons of *Body Measurements* (length), *In One Minute* (time), and *Weather Report* (temperature).

The take-away model for subtraction is illustrated in both *Money Comes, Money Goes* and *Billy Goes Shopping,* while the comparison model for subtraction is the focus of the other lessons in the collection. When students work on the *Comparing Storybooks* activity, their understanding of these two models can be assessed.

Attempting to cover the curriculum is frustrating and unrealistic. It is helpful to look for lessons that address more than one mathematical idea and help children make connections among mathematical ideas. While the activities in this collection focus on addition and subtraction, they involve other areas of the mathematics curriculum. Also, they promote communication and organizational skills through working together, class discussions, and the use of writing to explain mathematical thinking.

In order to help you with planning and teaching the lessons in this book, each is organized into the following sections:

Overview   To help you decide if the lesson is appropriate for your students, this is a nutshell description of the mathematical goal of the lesson and what the students will be doing.

Materials   This section lists the special materials needed along with quantities. Not included in the list are regular classroom supplies such as pencils and paper. Worksheets that need to be duplicated are included in the Blackline Masters section at the back of the book.

Time   Generally, the number of class periods is provided, sometimes with a range allowing for different-length periods. It is also indicated for some activities that they are meant to be repeated from time to time.

Teaching Directions   The directions are presented in a step-by-step lesson plan.

Teaching Notes   This section addresses the mathematics underlying the lesson and at times provides information about the prior experiences or knowledge students need.

The Lesson   This is a vignette that describes what actually occurred when the lesson was taught to one or more classes. While the vignette mirrors the plan described in the teaching directions, it elaborates with details that are valuable for preparing and teaching the lesson. Samples of student work are included.

Extensions   This section is included for most of the lessons and offers follow-up suggestions.

Questions and Discussion   Presented in a question-and-answer format, this section addresses issues that came up during the lesson and/or have been posed by other teachers.

GAMES AND WARM-UP ACTIVITIES

The games and warm-up activities included in the Additional Activities section are easy to do and require a minimum of materials and preparation. Each game or activity helps build or reinforce understanding of one or more key mathematical ideas for addition and subtraction. Developing strategies through logical reasoning, practicing basic facts, and doing mental computation are additional benefits. A brief summary and the key ideas involved precede the teaching directions for each activity.

CHAPTER ONE
TELEPHONE NUMBER TOTALS

Overview

Having children find the sum of the digits in a telephone number is a quick way to provide practice with basic addition facts. As students share their strategies for finding the totals, they learn that there is more than one way to put numbers together. Our goal is for students to find a way that works best for them.

One of the ways students can develop number sense is to look at numbers in the everyday world and play with them. They see numbers everywhere—on license plates, addresses, room numbers, grocery bills, and even phone numbers. This lesson provides a playful experience with numbers that is personally connected to each student.

Materials

▲ 3-by-3-inch sticky notes, 1 per student

Time

▲ one to two class periods

Teaching Directions

1. Discuss telephone numbers with the class. How many digits do they have? What's an area code? What is a prefix?

2. On the board, list the different prefixes of the students' phone numbers. Arrange them in numerical order with the students. Then have them find the sum of the digits in each prefix, calling on students to explain their addition strategies. Ask them what they notice.

3. Write a seven-digit phone number on the front board. Have students describe their methods for adding the digits together. Model for the class how you could

record how they reasoned and then have the children show their own ways of keeping track and recording.

4. Have each student find the total of his or her own telephone number, recording how he or she put the numbers together and then writing the sum of the digits of the phone number on a sticky note. Each of them then adds the digits of three additional telephone numbers that they know.

5. Observe students as they work to determine who knows the basic facts, who is developing a strategy, who can keep track of his or her procedures, and who records clearly.

6. When students have completed their papers, ask them to come to the front of the room and put the sticky notes with their telephone number totals in order.

7. Together, add the sum of the area code to each total.

Teaching Notes

At the beginning of the school year, teachers spend time getting to know their students and the skills they bring with them from their previous experiences. After adjusting to the realization that our new students in September are not like our students last year in June, we introduce to the class some of our favorite beginning-of-the-year activities.

Sometimes a class does not seem ready for some of the activities we typically do at the beginning of the year. This can require an on-the-spot adjustment or sometimes can trigger a creative lesson. The latter is what happened early one school year when Lynne decided not to pursue the *Name Values* lesson (see Chapter 9). She realized that many of the students did not have facility with mental arithmetic that involved working with two-digit numbers. She made the decision to postpone the lesson and instead had the children find the sums of their telephone numbers.

There seems to be a delicate balance between allowing students to struggle to figure things out and asking students to do something that they do not have the tools to pursue. We want students to feel that they have access to the task. When doing whole-class lessons, it is nearly impossible to find the perfect level of difficulty for each individual. We continually look for clues and assess both individuals and the class as a whole.

The Lesson

▲▲▲

DAY 1

"How many digits are in your phone number?" Lynne asked the class.

"I've got seven," Hannah said. There were nods of agreement from some of the other students.

"It's ten if you count your area code," Sandy replied.

"I get eleven," Greg said. "When I call my grandma, I have to punch a one first.

"For today, let's just look at our seven-digit phone numbers," Lynne said. "Each phone number is divided into two parts—a three-digit prefix followed by another group of four digits. If we look first at the prefix, what is the largest number possible?" asked Lynne.

"Nine hundred!" Johnny shouted.

"Are you sure?" Lynne asked.

"Whoops, it's nine hundred ninety-nine," Johnny corrected himself.

"What is the smallest number possible?"

"Zero zero zero," Mark answered, "but that would be a funny phone number."

"Let's see whose prefix is the smallest," Lynne suggested.

As the students told Lynne their prefixes, she wrote them on the board:

566   731   664   665   564   242   759

Some of the students seemed surprised that there were only seven different prefixes for the entire class.

"Which prefix is the smallest?" Lynne asked.

"Two hundred forty-two," the class agreed.

Lynne then had the class arrange the prefixes in numerical order.

242   564   566   664   665   731   759

"Mine is the largest!" Martha commented.

"Just for fun, let's add the digits of each prefix and see if they stay in the same order," Lynne suggested.

The students busily began adding the figures mentally. Lynne wrote down the totals under the prefixes and then had the class put them into ascending order.

242	564	566	664	665	731	759
8	15	17	16	17	11	21

"What do you notice?" Lynne asked.

"Six hundred sixty-five and five hundred sixty-six both add up to seventeen," Christina offered.

"Why?" Lynne asked Christina, who had good facility with numbers.

"Because they both have the same numbers, and it doesn't matter which way you add them, they always come out the same."

The commutative property of addition was obvious to a few of the students, but not to all. Most students were still building understanding of this concept, so Lynne wrote the two prefixes on the board.

"If you add six hundred sixty-five, how do you do it?" Lynne asked.

Most of the students added six and six because it was a double and then added the five.

"If you add five hundred sixty-six, what do you do?" Lynne continued.

Again, most students looked at six and six first, but not all. Some added five and six to get eleven, and then added the other six to get seventeen. One student changed the five to a six, added three sixes, and subtracted one. Even with this simple problem, students had a variety of ways to solve mentally.

"Look at five hundred sixty-six again," Lynne directed. "Can you think of another prefix that could add up to seventeen?"

The students offered several suggestions, and Lynne asked them to explain their thinking.

Sam went first with 82**7.** "Just find two numbers that make ten, and then add seven," he explained.

"Let's use Sam's strategy and find others," Lynne suggested.

The class came up with 737, 647, 557, 917, and 980 as examples of digits whose sums were seventeen.

"I did doubles," Christina said. She proceeded to give 449, 557, 665, 773, and 881 as examples.

"Why can't you use nine and nine?" Lynne probed.

"Nine and nine make eighteen, and that's too much," Robby explained.

Lynne tries to do this kind of informal practice in mental computation each day with her class. She feels that facility with small numbers is essential before pushing on to larger numbers. Doing daily warm-ups is one way to build both number sense and facility with numbers. Lynne used this activity as a warm-up and went on with the lesson she had planned. She returned to telephone numbers the next day.

DAY 2

The next day Lynne began class by writing a telephone number on the front board.

665-4213

"If we added up all seven digits in this telephone number, what sum would we get?" Lynne asked the class. "Take a look at these numbers and think about how you can figure out the total in a way that would make it easy. You might want to use paper to keep track of how you put the numbers together so you can share how you did it."

There was a scramble for scratch paper and pencils and quickly the students were recording how they put the numbers together. When most of the students had found a total, Lynne gave the following instructions: "Each of you should explain to the person sitting next to you how you figured out the total. See if you both did it the same way or if you did it in two different ways."

Lynne sat with Alan, who had no one sitting next to him, and asked him to explain how he had found the total. She explained to him how she had found the total.

"We had two different ways to find the total!" Lynne exclaimed. "Do you think you could find a third way?" she asked Alan before she went to check on the rest of the class.

At the beginning of the year, Lynne is continually checking to see if students have ways to talk and listen to each other. Much of their learning is enhanced by communicating with one another.

When it appeared that most students had talked to each other, Lynne asked them to gather in the front of the room to share some of their methods for finding the total.

Lynne invited Lydia to come up to the board and explain how she had found the total.

"I put the six and six together and got twelve," Lydia began pointing to the numbers, "Then I put five plus four and got nine. Then two plus one plus three makes six."

"Let me write on the board what you have so far," Lynne suggested.

6 + 6 = 12

5 + 4 = 9

2 + 1 + 3 = 6

"Then what?" Lynne asked.

"Then I put the nine and the six together and got fifteen and fifteen plus twelve makes twenty-seven," Lydia continued.

Lynne wrote on the board:

9 + 6 = 15

15 + 12 = 27

"The way that I wrote the numbers on the board is one way to record how Lydia put the numbers together, but I just noticed that she had a different way of keeping track on her paper. Maybe Lydia can show us on the board how she kept track of her subtotals," Lynne requested as she cleared a space on the board and wrote the telephone number again.

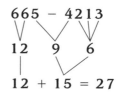

"Did anyone put the numbers together like Lydia did?" Lynne asked the class.

"I started like she did, but I didn't do it in order like that," Vincent reported.

"So you started with six plus six?" Lynne inquired.

"Yes. Then I put the five with the two and the three to make ten. That would make twenty-two. Then there's the four and the one, which makes five more. Twenty-two plus five makes twenty-seven," Vincent stated confidently.

"Did you record it like Lydia?" Lynne asked.

"No, I just circled the numbers and wrote the totals as I did them in my head," Vincent said.

"Show us on the board how you circled the numbers," Lynne said.

Vincent came up to the board, wrote the phone number, and circled the numbers as he explained again how he had added the numbers. "Two sixes make twelve," Vincent said as he circled the 6s and wrote the sum below.

6 6 5 – 4 2 1 3

12

"Five plus two and three makes ten," he continued, circling the three numbers and writing a 10 below the 12.

6 6 5 – 4 2 1 3

12

10

"Then there's just the four and one left," he said as he circled the numbers and wrote a 5 below the 12 and the 10.

6 6 5 – 4 2 1 3

12

10

5

Vincent next circled the 12 and the 10 and wrote *22*. He continued by connecting the 22 and the 5 with a line and writing *27*.

Lynne wanted to have one more student share a method of putting the numbers together, but she could tell that the students were eager to find out the totals of their own telephone numbers.

"You will each find the total of your own phone number," Lynne told the class. "First you will write your phone number at the top of your paper. Next you will find the total of the digits and record how you did it so that someone else can follow your thinking. Write the sum of the numbers in your phone number on a sticky note and place it on the front board. After that, write three more telephone numbers that you know and find the sum of each. Be sure to label whose telephone numbers you used."

Lynne asked if someone would repeat the directions so that everyone could hear them again. She called on Nancy.

Nancy began, "Put your phone number on the top of the paper, find the total and write down how you did it, then put your total on a sticky note."

"Can anyone add to Nancy's directions?" Lynne asked.

"You have to write three more telephone numbers and find the totals," Alan added.

On the chalkboard, Lynne wrote a sample to model how their paper should look.

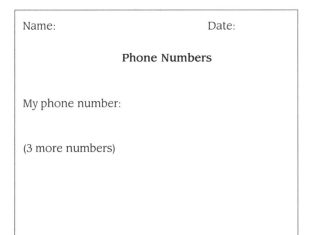

Lynne asked one student to pass out paper and another to give each student a sticky note. The class got to work quickly. Lynne told the children that if they needed an idea for a telephone number, they could refer to their emergency cards, which they had recently returned.

When Lynne began observing individual students, it was clear which ones relied on counting to find the totals. There were students who were more comfortable adding the first number to the next in order, one number at a time. Others added pairs of numbers and then added the sums of each pair in pairs until they got the total. Sandy added pairs of numbers that were not adjacent. She seemed to be adding a big number to a little number. She seemed to know that 6 + 4 made ten but ignored other sums that made ten like 9 + 1, 8 + 2, and even 5 + **5**. Lydia appeared to look for doubles when she added. Christina mentally added first the three numbers of the prefix, then the next four numbers, and finally, put the two partial sums together.

By observing the students as they worked, Lynne could informally assess who had a strategy, who had a way to keep track of his or her thinking, and who had access to basic facts. (See Figures 1–1 through 1–4.)

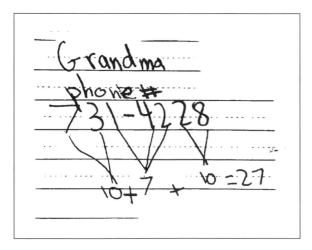

▲▲▲▲▲▲**Figure 1–1** *Greg added numbers in order.*

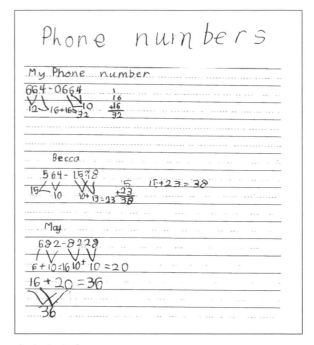

▲▲▲▲▲▲**Figure 1–2** *Elizabeth found pairs of numbers that made 10.*

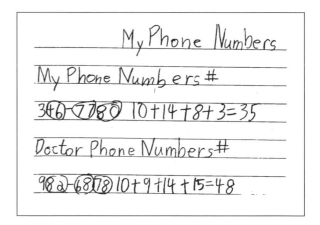

▲▲▲▲▲▲**Figure 1–3** *Kevin added pairs of numbers and then added the sums together.*

As students began to finish their papers, Lynne instructed them to sit on the rug near the chalkboard. She asked some to help her put the sticky notes in order from least to greatest. Lynne asked everyone to join the group and told the students that they would have time to complete their work after lunch.

After the totals were put in order, Lynne listed them in a column on the board under the heading "Sum of Phone Numbers." Then

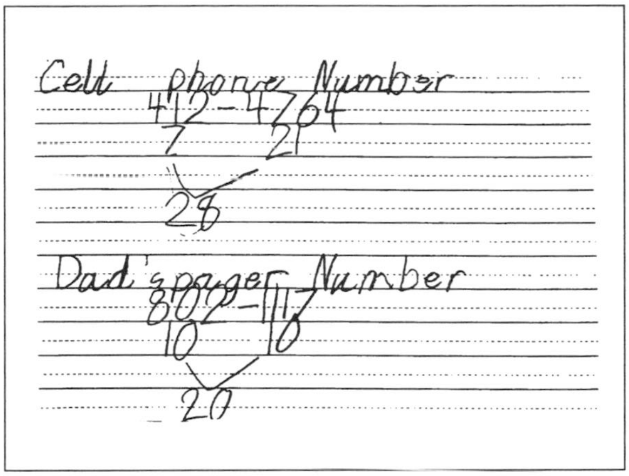

▲▲▲▲▲Figure 1–4   *Christina mentally added the sum of the prefix to the sum of the last four numbers.*

she posed the following question: "What if we added the area code to each of these numbers?"

"Everyone would have to add ten," Elizabeth reported.

"Why?" Lynne asked.

"Everyone has the four one five area code, and that makes ten," Vincent said.

"What would we get if we added ten to twenty?" Lynne began, pointing to the first sum.

"That would be thirty," Lydia told the class.

Lynne added a second column to the board and labeled it *Plus Area Code.*

"What do you get when you add ten to the other numbers?" Lynne asked.

"Ten plus thirty makes forty," Robby contributed.

The class continued to complete the chart. Lynne made a mental note to give the class more experiences adding ten to numbers since this was an important skill for mental arithmetic. She also thought she would give the class additional practice with other area codes that didn't add to ten by posing the question, "What if our area code was changed?"

Sums of Phone Numbers	Plus Area Code
15	25
20	30
25	35
30	40
31	41
32	42
33	43
35	45
36	46
37	47
40	50
44	54

Questions and Discussion

▲▲▲

▲ *How do you involve parents with helping students learn the basic facts for addition and subtraction?*

From the beginning of the year, we let parents know that it is important for them to be involved in their children's education. We also let them know that it is important for all second and third graders to know their basic facts for addition and subtraction. What we don't want is to put parents in the position of pushing or pressuring their children into memorizing the facts.

One way parents can help is by playing games with their children regularly. Once we have taught a game to the class we often send the rules and the necessary materials home so that the students can teach their parents how to play. We want students to have fun with mathematics and to learn to play with numbers. Playing with a parent who has this disposition is invaluable.

▲ *Do you suggest giving timed tests to encourage students to have quick recall of the basic facts?*

We have never seen the need for giving students a timed test. One of the things we reinforce all year is that students need to take their time to do things well and to try to make sense of mathematics in their own ways. Every child is different when it comes to math. Some feel confident about their skills and are not easily discouraged by errors or seeing that someone is faster than them. Others are easily discouraged when they make mistakes or do not finish when others do. We want to honor these differences and don't want to do anything that could discourage a single child.

We find that timed tests do not give us the information we need about our students. Those who already know the basic facts would show us once again that they know the facts, and those who do not know the facts would show us once again that they do not have this skill. This is information we already know from our daily interaction with our students.

CHAPTER TWO
MORE

Overview

The context of this lesson is a card game. Partners divide a deck of playing cards and compare the numerical values of two overturned cards. They decide who has more and how many more. The player with more takes cubes to represent the difference between the cards. After all the cards are played, each player counts his or her train of cubes and records that amount. The players find the difference between their scores. The students play and record another game and total their individual scores from the two games. Finally, they compare their total scores and show the difference. The lesson has students actively involved in basic fact practice as well as in the addition and the subtraction of two- and three-digit numbers.

Materials

- ▲ 1 deck of cards per pair of students
- ▲ *More* record sheets (see Blackline Masters), 1 per student
- ▲ 150 Unifix or interlocking cubes per pair of students

Time

- ▲ forty-five minutes to teach the game, fifteen to thirty minutes to play the game, ten to fifteen minutes for class discussion after playing

Teaching Directions

1. Have one student in each pair shuffle a deck of cards and deal twenty-six cards each to his partner and himself.

2. Each player turns over one card at the same time. For example,

Player 1 turns over a 7.

Player 2 turns over a 10.

3. The students compare the face value of the cards.

Who has more? Player 2

How many more? 3 more

Ace = 1   Jack = 11   Queen = 12   King = 13

4. The player with more takes cubes to represent the difference between the values (for example, three cubes).

5. The players continue playing, each snapping his or her cubes into a train.

6. When students have played all the cards, they compare their trains and record the difference.

Player 1   49

Player 2   66

Difference   17

7. The pair plays the game once again and records the scores.

Player 1   57

Player 2   73

Difference   16

8. The players total their points for both games, record the sums, and find the total difference.

	Player 1	Player 2	Difference
Game 1	49	66	17
Game 2	57	73	16
Total	106	139	33

9. Have the students show how they found their differences and totals.

10. On another day, have a discussion with the students about what they noticed about their scores and playing this game.

Teaching Notes

If arithmetic is taught in contextual situations, students will have opportunities to develop understanding of the various models of operations. They will be able to interpret distinct differences that occur in real-life situations. For example, when students are comparing two cards such as a 10 and a 6 in the game of *More*, the comparing model is being represented. The question is not how many is ten take away 6? but rather what is the difference between the two numbers? In the take-away model, only one set is being operated upon: If you have ten and take away six, how many are left? In the comparing model, two sets are being compared: What is the difference between a set of ten and a set of six?

To build background in this comparison model, students need many formal and informal comparing experiences. Asking questions like "How many more?", "How many less?", and "What's the difference?" can become part of the daily classroom routine.

Here are some examples of contextual situations that involve comparisons:

Comparing Heights, Weights, Daily Temperatures, and Capacity

▲ John's height is 49 inches. His father's height is 72 inches. What is the difference in their heights?

▲ The temperature in San Francisco is 61 degrees. The temperature in Chicago is 90 degrees. How much hotter is it in Chicago today?

Comparing Class Sizes and Daily Attendance

▲ The smallest class in our school has 19 students. The largest class has 32 students. How many fewer students are in the smallest class?

▲ Yesterday, our school had 23 students absent in all. Today, 15 students are absent. How many more students were absent yesterday?

Comparing Prices

▲ One brand of chocolate pudding sells for $.89. Another sells for $1.10. How much less is the first brand?

▲ Barbara bought a notebook for $.79. Her friend Jason bought the same notebook for $.50 more. How much was Jason's notebook?

Comparing Scores or Statistics

▲ The score of the basketball game was 95 to 79. The winning team scored how many more points?

▲ The home run record this year was 52. Last year the record was 70. What is the difference between the two years?

Comparing Time

▲ Kim jumped 65 times in one minute. Carl jumped 49 times in one minute. Who jumped more? How many more times did he or she jump?

▲ It takes the class 45 minutes to walk to the museum. The bus takes 12 minutes. How much longer does it take to walk?

The Lesson

▲▲▲

DAY 1

To introduce the lesson, Bonnie gathered the students in the front of the classroom as she held a deck of playing cards in her hand. "I know that many of you have used playing cards before," Bonnie said as she showed the deck to the class. "Today I am going to show you a math game that uses these cards. It's a game for two players that is called *More*."

"If I keep the jack, the queen, and the king of hearts in my deck, how many hearts are there in all?" Bonnie began.

"Thirteen," responded several members of the class. The students were familiar with playing cards and had used them since first grade.

"How many spades?" Again the class responded with thirteen.

"How many diamonds?"

"Thirteen."

"And how many clubs?"

"Thirteen."

"How many cards in all?" Bonnie asked.

There was a murmur of "fifty-two" when Mark responded, "It's fifty-two. Everyone knows that's how many cards there are in a deck."

"But how do you know that's correct?"

Francesca raised her hand "I know because they all have one through ten, and that makes forty. Then you have three plus three equals six, six plus three equals nine, and nine plus three equals twelve, and forty and twelve make fifty-two."

"You can just say thirteen times four," Alvin called out.

"Are you a calculator?" Bonnie said, laughing.

"I just know times," Alvin answered.

"I know another way," Jennifer said. "You make four piles of thirteen and add them up. You add all the ones and that gives you forty." Jennifer knew that the "ones" were not really ones, but tens, even though she couldn't communicate that idea verbally. "Then you add all the threes. So it's forty-three, forty-six, forty-nine, fifty-two." Jennifer started with the tens and then added the ones to the tens.

Max raised his hand after he heard Jennifer's method. "I do the same as Jennifer, but I add the threes first." Max then showed the class the standard algorithm for column addition on the board.

"I do it different," Carissa said. Carissa then carefully explained how she added thirteen and thirteen to get twenty-six. Then she added twenty-six and twenty-six by adding $20 + 20 = 40$ and $6 + 6 = 12$ and finally adding $40 + 12 = 52$.

Getting back to the game, Bonnie explained that each pair of students would be using a full deck of fifty-two cards. "In this game, the number cards are worth one to ten, starting with the ace. The jack is worth eleven, the queen is worth twelve, and the king is worth thirteen."

"First you shuffle the cards to get them mixed up, and then you deal out the deck." Bonnie demonstrated these first steps using Weslie as her partner.

"Then you each turn over a card. You decide who has more and then figure out how many more that player has." Bonnie turned over a 6 and Weslie turned over a king. "Weslie has thirteen and I have six. Who has more? How many more?"

The children answered correctly.

"Since Weslie has seven more than I do, she gets to take seven cubes."

Bonnie and Weslie continued playing, each one snapping her cubes onto their trains.

"When you finish playing all your cards," Bonnie continued, "you each count how many cubes you have in all and record that amount. Then you find the difference between your scores. After recording Game 1, you play again and record your scores. Your last job is to find the total scores of each player from both games." She demonstrated the recording procedure on the board, having the students figure out the totals and the differences.

	Player 1	Player 2	Difference
Game 1	76	54	22
Game 2	58	67	9
Total	134	121	?

"The last thing you do is compare your total scores and show the difference. How do these scores compare?" Bonnie asked, pointing to the recording data.

"Weslie won," Nicole said.

"How many points did she win by? Was it more than ten points?"

"I think it was three more than ten," Carissa said. "I added ten and got one hundred and thirty-one. Then I added three to the one hundred and thirty-one and got one hundred and thirty-four. So it's thirteen more."

"Did anyone else figure out the difference in another way?" Bonnie asked.

"I did," Alvin said. "I went back ten from one hundred and thirty-four and got one hundred and twenty-four. Then I counted back one hundred and twenty-three, one hundred and twenty-two, one hundred and twenty-one. That makes thirteen."

"I just knew that twenty-one to thirty-four was thirteen," Kenneth said. "And since they're both hundreds, it doesn't change anything."

Bonnie believes that children construct their own meaning for problems that are presented in the classroom. She allows time for students to verbalize their thinking to the whole group. Listening to others' strategies for solving problems allows students to realize that there are many ways to look at a problem.

Bonnie distributed playing cards to each pair of students and reviewed the instructions. "Play two games, record your scores, and find the totals and the difference. If you need to remember the rules of the game, I have copies of the instructions in a folder on the math table, or you may ask me."

The children went back to their tables and began playing the game. Figures 2–1 through 2–3 show how some students recorded their games.

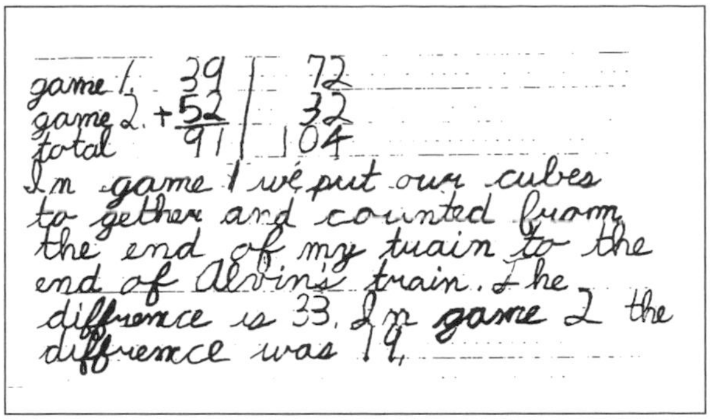

DAY 2

On another day, after all the students had played and recorded their games, Bonnie called them back together to discuss the activity.

She asked each student to put one of his or her individual game scores on a sticky note. The students then placed their sticky

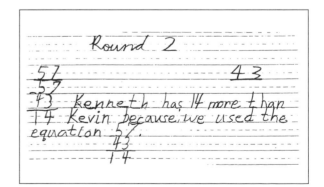

▲▲▲▲▲▲Figure 2–1 Nicole described how she and Alvin used cubes to find the differences in their scores.

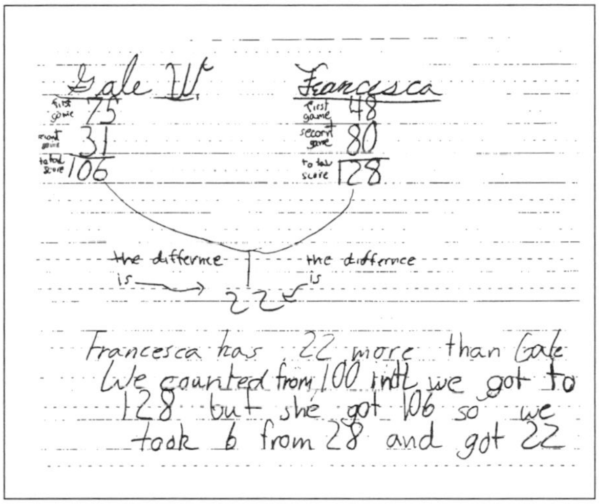

▲▲▲▲▲▲Figure 2–2 Using 100 as a landmark number, Francesca and Gale began with adding 28 to 100 and then subtracting 6.

▲▲▲▲▲▲Figure 2–3 Kenneth and Kevin showed the difference using a standard form of notation for subtraction.

notes on the board. "What do you notice about these scores?" Bonnie asked.

The students called out several observations.

"There are lots of fifties and sixties!"

"The biggest score was eighty-four."

"Lots of us had the same scores, especially sixty-three."

"Nobody got over one hundred."

"Thirty-eight was the smallest score."

"If you got thirty-eight, you would have been the loser for sure."

"Let's arrange them in a more organized way," Bonnie suggested, and the class arranged the scores in a bar graph from the lowest to the highest score.

38 39 48 49 50 52 56 57 59 63 66 69 70 72 75 84

57   63
*   63*
*   63*
*   65*

Bonnie confirmed their previous observations. "You were certainly right about those fifties and sixties. I also can easily see that the scores went from thirty-eight to eighty-four and that sixty-three was scored five different times."

"In mathematics when we talk about the results from lowest to highest, we call it the range," she explained. "So thirty-eight to eighty-four is our range of scores when we played *More*. Can anyone tell me the difference between the lowest and the highest scores of the game?"

"It's forty-six," Francesca said.

"What do you mean forty-six?" Bonnie asked to make sure Francesca really understood the concept.

"The highest score had forty-six more points than the lowest score," Francesca answered.

"How did you get that number?"

"I addcd fifty to thirty-eight and got eighty-eight, but that was too much, so I went back four to forty-six."

Bonnie then asked various children to compare their individual scores from Game 1 and Game 2 and give her the difference. Then she asked them to compare their differences with the range of forty-six. All of the students had differences less than forty-six. "Why do you think nobody had more than forty-six for a difference?" she asked.

Kevin, a thoughtful student, looked carefully at the data for a long time before he raised his hand. "We got forty-six because we compared the lowest number with the highest number. To get a bigger number, we would have had to have a lower low score or a higher high score. That didn't happen, so it couldn't be a bigger number."

Bonnie could see that Kevin understood the concept of range and its connection to the scores and the differences of the games that the students had played. Other students were still building their basic understanding of comparison and difference. In any group or class there is a range in the depth of mathematical understanding. Playing games more than once can help students gain a solid understanding of numbers. Having class discussions can help students make connections.

"Tomorrow I will teach you *Double More*," Bonnie concluded.

EXTENSIONS

In *Double More*, each player turns over two cards at one time, finds the total of the two cards, and then finds the difference between the two totals. Example: If Player 1 turns over a 6 and a 9, and Player 2 turns over a 3 and a 5, the totals to compare are fifteen and eight, with a difference of seven. Player 1 gets seven cubes.

Questions and Discussion

▲▲

▲ *What is the value of playing mathematical games in the classroom?*

Games are intrinsically motivating for children, and students often enjoy playing familiar games over and over again. Games provide situations where students can make sense of numbers in an informal setting. They also provide a natural time for working together with a partner. We have found that this more relaxed atmosphere gives us excellent opportunities to observe students both academically and socially. We are able to assess a student's facility with numbers and, depending upon the game, the student's use of strategies. When the class has a common experience of playing the same game, it is often a springboard to lively class discussions.

▲ *Is it worthwhile to have children explain their methods for mental computation to the whole class?*

There are two main reasons we like to have children report to the whole group. Mathematics is a way of thinking. Being able to explain your thinking verbally, as well as in writing, helps clarify meaning for yourself. By listening to the ideas of others, you begin to realize there is more than one way to look at a problem and that it is possible to deepen your understanding by looking at things from different perspectives.

CHAPTER THREE
ESTIMATE AND MEASURE

Overview

Measurement provides real-life contexts for making comparisons. The students begin measuring lengths with nonstandard units. Using interlocking cubes, they estimate and then measure the length of various objects in the classroom. They compare their estimates with their measurements and find the differences. In the second part of the lesson, students make comparisons between the lengths of the various classroom objects. These experiences introduce students to measuring length, give them practice in making comparisons, and provide computational practice in a context.

Materials

- ▲ 28 paper clips
- ▲ 2 pieces of string, measuring 8 and 20 paper clips in length
- ▲ copies of directions for *Estimate and Measure* and *Comparing Lengths* (see Blackline Masters)
- ▲ *Estimate and Measure* sheet (see Blackline Masters), 1 per student
- ▲ Unifix or other interlocking cubes, arranged into trains of 10, at least 50 cubes per pair of students
- ▲ 35 sentence strips cut into 3-by-8-inch strips OR 50 5-by-8-inch index cards cut in half into $2\frac{1}{2}$-by-8-inch strips
- ▲ 10 paper bags

Time

- ▲ three to four class periods

Teaching Directions

1. Review the meaning of length. Explain that height and width are also measures of length.

2. Explain that measurement is done with equal units. Show paper clips and interlocking cubes as two examples of measuring units.

3. Measure the two lengths of string with the paper clips and with the cubes. For each measuring unit, have students figure out the difference between the lengths of the shorter and longer strings.

4. Explain the directions for *Estimate and Measure*. Do a few examples with the students and model how to record on the worksheet.

5. Select four measurements from the students' record sheets and write them on sentence strips or index cards.

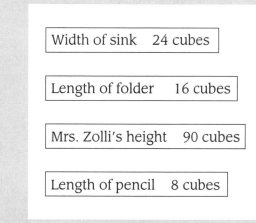

Width of sink   24 cubes

Length of folder   16 cubes

Mrs. Zolli's height   90 cubes

Length of pencil   8 cubes

6. Put the four strips in a bag. Remove two strips, show them to the class, and ask the students to compare their lengths. For example, ask: "How much longer is the sink than the pencil?" Have students explain their reasoning. Then remove the remaining two strips. "What is the difference between my height and the length of the folder?"

7. Ask each student to select five measurements from his or her *Estimate and Measure* record sheet and write the names of the objects and their actual measurements on individual sentence strips or index cards.

8. Collect the students' strips, mix them, and put ten strips into each paper bag.

9. Explain to the students that they will work in pairs pulling out two sentence strips from a bag at a time. For each pair of strips, they should record the names of the objects and the measurements and the difference, as you modeled before. Have them repeat this four more times until the bag is empty. Then have them put the strips back in the bag and repeat, or use a different bag. You may want to post the directions or duplicate and distribute them.

Teaching Notes

Students need many opportunities to explore their environment through measurement. Before students learn about standard measures and measuring tools, they need to do direct comparisons: Is it colder today than it was yesterday? Is the red ribbon longer than the yellow one? Do these two books weigh the same? They also can work with nonstandard units: How many paper clips measure across the desk? How many beans weigh the same as five crayons? How many more marbles will it take to fill the jar?

Comparing measurements involves finding the difference between two sets: How much longer? How much heavier? How many more? Comparison words such as *hotter/colder, longer/shorter, heavier/lighter,* and *faster/slower* are often used to describe the difference between measurements. "What's the difference?" is answered not by the amount left in the set after some are taken away, as is the case for many subtraction problems, but rather by the number that represents the numerical distance between the two sets. In *Estimate and Measure,* students can build visual models to show differences.

Estimated: 10 cubes

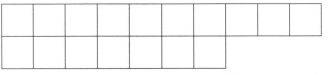

Actual Measurement: 7 cubes   Difference: 3 cubes

The Lesson

▲▲▲

DAY 1

"Today we are going to be measuring the length of things in our classroom," Lynne said to the class. "What do I mean when I say length?" she asked.

"It's how long something is," Jeffrey answered.

"It's also how wide or how tall something is," Lynne continued, using her hands to demonstrate. "If I measured the door, I could measure how tall it is, which is the height of the door, or I could measure the width of the door, which is how wide it is. Length and width are measured in the same way."

"Today we're going to measure the length, the width, or the height of various things around the classroom." Lynne held up a train of ten interlocking cubes and a hand-ful of individual cubes. "You will be using these cubes as your measuring tools today."

"But those aren't rulers," Diana protested.

"You're right," Lynne responded. "When we measure things, we can use any unit of measure. Let me show you how I could use paper clips to measure."

Lynne then linked paper clips together and used them to measure the lengths of two pieces of string. She began with the shorter piece, which was 8 paper clips long.

Lynne held up the second piece of string so that the students could compare it with the first piece. "Is this piece longer or shorter than the one I just measured?"

"It's longer," the class agreed.

"How much longer?" Lynne asked.

"It's more than twice as long," Maria said.

"If that's true, how many paper clips long do you think it will be?"

"Sixteen and maybe two more clips," Maria replied.

"Let's measure it to find out exactly how much longer," Lynne suggested.

Lynne asked Gina to do the measuring. The string was 20 paper clips long. "That was very close to Maria's estimate," Lynne said.

"She was off by two," Collin said.

Lynne then wrote on the chalkboard:

8 clips   20 clips

"How much longer was the second string?" she asked the class.

"That's easy," Susan said. "It's twelve. I just added eight and then four." Susan had used Maria's estimating strategy to help her find the difference.

"The second string is twelve paper clips longer than the first string," Lynne said, rephrasing the comparison in a sentence to model the correct mathematical language. "You could also say that the first string is twelve paper clips shorter than the second string."

"What if we measured the strings with these cubes?" Lynne asked. "Would the second string still be longer?"

The class laughed.

Lynne then had two students measure the strings with the interlocking cubes. The first string was 11 cubes long, and the second was 27 cubes long. Lynne wrote on the board:

11 cubes   27 cubes

The students figured out that the second string was 16 cubes longer than the first.

"We can make comparisons as long as we use the same measuring units," Lynne reiterated. "If we use paper clips, the strings have a difference of twelve paper clips. If we use cubes, the difference is sixteen cubes."

Lynne then explained what the students would do. "You are going to do an activity called *Estimate and Measure.* In this activity, you are going to use interlocking cubes as your measuring tool. You will select something in the classroom to measure. Does anyone have an idea of something we could measure?"

Many students had ideas. Lynne called upon Kelly, who suggested the bookcase.

"Do you want to measure how high it is or how wide it is?" Lynne asked, using her hands to show the difference between height and width.

"I want to see how tall it is," Kelly said.

Lynne took a train of 10 cubes and showed them it the class. "Use this train to make an estimate of the height of the bookcase," Lynne said. "Kelly, what is your estimate?"

"I think it's fifty cubes," she replied.

Lynne then asked Kelly to measure the actual height, which was 42 cubes.

"I was pretty close!" Kelly cried.

"Exactly how close?" Lynne asked.

Kelly thought a minute and then said, "Eight. I counted three to forty-five, and then added five to get to fifty."

Lynne then modeled the record sheet for the class (see below).

After Lynne did a few more examples with the students to make sure they understood the task, they set to work. Most of the class worked in pairs, but a few students chose to work independently. The class was totally engaged. They measured a wide variety of things including the door, the sink, their backpacks, and even each other. No one had completely finished the activity when it was time for recess.

"We need to stop for today," Lynne said. "It's important that we put the cubes neatly away in groups of ten so they'll be ready when we continue tomorrow."

DAY 2

The following day Lynne began the math period by asking the students to bring their *Estimate and Measure* papers to the front of the class.

"But I didn't finish," Albert said.

"That's OK. We're just going to spend a few minutes talking about the activity and then I'll let you finish up your work."

Object Being Measured	Estimated # of Cubes	Actual Measurement	How Far Off?
Height of bookcase	50	42	8

After the children were settled, Lynne continued, "Was anyone surprised about a measurement?"

"I didn't think you would be ninety cubes long," said Jane, who had measured Lynne the day before.

"Why were you surprised?" Lynne asked.

"It just seems like a big number of cubes," Jane answered. "You were more than twice the height of the bookcase." Jane loved working with numbers, had excellent number sense, and was always connecting one experience with another.

"Look at your papers," Lynne directed. "Did anyone have a measurement exactly the same as the estimate?"

Several students raised their hands and told the class the objects they had estimated correctly.

"I notice," Lynne commented, "that you were more accurate with smaller objects than you were with longer things. Why do you think this is true?"

"It's because we put the cubes into tens or in ones," Josh said. "So if the object is close to one cube or to ten cubes long, it's easier to figure out."

"The more you measure things," Lynne added, "the better you get at estimating. If you know how long one object is, it's easier to estimate the length of something else. Josh was right when he explained how knowing the length of one cube or of ten cubes helps us measure other things. Today, I want you to complete your *Estimate and Measure* worksheets. If you're finished, practice estimating with a few more things, remembering to think of lengths of ten to help you."

As the students worked, Lynne observed which students were making reasonable estimates by using prior experiences to help them with their next measurements. She also talked with students about how they compared measurements and estimates.

DAY 3

"We are now going to make some comparisons between the measurements you made," Lynne began.

She held up a paper bag into which she had put four sentence strips, each with the length of a classroom object measured in cubes written on it.

"In this bag are some sentence strips. On each strip is the name of a classroom object and its length in cubes." Lynne opened the bag and pulled out two sentence strips to show the class.

Width of sink 24 cubes		Length of pencil 8 cubes

"How much longer is the sink than the pencil?" Lynne asked. "When you answer, be ready to tell me how you figured it out."

Lynne waited while the students computed. As each explained, she recorded their explanations on the board (see below). Some students had used the 0–99 chart, which was easy for them to see from where they were seated.

Lynne pulled out two more strips from the bag:

Length of eraser 7 cubes		Length of Brian's hand 6 cubes

Jeffrey	Eric	Patricia	Kim
8 + 2 = 10	8 + 20 = 28	(using fingers to count back 8)	8 + 10 = 18
10 + 14 = 24	28 − 4 = 24	23 22 21 20 19 18 17 16	18 + 2 = 20
2 + 14 = 16	20 − 4 = 16		20 + 4 = 24
			10 + 2 + 4 = 16

"That one is too easy," Dylan said, laughing. "The eraser is one cube more."

"Sometimes that happens," Lynne commented. "When *you* do this activity, you will have a paper bag with ten measurements inside. Pull out two at a time and compare them. Write down the two objects being compared and find the difference between the two. Continue pulling out strips two at a time until the bag is empty. If you finish, put the strips back in the bag and try it again or exchange your bag with someone else to use different strips."

Lynne had the students use their *Estimate and Measure* record sheets to help get the bags ready. Each student selected five measurements and recorded the objects and their lengths on individual strips. Lynne mixed the strips and put ten in each bag. Each pair of students selected a bag and they set off to do their comparisons. Figures 3–1 through 3–3 show some students' work on this activity.

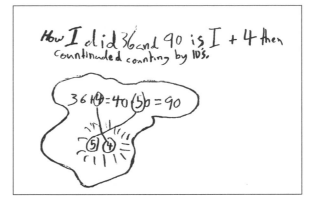

▲▲▲▲▲▲**Figure 3–2** *Brian found the difference between the length of a table and his teacher's height. He added 4 to 36 to get to 40 and then counted by tens until he reached 90.*

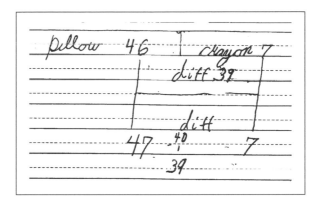

▲▲▲▲▲▲**Figure 3–3** *Thomas found 47 – 7 an easier problem than 46 – 7 and adjusted his computation by subtracting 1 from 40.*

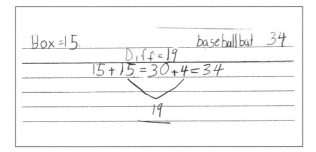

▲▲▲▲▲▲**Figure 3–1** *Gina first added 15 to get to 30 and then 4 more to get to 34. She added the 15 and the 4 to show the difference of 19.*

Questions and Discussion

▲▲

▲ *Why is working with nonstandard measurements important?*

One of the important aspects of measurement is understanding the unit of measure. By working with familiar units such as paper clips, Popsicle sticks, or interlocking cubes, students can begin to understand that quantities are measured in equal units. When making measurement comparisons, it is important for students to see that the quantities must be measured with the same unit. Students are able to see that the length of one pencil measured in paper clips cannot be compared to the length of another pencil measured in cubes. Moving too quickly to rulers or measuring tapes can confuse students because of the fractional markings on those tools. By starting with counting nonstandard units such as cubes, students are better able to move to the more abstract units of measurement represented by the numbers on rulers and tapes. If students measure an object in cubes, they count the number of cubes, but when using a ruler or a measuring tape, they often make the mistake of starting with 1 rather than starting at the end of the ruler or the tape. Using nonstandard units can help students understand these basic measurement concepts.

▲ *How can you get students to work well with partners?*

Students work well with others when they are given opportunities to work together daily. Students cannot be expected to work together effectively without practice. When first starting partner work, it is important to design partner tasks that are of short duration and will ensure success. Taking the time to discuss how to work together, how to be a good partner, and what to do when a partnership is not going well is essential.

CHAPTER FOUR
HOW MANY POCKETS?

Overview

This lesson uses the number of pockets that children are wearing to give them experience with estimation, addition, and subtraction. To begin the activity the students estimate the total number of pockets in the class. Then each child records on a sticky note the number of pockets he or she has, and the students organize the sticky notes into a class graph. Each student builds a train of interlocking cubes to represent his or her own number of pockets, and small groups find the total number of pockets at their own tables. Finally, children figure the total number of pockets in the classroom and compare the actual amount with their estimates. The activity can be revisited and extended, and children can make comparisons about the total number of pockets on different days. You can also use the children's book *Chrysanthemum*, by Kevin Henkes, with this activity.

Materials

▲ interlocking cubes, 30 per group of four students
▲ 3-by-3-inch sticky notes, 1 per student
▲ optional: *Chrysanthemum*, by Kevin Henkes (New York: Greenwillow Books, 1991)

Time

▲ one to two class periods, then fifteen to thirty minutes for each revisit

Teaching Directions

1. Ask the students to estimate how many pockets the whole class is wearing today. If you've previously read *Chrysanthemum* to the class, ask students to recall how many pockets were on the outfit Chrysanthemum wore to school. Show the page from the book to verify that she had seven pockets.

2. Have each student count the number of pockets he or she is wearing.

3. Have each student record his or her number of pockets on a sticky note and post it on the board.

4. Ask the students to help you organize the data. Find out who has the least and the most number of pockets. Discuss the range. Ask which number of pockets came up the most; tell the children that this number is called the mode.

5. Ask the students to think about their original estimates, decide if they would like to change them, and explain their reasoning.

6. Have the students build trains of interlocking cubes to represent their pocket numbers and organize themselves into a circle starting with those with zero pockets and ending with those with the most number of pockets.

7. Have the students figure out the total number of pockets at their tables.

8. Record the total for each table on the board. Ask students for their ideas for adding the numbers for each table to find the total number of pockets for the class. As children explain their strategies, record their methods on the board and figure the total.

9. Ask groups to organize their cubes into trains of ten. Collect the tens and count them aloud with the class—"ten, twenty, thirty," and so on. Combine the remaining cubes from tables into tens and then add on the extras. This total should match the total number of pockets from the previous step.

10. For another check, have the students individually add the amounts on the sticky notes on paper. Ask them to show their methods.

Teaching Notes

How Many Pockets? is an engaging lesson that can be taught on the first day of school and then repeated many times throughout the school year. The context of the lesson is something students can personally relate to, the mathematics is accessible, and there are many opportunities to connect this activity with other areas of mathematics. Finding the total number of pockets the class is wearing on any particular day can be done in a variety of ways. At first, the activity can be done concretely, using interlocking cubes to represent pockets. The students make individual cube trains showing the number of pockets they are wearing, combine their trains by grouping them into tens, and then count the total number. This helps students move away from counting by ones and can reinforce place value. Students can also write their pocket numbers on individual sticky notes and organize the notes in a graph that can be used to find the total. Using a sticky note graph can help children see that numbers can be combined in many different ways. It is also a good visual model for skip-counting. The graph can also be used to discuss range and mode. The total number of pockets can also be found using mental computation, with each student adding on to the subtotal until everyone has been counted. If this lesson is repeated many times throughout the year, students can become familiar with looking at statistics over time and begin to develop an intuitive sense of what might be typical or atypical for pockets on any given day. They can predict what might happen the next day or compare the totals of different days.

The Lesson

▲▲▲

After gathering the class in a circle at the front of the room, Lynne asked, "Do you remember when we read *Chrysanthemum?* Do you recall that Chrysanthemum wore her outfit with lots of pockets to school one day?" Most of the students in the class nodded their heads.

"She loaded all the pockets with good luck charms," Kelly recalled.

"Well, I'll really test your memory now. Do you remember exactly how many pockets were on her outfit?" The students called out several different numbers, but most weren't really sure how many there were.

"I know there were seven pockets, because it's a lucky number," Sonja told the class.

"You're right," Lynne said as she showed the class the page from the book. "Is anyone wearing seven pockets today?" The children began to count their pockets.

"I've got four," Maria yelled.

"So do I," Diana added.

"I've got ten," bragged Kim, who was wearing overalls that day.

Lynne interrupted the students by saying, "We're going to find out how many pockets each of you has today and we're also going to find out how many pockets we have in all."

"I don't have any pockets," lamented Brian who was wearing sweats.

"That's OK," Lynne said. "We're going to be doing this activity on other days and you might have pockets then. But even if you have no pockets, you will still be able to participate."

Lynne then asked the class to estimate how many pockets the children might have altogether that day. She recorded the numbers on the board as the students called them out. The estimates ranged from ten to three hundred pockets. "What do you think about this range of estimates?" she asked.

"I know there's a lot more than ten," Kim said, "because I already have ten."

"I don't think there are three hundred," Diana said. "If everyone in the class had ten pockets it would be about three hundred, and nobody except Kim has ten."

Lynne then said to the students, "Count again to check exactly how many pockets you are wearing. Then you'll write the number on a sticky note." Lynne showed them the pad of 3-by-3-inch sticky notes she had.

"What do I do if I have no pockets?" Brian asked.

"You write a zero on your sticky note," Lynne said.

After the students stuck their notes on the chalkboard, Lynne asked them to help her rearrange the data in a more organized way. The students suggested placing the data from the smallest to the largest number of pockets across the board horizontally, putting numbers that were the same in columns.

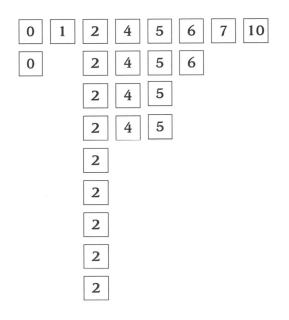

The number of pockets ranged from zero to ten. "Which numbers came up the most?" Lynne asked.

"Four and five have a lot," Jennifer said.

"Two has even more," Brendan offered. "It has the most, with nine."

"The number with the most responses is called the mode," Lynne instructed.

"What if two of them are the same and the most?" asked Susan, who was always extremely inquisitive about numbers.

"Then our graph is called bimodal," Lynne answered.

"Then three the same would be trimodal, right?" Susan asked.

"I'm not sure, but that certainly makes sense. I'll have to check with a mathematician," Lynne said, laughing.

Continuing with the lesson, Lynne asked, "Looking at this data on the board, how many of you would change the estimates you first made about the number of pockets in the entire class?" Several students raised their hands.

Lynne added, "Why did you change? Who can explain his or her thinking?"

"My guess was much too small," Gina said.

"How do you know it's too small?" Lynne probed.

"I guessed forty, and I can already see that there are nine people with two pockets and that's eighteen, and there are four people with five pockets and that's twenty. Together, that's thirty-eight, and I haven't even added the other numbers like the fours and the sixes."

"What about the estimate of three hundred?" Lynne asked the class. "Do you think that is a reasonable estimate?"

"I was the one who guessed three hundred," Ben admitted. "Now I don't think we'll even make one hundred."

"Why not?" Lynne continued.

"I just did part of it in my head, and it only came out to be sixty-five and there are only three more things to add."

"What did you add?"

"I added the one and the eighteen from the twos to make nineteen. Then I added the sixteen from the four fours and got

thirty-five. Then I added the four fives and got fifty-five and the one ten to get sixty-five. I only have two sixes and one seven left," Ben explained.

"It's important to be able to change your estimates as you get more information," Lynne added. "Estimates are only guesses, but some estimates can get closer to the actual amount as we gather more data."

Lynne had a container of interlocking cubes and asked the students to take one cube for each pocket they were wearing.

"But I don't have any pockets," Brian complained.

"If you have zero pockets, don't take any cubes," Lynne answered.

After all the students with pockets had their cubes, she asked them to connect the cubes and hold up their trains.

"Now I want you to rearrange yourselves in a circle," Lynne instructed. "Everyone with no pockets will start here by me, and then the people with one pocket will sit together. Next to them will be the people with two pockets, three pockets, and so on, until we get to Kim with ten pockets. Don't forget to bring your cube trains with you."

After the students moved, Eric commented, "Look at all the people with two pockets."

"I'm not the only one with zero pockets," Brian said.

"I know there aren't over a one hundred pockets today. I agree with Ben," Jeffrey said.

Lynne then instructed the children to return to their seats with their trains of cubes and find the total number of pockets at each table. As Lynne went from group to group, she saw that children at some tables were adding the numbers of cubes in the trains while others were counting cubes one by one.

"Leave your cube trains at your tables, and come up to the front of the room so we can write down the table totals," Lynne said. When the children gathered, she wrote the totals they reported horizontally on the board.

Table 1	Table 2	Table 3	Table 4	Table 5
14	18	14	26	12

Lynne said, "Let's add these numbers together and see how many pockets we have altogether. Does anyone have a way to begin?"

As the students suggested and tried various strategies, Lynne recorded their thinking on the board.

Gina, for example, added the tens first and got sixty. Then she added the ones and got twenty-four. Lynne wrote:

10 + 10 + 10 + 20 + 10 = 60

4 + 8 + 4 + 6 + 2 = 24

60 + 24 = 84

Thomas looked for friendly numbers. He added twelve plus eighteen to get thirty, then twenty-six plus fourteen to get forty. He added those subtotals to get seventy, and then added on the fourteen to get eighty-four. Lynne wrote:

12 + 18 = 30

26 + 14 = 40

30 + 40 = 70

70 + 14 = 84

After a few more students explained their methods, Lynne commented, "It looks like eighty-four is the correct total, but is there a way we can check?"

"We could count all of our cubes," Luis said.

"Let's do that," Lynne said. She had the students go back to their tables and put their cubes into groups of ten. She collected the groups of ten as the class counted. "Ten, twenty, thirty, forty, fifty, sixty."

After the tens were collected, Lynne took the four extra cubes from Table 1 and

asked, "How many more do I need to make a ten?"

"Six," the class called out.

"We have six left over," Jennifer shouted at Table 4.

Lynne continued, "That makes seventy so far. I see that Table 2 has eight cubes."

"We have two cubes to make ten," Diana said at Table 5.

"That makes eighty. Are there any cubes left?" Lynne asked.

"We've got four more," Maria said at Table 3.

"That makes eighty-four, so we've double-checked ourselves," Lynne said. "But I have one more way for us to be sure. See if the numbers on the sticky notes add up to eighty-four. Record how you add these numbers on a piece of paper."

The students got out paper and pencils and went to work. Lynne went to each table as the students worked, noting the addition strategies they used to find the total number of pockets. (See Figure 4–1 for one student's strategy.)

As the students finished, Lynne asked them to compare their original estimates with the actual number of pockets the class was wearing that day. (See Figure 4–2 for one student's comparison.)

While the students were getting ready for recess, Lynne told the class, "We'll be doing *How Many Pockets?* a lot this year. I want you to think about this question as you are walking outside: Will we always

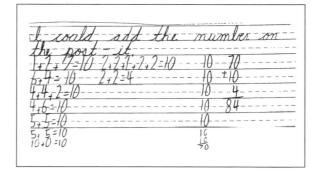

▲▲▲▲▲▲**Figure 4–1** *Thomas made tens in all the ways he could.*

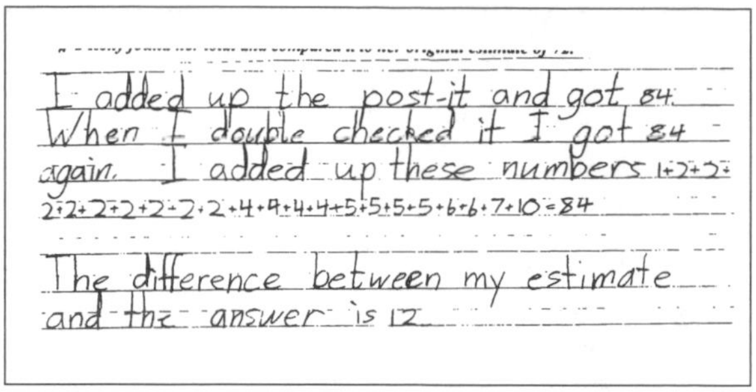

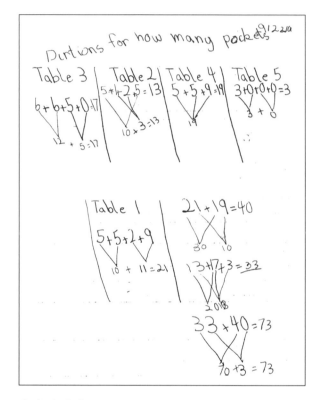

I added up the post-it and got 84.
When I double checked it I got 84
again. I added up these numbers 1·2·2·
2·2·2·2·2·2·2·2·4·4·4·4·5·5·5·5·6·6·7·10=84

The difference between my estimate
and the answer is 12.

▲▲▲▲▲▲Figure 4–2 *Kelly found her total and compared it to her original estimate of 72.*

▲▲▲▲▲▲Figure 4–3 *On another day, Sonja first found the total number of pockets at each table and then combined those subtotals by adding the tens and the ones separately.*

have eighty-four pockets?" (Figure 4–3 shows one student's work when the class revisited the activity.)

EXTENSIONS

1. After doing *How Many Pockets?* the second time, begin a record of each time the class counts pockets. Record the data on a chart or a graph. See how the number of pockets changes throughout the year. Ask some of the following questions as new data is collected:

How many more or fewer pockets did we have today than the last time we counted pockets?

What is the difference between the least amount of pockets and the greatest amount of pockets we have ever counted?

Do you think another class might have the same amount of pockets as we have today?

Do you think the weather has anything to do with the number of pockets we are wearing?

How many more pockets will we need to wear to reach one hundred? five hundred? one thousand?

If I told you we were counting pockets tomorrow, how would you be able to influence the results?

2. For practice with adding mentally, have students sit in a circle with their cube trains. Go around the circle adding on to the number of pockets each time. Have each student verbalize the adding as follows:

There are thirty-two pockets. I have five. Now there are thirty-seven.

There are thirty-seven pockets. I have four. Now there are forty-one.

Continue in this way until everyone has been counted.

3. Have the students write a plan with directions for figuring out the number of pockets the class is wearing. The students can then collect the data they need to actually solve the problem. Having students describe strategies in their own words is a useful assessment tool and gives them an opportunity to communicate mathematically. Figures 4–4 through 4–6 shows three students' strategies.

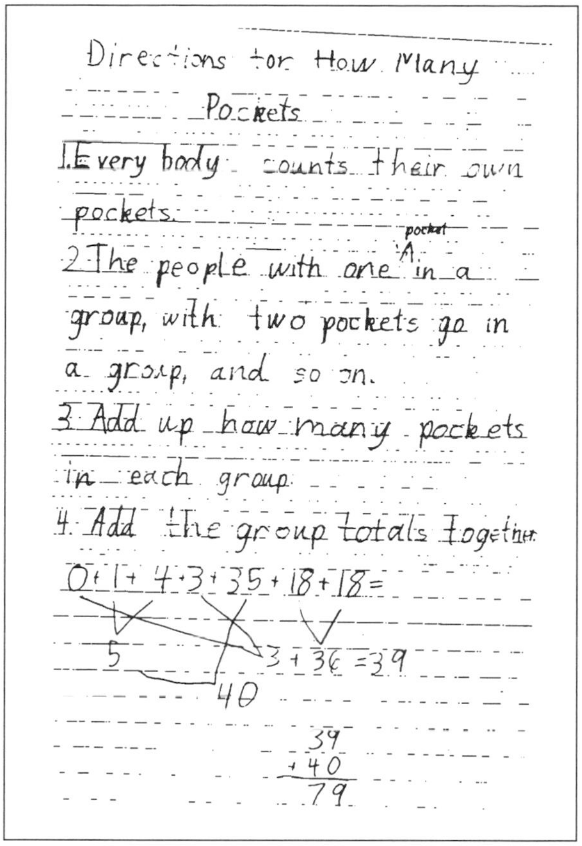

Directions for How Many
Pockets

1. Every body counts their own
pockets.
2 The people with one ^pocket in a
group, with two pockets go in
a group, and so on.
3 Add up how many pockets
in each group
4. Add the group totals together
0 + 1 + 4 · 3 + 35 + 18 + 18 =

5   3 + 36 = 39
     40
              39
            + 40
              79

▲▲▲▲▲▲Figure 4–4 *Dylan followed his own plan to find the total number of pockets.*

Directions For How Many Pockets
First, everybody takes some cubes in
the same amount of their pockets. If you
don't have any don't take any. Then everybody
adds them around people in a circle Then
to double check. put the cubes in tens. Then count
them by tens. If there are leftovers add
them together.

▲▲▲▲▲▲Figure 4–6 *Brian described a method of finding the total number of pockets using cubes and then explained a method for double-checking his work.*

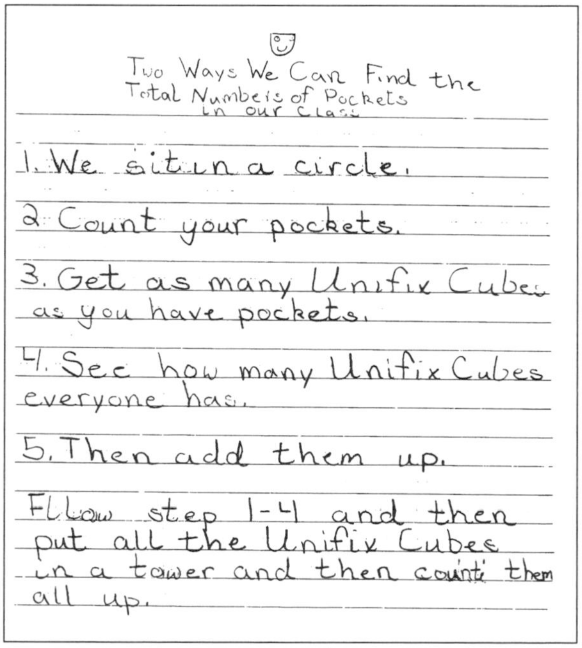

Two Ways We Can Find the
Total Numbers of Pockets
in our class

1. We sit in a circle.

2 Count your pockets.

3. Get as many Unifix Cubes
as you have pockets.

4. See how many Unifix Cubes
everyone has.

5. Then add them up.

Fllow step 1–4 and then
put all the Unifix Cubes
in a tower and then count them
all up.

▲▲▲▲▲▲Figure 4–5 *Gabi explained two ways to find the number of pockets in the class.*

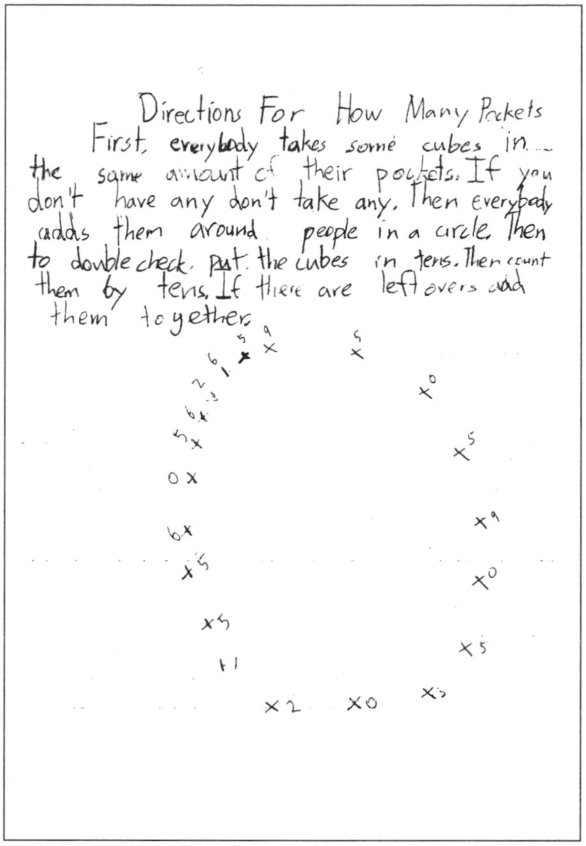

Questions and Discussion

▲▲▲

▲ *Don't students get tired of doing the same lesson over many times?*

Teachers often worry that children resent repeating an activity. It has been our experience that if the activity is engaging and holds some personal interest, students look forward to doing it again. There is a certain comfort level in being familiar with an activity. With *How Many Pockets?* students soon realize that the number of pockets always varies. Not knowing the final answer on any day until the data is collected keeps the lesson interesting and fresh. Also, by repeating the activity, students fine-tune their estimation skills.

▲ *When the children were figuring the number of pockets at their tables, Lynne saw some children adding the numbers of cubes in the trains while others were counting cubes one by one. Is this a concern, and is there something a teacher should do to help all children think about combining numbers, not just counting?*

Children need lots of counting experiences to develop a sense of numbers. As students begin working with addition, however, they need to develop strategies other than counting by ones to find an answer. Spending time with basic facts less than ten and with those combinations that make ten builds the foundation for adding all other numbers. Recognizing and practicing strategies for addition of both small and large numbers is also important and enables students to develop speed and efficiency. The following are some examples of useful addition strategies:

Building from a Knowledge of Doubles (6 + 6 = 12, 7 + 7 = 14, etc.)

   Doubles + 1: 6 + 7 = (6 + 6) +1

   Doubles − 1: 6 + 7 = (7 + 7) − 1

Going to the Nearest Ten

   8 + 7 = 10 + 5 (Take two from the seven and add to the eight)

Adding the Smaller Number to the Larger Number

   9 + 2 instead of 2 + 9

Applying One-Digit Facts to Addition of Larger Numbers

   3 + 6 = 9

   13 + 6 = 19

   53 + 26 = 79

   30 + 60 = 90

Rounding to Landmark Numbers Such as the Nearest Ten, to Twenty-Five, or to One Hundred and Then Compensating for the Difference

   39 + 56 = (40 + 56) − 1

   23 + 75 = (25 + 75) − 2

   60 + ? = 105 (Add forty to make one hundred and add five more to make one hundred five; 40 + 5 = 45, so missing addend is forty-five.)

▲ How can we help develop children's facility with mental computation?

Students get better at doing mental computation by doing it often. Writing numbers horizontally is useful for helping students focus on the quantities at hand and make use of their knowledge of place value. When considering numbers written horizontally, students typically combine the tens first. When students see numbers written vertically, however, they often begin adding or subtracting in the ones column and lose all sense of the quantities.

▲ Why do you record the ways students compute?

There are two main reasons for recording the ways in which students explain their computational strategies. The first is to ensure that you are following the student's thinking. Take the example of 16 + 49:

Luis' explanation: "Take one from the sixteen and add it to the forty-nine to make fifty. Then add fifteen and fifty to get sixty-five." Record:

$16 - 1 = 15$

$49 + 1 = 50$

$15 + 50 = 65$

Gina's explanation: "Add the tens and then add the ones." Record:

$10 + 40 = 50$

$6 + 9 = 15$

$50 + 15 = 65$

Jennifer's explanation: "Add the tens. Then start adding on the ones."

$10 + 40 = 50$

$50 + 6 = 56$

$56 + 9 = 65$

Although Gina and Jennifer have similar methods, the actual account of their mathematical thinking differs.

The second reason for recording computation is to give visual models of students' thinking to their peers as they listen to their strategies. By tapping into the visual as well as the auditory learning mode, you'll give students greater access to understanding and accepting the various ways computation can be done.

▲ Why do you introduce vocabulary that may be above the level of most of the class?

Introducing mathematical vocabulary informally helps lay the groundwork for more advanced mathematics at a later date. When students hear these terms in the future, they are not totally alien or intimidating. The danger lies in expecting complete understanding of the terms or requiring students to memorize definitions of the vocabulary too soon. There is always a range of abilities and interest in any class and not every child takes the same meaning or understanding away from a lesson. However, using precise mathematical terms when answering a question, presenting a lesson, or discussing student work can be beneficial.

CHAPTER FIVE
BILLY GOES SHOPPING

Overview

For this activity, students go shopping for Billy. This imaginary character has one dollar to spend on a variety of school supplies, which are listed on a price list. Once students select their purchases, they find the total cost and figure out how much change Billy would get from his dollar. Students have an opportunity to act out the shopping situation, taking turns being Billy and the shopkeeper. They use coins to help them figure their solutions and they keep track of the transactions on receipt forms.

Materials

▲ price lists of items to buy (see Blackline Masters), 1 per pair of students
▲ small baggies with 10 dimes and 10 pennies each, 1 per pair of students
▲ play dollar bills, 1 per pair of students (see Blackline Masters)
▲ copies of directions for *Billy Goes Shopping* (see Blackline Masters)

Note: We used real dimes and pennies because we already had them in baggies from previous activities and found that coins were rarely missing from them. Play money will work just as well. We duplicated the play dollars on green copier paper and cut them out. Sometimes we have presented this activity as an independent choice activity. This means not all students would be doing the activity at the same time, so fewer baggies of coins would be necessary.

Time

▲ two class periods

Teaching Directions

1. Introduce the activity to the class. Tell the class that Billy has one dollar to spend and has to buy some school supplies. They will each help Billy select items from the following price list:

Eraser	$.10
Ruler	$.29
Pencil	$.25
Pen	$.39
Book cover	$.20
Key chain	$.32
Marking pen	$.28
Glue stick	$.30

2. Tell the students that they will do this activity with partners. Partners will take turns being the shopkeeper and Billy. Billy chooses some things to buy. He can buy different things or more than one of the same thing. However, this store allows customers to buy no more than two of each item. The shopkeeper writes a receipt to record the items purchased, the price of each item, and the total cost. Once Billy decides what he will purchase, he gives the shopkeeper his dollar, and the shopkeeper records the transaction and gives the change needed. After one shopping transaction is completed, partners change roles. Each student should go shopping at least two times.

3. Once you have described the directions to the class, have two students model doing the activity as partners. Have students show how they would decide who will be Billy and who will be the shopkeeper for the first transaction. Give the shopkeeper a bag of dimes and pennies and the receipt form. Give Billy a dollar and the price list.

4. Guide the two students through a sample shopping trip. Billy decides what to buy, and the shopkeeper writes down what Billy purchases. The shopkeeper figures out the total, Billy gives him the dollar, and the shopkeeper gives Billy the change.

5. Show the class how to complete the receipt form by recording the transaction on the chalkboard:

Customer:

Shopkeeper:

Date:

Quantity	*Item*	*Cost*
1	*key chain*	*$.32*
1	*marking pen*	*$.28*
2	*erasers*	*$.20*
	Total	*$.80*
	Change	*$.20*

You may want to post the directions somewhere in the classroom for students to refer to or hand out copies to each pair.

6. After all the students have completed the activity, lead a class discussion as follows:

▲ First, ask for volunteers to explain how they calculated the amount they spent and the change they received.

▲ Ask if any students spent exactly one dollar. Ask them to report what they bought.

▲ Ask students to think of other ways Billy could have spent exactly one dollar.

▲ Pose another problem: *If you could buy more than two of each item on the price list, what other ways could you spend exactly $1.00?*

▲ Ask students to report how much they spent and the change they received. Record on a class chart, for example:

Spent	Change
$.95	$.05
$.98	$.02
$.92	$.08

▲ Ask students to look for and describe patterns they see in the amounts spent and change received.

Teaching Notes

The context of this experience draws upon students' interest both in money and in play-acting. The activity gives students an opportunity to practice writing dollars and cents in proper notation while finding the total amount spent and figuring out how much change they would get from a dollar.

Having coins to help them find the totals and figure out the change gives students a tool for finding solutions. The coins also provide the props to complete the playacting scenario. However, the coins do not guarantee that students will learn to use numbers confidently in real situations. It is through the activity itself and the follow-up discussions that they will develop a flexibility with numbers that will serve them in new situations.

We want to encourage students to look at patterns in the numbers and to see how numbers are related. Students need to recognize that knowing these relationships will help them solve problems and that every problem is not a new situation. During the discussions about students' strategies and solutions it is important to ask questions that allow students to think and reflect on their understanding. It is also critical to encourage all students to talk and be engaged in thinking and reflecting. We continually try new ways to increase involvement so more students have a chance to engage in thoughtful dialogue. Sometimes we have partners talk to each other before we hear from a few. At other times we have students work in small groups and write their responses prior to sharing with the class. Whenever possible, we interact individually with students to hear their thinking.

The Lesson

▲▲▲

DAY 1

"Today you will learn how to do an activity that requires you to be a customer and a shopkeeper," Bonnie told the class.

Bonnie posted an enlarged version of the price list on the front board.

"The name of the activity is *Billy Goes Shopping*," Bonnie told the class. "For this activity you need a partner, a baggie of coins, a dollar bill, and paper for the receipt. First you will decide who will be Billy and who will be the shopkeeper. Then Billy looks at the price list and decides what to buy. He tells the shopkeeper what he will buy and how many of each. He can buy up to two of each item. The shopkeeper makes a receipt to record what Billy buys and figures the cost. Remember, Billy only has a dollar to spend. After Billy is finished with his shopping, the shopkeeper figures out the total cost and how much change Billy will get. After this transaction is completed, you change roles. The shopkeeper will be Billy and Billy will be the shopkeeper."

The class was eager to get started with this activity.

"Before you go off on your own to do this activity, let's do a sample so you all are clear on what to do," Bonnie suggested. "Let's have Carissa and Louise show us how to be partners for this activity," she continued as she provided the baggie of coins and paper for the receipt.

"What's the first thing Carissa and Louise need to do?" Bonnie asked the class.

"Decide who will be Billy," Francesca told us.

Carissa and Louise looked at each other and whispered something.

"Show us how partners could decide who will be Billy," Bonnie urged.

"Do you want to be Billy or the store-keeper?" Carissa asked Louise.

"The storekeeper," Louise replied, picking up the paper and a pencil.

"Now what?" Bonnie asked the class.

"Billy should buy something and give her some money," Ronald called out.

"I think I'll buy a pen," Carissa began.

"As Carissa decides what to buy, I'll write it on the board so you will all know how to make a receipt," Bonnie told the class. She wrote:

1 pen $.39

Carissa then selected two erasers, a book cover, and a pencil. Bonnie continued recording:

1 pen $.39

2 erasers $.20

1 book cover $.20

1 pencil $.25

"That's more than a dollar," Kyle called out.

"How do you know?" Bonnie asked.

Kyle came up to the board as he explained, "Thirty-nine cents is almost forty, plus twenty is sixty, twenty more is eighty, and twenty-five more would be over a dollar."

"I think I won't buy the pencil," Carissa suggested.

"Let's figure out the total now," Bonnie said as she erased the pencil from the receipt. "While we're figuring it out in our heads, Carissa and Louise can use the money to find the total."

After giving Carissa and Louise a chance to find the total, Bonnie asked for volunteers to tell how they had found the total.

"I added the two twenties and got forty," Alan began, "then I put the forty with thirty-nine and got seventy-nine."

Julian explained his approach next, "I thought of thirty-nine as forty and added forty plus twenty equals sixty then sixty plus twenty is eighty. But I have to take off one because I added one to the thirty-nine."

"For this transaction, Billy spent seventy-nine cents," Bonnie stated as she wrote the total on the board. "How much change should Louise give to Carissa?"

"She should get twenty-one cents," Alexei offered.

"How do you know?" Bonnie asked.

"It's just one more to get to eighty, plus ten to ninety, and ten more to one hundred. That's twenty-one cents left," he explained.

Bonnie wrote on the board:

79 + 1 = 80

80 + 10 = 90

90 + 10 = 100

"One hundred what?" she asked.

"It's really a dollar," Nichole said.

"On the receipt, I have to make sure I let the customer know what that one hundred means," Bonnie instructed as she added this information to the sample receipt form.

1 pen	$.39
2 erasers	$.20
1 book cover	$.20
Total	$.79
Change	$.21

Partners picked up their materials before returning to their seats to begin the activity. Before long there was a hum of enthusiasm. The whole class was quickly engrossed in shopping and playing store-keeper. Some even wrote on their receipt forms: *Thank you, come again*. Figures 5–1 and 5–2 show how two pairs recorded their transactions.

DAY 2

The next day, Bonnie gave the class enough time for each person to complete at least

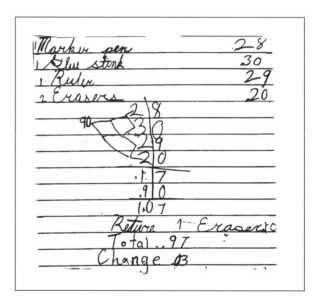

▲▲▲▲▲▲Figure 5–1   *Nichole and Kyle figured out the change mentally.*

▲▲▲▲▲▲Figure 5–2   *When Jennifer and Max figured their total, they added the tens and the ones separately.*

two transactions. She encouraged them to check their totals and be sure they had listed the change. By circulating among the partners and reviewing their work, Bonnie found some examples that would provide starting points for discussion.

When the students had each completed at least two shopping transactions, Bonnie asked them to come to the front of the classroom with their partners and their shopping receipts.

"What did you think of the activity *Billy Goes Shopping?*" Bonnie asked the class.

"It's pretty mathematical," Francesca offered.

"How was it mathematical?" Bonnie probed.

"We were working with money and you had to figure out the change," Kyle responded.

"It was fun," Alvin added.

"How many of you enjoyed this activity?" Bonnie inquired.

There seemed to be a consensus that spending money was enjoyable.

"Now I'm interested in hearing how some of you spent Billy's money," Bonnie said. "I wonder if Billy could have spent exactly one dollar."

"We did it!" Alvin told us enthusiastically.

"Come up and show us what you spent and how you know it was exactly one dollar," Bonnie directed.

Alvin and his partner, Maxim, came up and worked together to show what they had spent:

$.32

$.28

$.20

$.20

Alvin showed how he knew it was one dollar by writing on the board:

30 + 20 = 50

2 + 8 = 10

50 + 10 = 60

20 + 20 = 40

60 + 40 = 100

"Where did Alvin get all those numbers?" Bonnie wondered aloud. "Where did the thirty plus twenty come from? Talk to the person next to you and see if you can explain why Alvin wrote thirty plus twenty."

After giving the students a chance to talk to each other, she called on Jennifer.

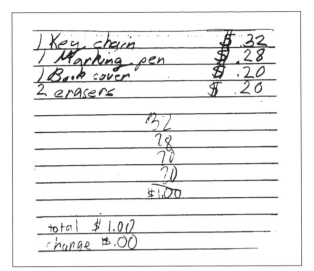

▲▲▲▲▲Figure 5–3 *Alvin and Maxim made sure their purchases came out to exactly $1.00.*

"The thirty is from the thirty-two cents and the twenty is from twenty-eight cents," she stated clearly.

"What about the fifty plus ten?" Bonnie continued.

Kevin raised his hand. "He took the fifty from here," he explained while coming to the board to point to the numbers, "and the two and eight from this part he didn't add before and made the ten."

"What did Alvin do next?" Bonnie asked.

"He put the two twenties with the sixty and got one hundred," Jennifer said quickly.

Maxim proceeded to show how he figured the total by doing the traditional algorithm, adding the numbers in a column.

"Did anyone else spend exactly one dollar?" Bonnie continued.

Kenneth raised his hand and shared how he and Kyle had bought two erasers, two glue sticks, and one book cover.

"Two twenties makes forty, plus sixty equals exactly one dollar," Kyle explained concisely.

Eager to have more students involved in finding sums that add to exactly one dollar, Bonnie posed the following, "What if you can buy more than two of one item on the price list; are there other ways to spend exactly one dollar?"

Billy Goes Shopping **37**

Bonnie gave them a minute to think about this question, then asked students to tell each other what they had found before asking students to share their ideas.

"You could buy ten erasers," Jennifer told us.

"Five book covers would be five twenties," Eric suggested.

"Four pencils would cost one dollar," Louise piped in.

"Let's collect some of the other totals Billy spent," Bonnie said while starting a chart on the board. "Did anyone spend ninety-nine cents?" she asked.

Maxim raised his hand.

"What change did you get?" Bonnie asked.

"One cent," he responded.

Bonnie continued collecting the information in this way:

Spent	Change
$.99	$.01
$.98	$.02
$.95	$.05
$.92	$.08
$.90	$.10

After collecting several pairs of totals and change, Bonnie continued by asking, "What if Billy spent eighty cents? How about seventy cents?"

She added these to the list.

$.80	$.20
$.70	$.30

"What if he spent fifty-five cents? What if he spent forty-five cents?" Bonnie asked as she added these numbers to the list.

$.55	$.45
$.45	$.55

"When you look at these numbers, what are some things you notice?" Bonnie asked.

"When the total ends in a zero, the change ends in a zero," Kyle offered.

"Who can give an example of what Kyle sees?" Bonnie asked.

"When the total is ninety cents, the change would be ten cents and the same with eighty cents and twenty cents," Kevin explained.

Bonnie started a new list on the board:

$.90	$.10
$.80	$.20
$.70	$.30

"What other pairs of numbers belong on this list?" Bonnie asked. "Take a minute to think about it and then I'll hand the chalk to some of you so you can add to the list."

After seeing that most students had an idea, Bonnie handed the chalk to Alan, who wrote *sixty cents* and *forty cents*. She instructed Alan to give the chalk to a new person so someone else could add another pair. This continued until the list was complete.

$.90	$.10
$.80	$.20
$.70	$.30
$.60	$.40
$.50	$.50
$.40	$.60
$.30	$.70
$.20	$.80
$.10	$.90

Bonnie decided to have students talk about the patterns in these numbers another time and made a note to also explore the patterns in number pairs like $.55, $.45 and $.45, $.55.

Before ending the discussion, Bonnie asked one more question.

"When you're shopping for Billy, how can you tell if what you bought is less than a dollar or not? Look at your receipt forms and see if you can remember how you knew you had bought too much or were still under a dollar for your total."

Jason and Kenneth offered their system for making sure they were under a dollar when they finished shopping. "We would each buy four or five things. Then we'd add them up and if it was more than a dollar, we'd give something back," Jason explained.

"Could you give us an example?" Bonnie asked.

"Like one time we got a total and it came out to one dollar and four cents. So we gave one eraser back and subtracted ten cents from the total and got ninety-four cents." (See Figure 5–4.)

"Did anyone do it like Kenneth and Jason?" Bonnie inquired.

"We usually only bought three things," Jennifer reported. "Especially if you buy a pen or a glue stick, you might go over a dollar."

"We added them up as we wrote them down," Alvin explained.

"You'll have a chance to go shopping with Billy again this year," Bonnie told the class.

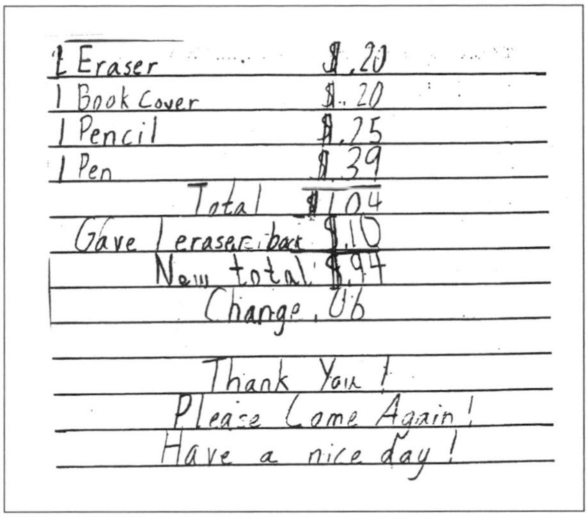

▲▲▲▲▲**Figure 5–4** *Jason had to return an item when he spent more than $1.00.*

"Can we do it again and have Billy spend two dollars?" Kenneth asked.

"Good idea," Bonnie responded, thinking that this would be a good homework assignment.

Questions and Discussion

▲▲

▲ *Is it OK for students to write thirty cents as 30¢, or should they write $.30?*

When students enter third grade, they have often learned the dollar sign and the cent sign. We decided that in third grade, we would encourage students to use the dollar sign and a decimal point for their work with money. This would be useful when they used the calculator and would give students a base to build on when they learned about decimal remainders in division later in the year.

▲ *Is it appropriate for students to use mental arithmetic for large numbers?*

Just as students can be fluent with basic facts for addition and subtraction, they can be fluent with sums to one hundred. All of the relationships in the sums of single-digit numbers can be found in the sums of numbers to one hundred. If students have access to the relationships for small numbers, they will be more able to do mental arithmetic with larger numbers.

▲ *How do you monitor whether students are calculating accurately?*

We usually ask students to check their answers using a second method. If they get a different answer, it causes them to go back and check their work. While students are working on problems, our goal is to check with individuals and ask questions when we see a student getting offtrack. However, with an activity like *Billy Goes Shopping*, where individuals are recording their transactions, we cannot always check each child's work immediately. We ask students to check each other, and we discuss some of their findings as a whole class.

It is very important to develop a classroom community that helps one another find where one's thinking or recording caused an error. When we look over finished work, we see that some students make computation errors. This gives us further information to use for conversations with individuals or in our whole-class discussions.

▲ Do you always model how you want the students' recording to look?

We often model how we want students to record so that when they go off to do an activity, they can get started more easily. Not all students need this kind of modeling, but for those who do, it gives them a place to start. We try to give the message that our model is one way to record, but that students may have another way to do it that makes more sense to them.

We give students a format for *Billy Goes Shopping* so that the focus is not on creating the form but rather on the number ideas we want them to explore. The decision about whether to model exactly how the paper should look is really based on what you want your students to learn in the time you have. When working with money, neatness and lining up the numbers often increases accuracy, but we also give students opportunities during the year to learn on their own that neatness and order are important.

CHAPTER SIX
MONEY COMES, MONEY GOES

Overview

This lesson gives children practice with the take-away model for subtraction. After reading *Alexander, Who Used to Be Rich Last Sunday,* by Judith Viorst, each student creates a story modeled after the book, using him- or herself as the main character. Each student begins with one, two, three, four, or five dollars and loses or spends the entire amount over the period of a week. The completed stories are rewritten or published into accordion-folded books. These stories give students practice with the take-away model of subtraction, the inverse relationship between addition and subtraction, and with monetary notation.

Materials

▲ *Alexander, Who Used to Be Rich Last Sunday,* by Judith Viorst (New York: Aladdin Books, 1988)

▲ 4-by-18-inch drawing paper, 3 pieces per student (Accordion fold each paper into $4\frac{1}{2}$-inch sections.)

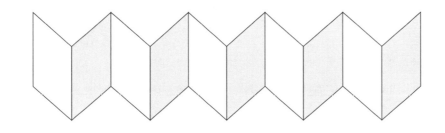

Time

▲ three to five class periods

Teaching Directions

1. Read *Alexander, Who Used to Be Rich Last Sunday* to the class.

2. Ask the students to figure out how much money each of Alexander's brothers had when the story began. (Anthony had $3.38; Nicholas had $2.38.)

3. Reread the story. During the reading, pause to write the following mathematical equation on the board, and ask the students how this equation relates to the story.

$.1.00 − $.15 = $.85$

4. Continue reading the story and writing the events mathematically.

$.85 − $.15 = $.70$

$.70 − $.12 = $.58$

$.58 − $.10 = $.48$

$.48 − $.03 = $.45$

$.45 − $.05 = $.40$

$.40 − $.11 = $.29$

$.29 − $.04 = $.25$

$.25 − $.05 = $.20$

$.20 − $.20 = 0$

5. Ask the students to use their imaginations to think of ways they could receive a dollar: receiving it as a gift from a relative, finding it on the ground, earning it, winning a bet, and so on.

6. Give them directions for creating their own Alexander stories:

▲ Each student will start with one, two, three, four, or five dollars. The student will pick a day of the week on which to receive the money. This will become the title of the book. For example: *Sandy, Who Used to Be Rich Last Tuesday* or *Justin, Who Used to Be Rich Last Saturday.*

▲ For each day of the week, the student will spend or lose a portion of the money received. The student will explain what happened to the money each day and write a subtraction sentence indicating how much money remains. When the week has gone by, there will be no money left.

7. Model a story on the chalkboard. Have the students help create the events of the story.

Jane, Who Used to Be Rich on Tuesday

On Tuesday I found $2.00 on the ground.

On Wednesday I bought used books for $.59.

($2.00 − $.59 = $1.41)

On Thursday I bought a pencil box for $.41.

($1.41 − $.41 = $1.00 left)

On Friday I bought a pencil for the pencil box for $.04.

($1.00 − $.04 = $.96 left)

On Saturday I bought some gum for $.11.

($.96 − $.11 = $.85 left)

On Sunday I lost a dime and two pennies ($.12).

($.85 − $.12 = $.73 left)

On Monday I bought a board game for $.73.

($.73 − $.73 = 0)

Tuesday: Last Tuesday I was rich, but this Tuesday I'm poor.

8. Pass out writing paper. Have each student write a title and his or her week's events in complete sentences. Below each event they should write a corresponding mathematical equation.

9. Pairs of students can do a check on each other's stories by adding the amounts lost or spent together. The sum should equal the amount originally received on the first day. Demonstrate by going back to the story and adding Alexander's losses, which should equal one dollar.

10. Give the stories a final check for grammatical and mathematical errors.

11. Have students transfer their corrected stories into accordion-folded books. The first page is the title page. The following eight pages should show the week's events from Tuesday to Tuesday (or whichever day the story begins). The tenth page is for "The End." Have students illustrate each page.

Teaching Notes

Students need many experiences with subtraction. The take-away model is commonly used to demonstrate subtraction and is probably the easiest model for most students to understand. In the model, there is one quantity. This quantity is changed by removing a part of the amount. Something leaves, something gets lost, or something is used or spent. The answer in the take-away model is what is left from the original set. For example, if you had fifty dollars and spent thirty-four dollars, the sixteen dollars represents what is left from the original set of fifty dollars. Money is a useful context for teaching the take-away model.

The Lesson

▲▲

DAY 1

"That Alexander wasn't very smart," Jennifer said laughingly as Lynne finished reading *Alexander, Who Used to Be Rich Last Sunday* to the class.

"What did the rest of you think about him?" Lynne asked.

The class had a lot to say about the character.

"He always got himself into trouble."

"He never had money because he was always making silly bets."

"His big brothers picked on him and played jokes on him."

Lynne then reminded the class that the book started with Alexander complaining that it wasn't fair that his two brothers had money and he didn't have any.

"Does anyone remember how much money his brothers had?"

Maria was the only one who raised her hand.

"I don't remember how much, but it was a lot of different coins."

"I'll read the amounts again and write them on the board," Lynne said.

Anthony	Nicholas
two dollars	one dollar
three quarters	two quarters
one dime	five dimes
seven nickels	five nickels
eighteen pennies	thirteen pennies

"Who had more money, Anthony or Nicholas?" Lynne asked.

"Anthony for sure," Eric answered.

"How do you know?"

"You can just look at the amounts," Eric explained. "The only thing Nicholas has more of is dimes and that's only forty cents more." Eric was able to look at numerical information and quickly make sense of it.

"What a good way to analyze the data," Lynne commented. "Now let's see exactly how much each brother had. See if you can figure out the amounts mentally or with paper and pencil. Start with whichever brother you wish."

"I'll start with Nicholas; he's easier," Ben said.

The students began calculating mentally. Some decided to use paper and pencil

to help them find the totals. Most of the students began with Nicholas.

After several minutes, Lynne stopped them and asked if anyone had a total.

"I do," Ben said.

Lynne had Ben share his paper with the class (see Figure 6–1).

Most of the students had figured out that Nicholas had $2.38, but no one had come up with Anthony's total.

"What would help you find the total?" Lynne asked.

"If we could keep track on the board," Brendan suggested.

"OK, let's do that," Lynne said. "Would you like to explain a way?"

"Sure," Brendan said. "If I add the two dollars and the seventy-five cents together and then add the dime, I get two dollars and eighty-five cents." Lynne wrote $2.85 on the board.

"Then I can use the nickels and count by fives: two ninety, two ninety-five, three, three ten, three twenty." Lynne continued keeping track on the board.

"Then I just add three twenty and eighteen and get three thirty-eight." Brendan understood that adding money can be done without the decimal points and converted his total to dollars and cents at the end of his calculations.

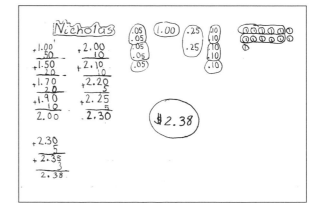

▲▲▲▲▲▲Figure 6–1 *Brendan found his total by drawing and circling groups of coins before adding.*

"Let's make sure that Brendan's answer is correct by doing it again another way," Lynne said.

The students went back to work. After several students had found a total, Lynne asked for volunteers to share their thinking.

Jeffrey began by showing how he subtotaled his dollars, quarters, nickels, dimes, and pennies (see Figure 6–2).

Gina offered her strategy. "Just put the dollars and the quarters together to get two seventy-five. Take five of the seven nickels to make a quarter and add that to the two seventy-five and you'll have three dollars. That leaves one dime, two nickels, and eighteen pennies, which adds up to thirty-eight cents. Altogether that makes three dollars and thirty-eight cents."

"Nicholas had two thirty-eight," Jennifer called out. "Anthony had exactly a dollar more."

"I wonder if the author did that on purpose," Lynne said.

"If she did do it on purpose, Alexander should have had one dollar and thirty-eight cents to make a pattern," Thomas offered.

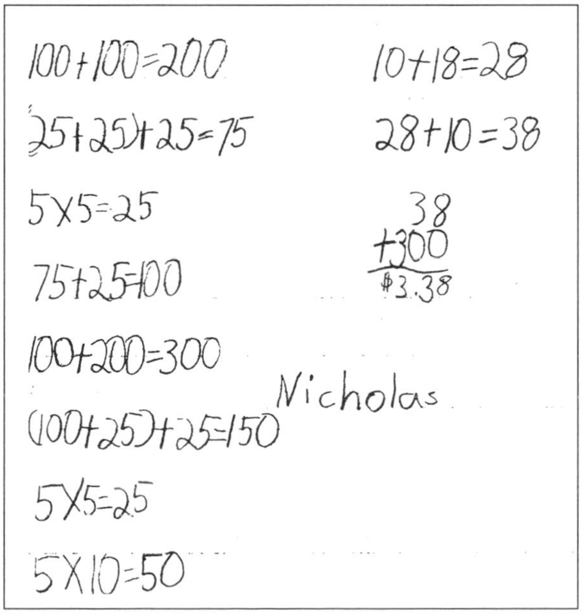

$$100+100=200$$
$$25+25+25=75$$
$$5 \times 5=25$$
$$75+25=100$$
$$100+200=300$$
$$(100+25)+25=150$$
$$5 \times 5=25$$
$$5 \times 10=50$$

$$10+18=28$$
$$28+10=38$$
$$\begin{array}{r} 38 \\ +300 \\ \hline \$3.38 \end{array}$$

Nicholas

▲▲▲▲▲▲Figure 6–2 *Jeffrey didn't use the dollar sign or a decimal point as he added, but he remembered to include them in his total.*

"She could have given him a dollar, one dime, three nickels, and thirteen pennies."

"He would have lost that money, too!" Ben added.

DAY 2

"Let's review how Alexander ended up with no money in the book we read yesterday," Lynne said as she continued the lesson from the day before.

Lynne began to reread the story and stopped after Alexander had spent fifteen cents on gum. She wrote $\$1.00 - \$.15 = \$.85$ on the board.

"What does this mathematical sentence mean?" she asked.

Lynne called on Albert, who explained, "Alexander started with one dollar, he spent fifteen cents, and now he has eighty-five cents left."

Lynne continued reading and the class reconstructed the entire story using mathematical sentences.

$$\$1.00 - \$.15 = \$.85$$
$$\$.85 \quad \$.15 = \$.70$$
$$\$.70 - \$.12 = \$.58$$
$$\$.58 - \$.10 = \$.48$$
$$\$.48 - \$.03 = \$.45$$
$$\$.45 - \$.05 = \$.40$$
$$\$.40 - \$.11 = \$.29$$
$$\$.29 - \$.04 = \$.25$$
$$\$.25 - \$.05 = \$.20$$
$$\$.20 - \$.20 = 0$$

"Today you are going to begin writing your own Alexander-type books," Lynne continued. "Your book will have *you* as the main character. You will receive an amount of money. It can be one dollar, two dollars, three dollars, four dollars, or five dollars. Use your imaginations to think of ways you could get that money."

The students suggested several ways they could receive the money. They said the money could be a gift, could fall from the sky, could be an allowance, or could be a contest prize.

"Next you will pick any day of the week to receive that money. You'll start your story on that day. Each day after that, you will spend or lose a part of your money in any way you choose. When the week is over, all your money will be gone. If you received money on Friday, you will lose some of your money on Saturday, some on Sunday, some on Monday, some on Tuesday, some on Wednesday, and the rest on Thursday. When it's Friday once again, you will be broke."

Lynne continued, "I will give you each a piece of paper. The title will be ______, *Who Used to Be Rich Last* ______. Put your name in the first blank. In the second blank, write the day of the week in which your story will start." Lynne wrote her name and *Wednesday* in the blanks on the board. "Then you will write what happened on each day. Be sure to keep track of how much money you have left."

"Before you start your stories, let's work together to create a story." The students volunteered ideas and together wrote the following story:

> *Mrs. Zolli, Who Used to Be Rich Last Wednesday*
>
> *On Wednesday, when I opened the front door to get my newspaper, I found two one-dollar bills on my doorstep.*
>
> *On Thursday I paid back $.65 that I owed my friend.*
>
> *$2.00 – $.65 = $1.35*
>
> *On Friday I had a hole in my pocket. I lost two dimes and six pennies.*
>
> *$1.35 – $.26 = $1.09*
>
> *On Saturday I went to a garage sale and spent $.50.*
>
> *$1.09 – $.50 = $.59*
>
> *On Sunday I gave my neighbor 15 pennies for her penny collection.*
>
> *$.59 – $.15 = $.44*
>
> *On Monday I made a wish and threw $.17 in a wishing well.*
>
> *$.44 – $.17 = $.27*
>
> *On Tuesday I went to the copy store and made three copies that cost $.09 each. I spent $.27.*
>
> *$.27 – $.27 = 0*
>
> *I used to be rich last Wednesday. Now I am broke.*

The students got to work, titling their stories, selecting the amount of money they wanted to receive, and beginning their stories. For the rest of the class period and during the next two days, the students wrote their stories and Lynne checked them. (See Figures 6–3 and 6–4.)

Then Lynne gathered the class together for a discussion. "Let's go back to the Alexander book," Lynne said, "and let's find all

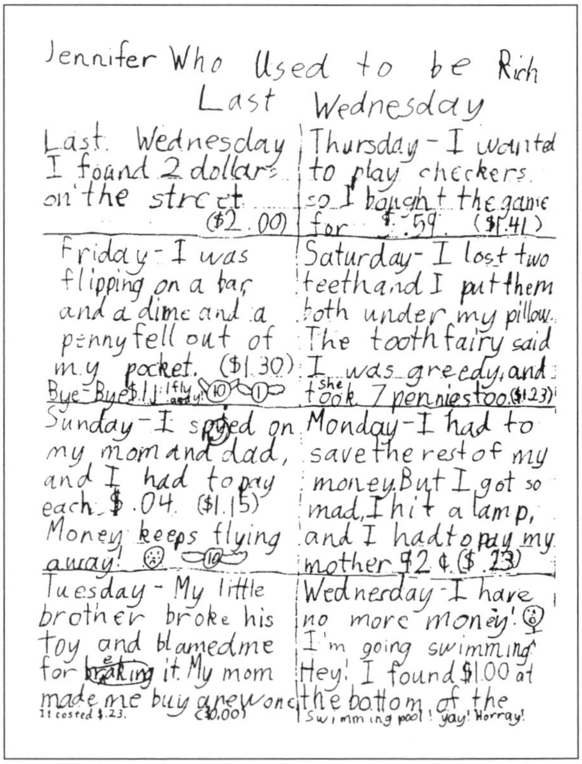
Jennifer Who Used to be Rich Last Wednesday

Last Wednesday I found 2 dollars on the street ($2.00)	Thursday - I wanted to play checkers so I bought the game for $.59. ($1.41)
Friday - I was flipping on a bar and a dime and a penny fell out of my pocket. ($1.30) Bye-Bye $.11! fly away!	Saturday - I lost two teeth and I put them both under my pillow. The tooth fairy said I was greedy, and she took 7 pennies too. ($1.23)
Sunday - I spied on my mom and dad, and I had to pay each $.04. ($1.15) Money keeps flying away!	Monday - I had to save the rest of my money. But I got so mad, I hit a lamp, and I had to pay my mother 92¢. ($.23)
Tuesday - My little brother broke his toy and blamed me for breaking it. My mom made me buy a new one. It costed $.23. ($0.00)	Wednesday - I have no more money! I'm going swimming. Hey! I found $1.00 at the bottom of the swimming pool! yay! Horray!

Figure 6–3 ***Jennifer wrote a rough draft and checked her work with Lynne before making her book.***

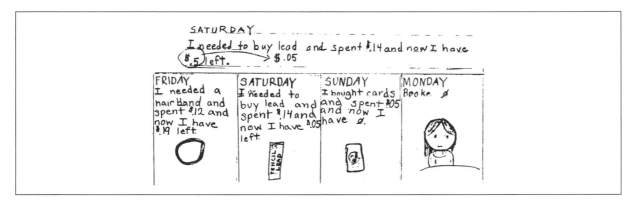

Kim originally used incorrect notation for five cents but made the correction after her draft was edited.

the ways Alexander lost his money." Lynne wrote a list on the board.

buying gum	*$.15*
losing bets	*$.15*
renting a snake	*$.12*
using bad swords	*$.10*
flushed coins	*$.03*
lost nickel	*$.05*
Anthony's candy	*$.11*
magic trick	*$.04*
kicking things	*$.05*
garage sale	*$.20*

"If I added up all of the ways Alexander spent or lost his money, what would I get?"

"You'll get a dollar because that's what he started with," Susan answered.

"That's correct," Lynne confirmed. "We've been taking away, or subtracting, money. Addition is the reverse of subtraction, so if we put the money back, we should get back to the original amount. To show you how subtraction and addition are related I would like some of you who have finished your stories to share the amounts you spent or lost."

Collin, who had started with one dollar, read off his amounts and Lynne wrote them on the board.

$.25 $.16 $.25 $.11 $.13 $.10

Lynne then asked Collin to help her add the amounts.

Collin explained, "Add the twenty-five and twenty-five to get fifty. Add the ten to get sixty. Add the sixteen and eleven to get twenty-seven and then add the thirteen to get forty. Add the sixty and the forty together and you get one dollar."

"Collin started with a one-dollar bill, so we've checked his work," Lynne added. (See Figure 6–5.)

Next, Susan read off her amounts, and Lynne wrote them on the board.

$.35 $.12 $.19 $.06 $.22 $.07

Susan explained how she had added. "Take the nineteen and six and get twenty-five. Take the twenty-five and thirty-five and you get sixty. Take twelve and twenty-two and get thirty-four. Take the thirty-four and seven and get forty-one. Then add the sixty and the forty-one and get . . . whoops! I should get one hundred, not one hundred one."

Lynne asked Susan to go back to her work and check her subtraction while other students shared their work.

"I found it! I found it!" Susan shouted. "I subtracted wrong. I bought a book for nineteen cents and wrote that fifty-three minus nineteen was thirty-five but it was really thirty-four."

"Can you think of a way to fix your story without changing the whole story?" Lynne asked.

Susan thought about the question for a little while, and then responded, "If I

▲▲▲▲▲▲Figure 6–5 *After Collin's rough draft was checked, he made his book.*

changed the price of the book to $.18, I'd only have to change one thing."

"That's a great idea," Lynne said, and Susan went back to correct her paper. (See Figure 6–6.)

To reinforce the inverse relationship of addition and subtraction, Lynne had pairs of students check each other's stories by adding up the amounts spent or lost to see if they got back to the amount received on the first day. Students then copied their stories into accordion-folded books and illustrated them. The completed books were displayed in the classroom and used from time to time for a practice lesson, as Lynne had done with the original Alexander book.

EXTENSIONS

1. One extension or alternative lesson is to have students spend one dollar in two, three, four, and five transactions instead of a week's transactions. A different amount of money should be spent each time.

Examples

Two transactions:

$.60, $.40   OR $.26, $.74

Three transactions:

$.35, $.15, $.50   OR $.46, $.31, $.23

Four transactions:

$.23, $.45, $.12, $.20   OR
$.25, $.52, $.04, $.19

▲▲▲▲▲▲Figure 6–6 *Susan found her mistake and corrected her work.*

Five transactions:
$.09, $.38, $.10, $.17, $.26   OR
    $.47, $.15, $.02, $.07, $.29

2. Have students find how many items at one price could be bought with one dollar and how much would be left over. For example, if one item cost twenty-five cents, you could buy four and have no money left over. If one item cost twenty-nine cents, you could buy three and have thirteen cents left over. Students can record these transactions using one operation or a combination of operations.

Examples

$.47 cents @

$1.00 − $.47 = $.53

$.53 − $.47 = $.06

OR

$.47 + $.47 = $.94

$.94 + $.06 = $1.00

OR

2 × $.47 = $.94

$1.00 − $.94 = $.06

3. Ask students to find possible combinations of coins for whatever amount was originally received in each story. For example, if two dollars was the original amount, here are four possibilities:

8 quarters

6 quarters, 5 dimes

2 quarters, 7 dimes, 16 nickels

3 quarters, 10 dimes, 2 nickels, 15 pennies

Questions and Discussion

▲▲▲

▲ *Why is decimal notation of money important?*

Decimal notation is important so that students understand money in the real world. Using the cent sign does not provide a real-life context and does not foster the understanding of our place value system. Students need many experiences with money in the primary grades. Using play or real money to show equivalencies is helpful. One dollar is the same as one hundred pennies, ten dimes, twenty nickels, or four quarters. Writing amounts of money using decimal notation should be an ongoing activity during the school year to help prepare students for numerical operations with decimals. Show students catalogs, newspapers, order forms, and receipts to help them realize how monetary amounts are written in the real world. Calculators provide still another way to represent monetary notation.

▲ *How can you help keep children from becoming confused when they are adding or subtracting money using decimal notation?*

By doing a great deal of mental computation in the classroom, students become more flexible with numbers by being able to look at a number in different ways. If you were asked to add $.26 and $1.25, you might think of these numbers in more than one way. First, you might look at the dollar and then look at the cents. You might think of the twenty-five cents and the twenty-six cents as two quarters and one penny to make fifty-one cents and then add the fifty-one cents to the dollar. You might also look at the dollar as one hundred cents and add fifty-one cents cents to make one hundred fifty-one cents, which can be converted to $1.51 in decimal notation. You might also think of it as $1.00 + .20 +. 20 + .11 = $1.51. Depending on the numbers or the circumstance, it is important to have flexibility in looking at numbers in many ways. By working with numbers in different ways, students can gain a greater understanding of decimals.

CHAPTER SEVEN
LETTERS IN NAMES

Overview

The book *Chrysanthemum*, by Kevin Henkes, gives the context for this series of activities that engage children with strategies for adding and comparing numbers. Chrysanthemum is a mouse eager to start her first day of school. It isn't long before her perfect world crumbles as her classmates make fun of her name. It's so long, it scarcely fits on a name tag, and with thirteen letters, it's the same as half the alphabet. Things go badly until Mrs. Delphinium Twinkle, the new music teacher, saves the day.

After reading the book, children investigate how many letters are in their own first names. They graph the results of their individual name lengths and with guidance find various ways to determine how many letters are in all the first names of the class. Later, students work independently or with partners to figure out how many letters are in all of their last names. They find out if there are more letters in their first names or more in their last names. Later they compare the total number of letters in their class names with the total number of letters in other classrooms, including Chrysanthemum's class.

Materials

- ▲ *Chrysanthemum*, by Kevin Henkes (New York: Greenwillow Books, 1991)
- ▲ 3-by-3-inch sticky notes, 2 per student
- ▲ 2-by-12-inch strips of one-inch squares, 1 per student (see Blackline Masters)

Time

- ▲ four to five class periods

Teaching Directions

Day 1

1. Read *Chrysanthemum* to the class. Ask the children if they remember how many letters are in Chrysanthemum's name. Have them compare the length of her name with their own first names.

2. Have children discuss the number of letters in their first names. Say: "Who has zero letters in his or her name? Who has the shortest first name in the class? Stand up if your name has three (four, five, etc.) letters. Who has the longest name? Can you think of a name that's longer?"

3. Have students return to their tables and write their first names on sticky notes.

4. On the front board, organize the sticky notes into a graph by the number of letters in the names. Have students discuss the results. Talk about the range of letters in their first names.

Day 2

1. Ask children to report what they remember learning the day before about the letters in their first names.

2. Tell the students they will be figuring out the total number of letters in all of their first names.

3. Ask them if they can think of ways to figure out the total.

4. Have students work with partners to use the information on the graph to find the total. Have students record their work and describe their methods in writing. Assist those students who are having difficulty explaining their strategies by asking them questions.

5. Collect papers and review them for discussion the next day. Are they complete? What strategies are the students using? What might they add to their papers to enhance communication?

Day 3

1. Gather the children together to share results of how many letters are in their first names. Make a list of various strategies students used.

2. Engage students in a discussion about how they can improve their papers. What can they add that will help others know what they did, what the numbers mean, and what they found out?

3. Have partners add to their written reports to improve the quality of the communication.

Day 4

1. Make a three-column chart like this:

First name is shorter than last name	First name is same length as last name	First name is longer than last name

2. Give each student a 2-by-12-inch strip of one-inch squares. Demonstrate how they are to write their first and last names, cut off extra squares, and post their names in the correct column on the chart.

3. Have students look at the chart to predict whether there will be more letters in their last names or in their first names. Ask students how they could find out for sure.

4. As you did with their first names, make a sticky note graph of the students' last names. Review the methods students used to find the total number of letters in their first names. Have each student independently find the total number of letters in all of their last names.

Teaching Notes

In this lesson students use various addition strategies to find the total number of letters in all the names of the class. They may add on to subtotals, skip-count, make groups, tally, multiply, make use of landmark numbers, or use calculators.

There are opportunities to compare numbers in these lessons: "Are there more letters in your first name or in your last name? How many more?" When children first encounter this question, they often look at you quizzically. Teachers can respond in a variety of ways to help children learn how numbers can be compared. For example, we can restate the question: "How far is this number from that number?" "How far off is this number from that number?" or we can try modeling with cubes: "Here's a train with twelve cubes and a train with seven cubes. How many more cubes does the short train need in order to be the same as the longer train?"

Once students understand the idea of how many more, they can find their own strategies for figuring out differences. A common strategy is counting up by ones or by tens. Another is to count back. It is rare for a student to use subtraction to figure the difference in second or third grade.

The Lesson

▲▲

DAY 1

After reading *Chrysanthemum* to the class, Lynne asked, "How many letters are in Chrysanthemum's name?"

"Thirteen," the class called out.

"My first name has five letters," Lynne stated. "Chrysanthemum's name has eight more letters than my name."

"Each of you should figure out how many more letters Chrysanthemum's name has than your name," Lynne directed the class. "Be ready to tell us in a complete sentence." Lynne had decided to take the time to have each student say how many more letters Chrysanthemum's name had than his or her name. She felt that many would benefit from this oral practice.

"Who would like to start?" Lynne asked.

Lynne called on Elizabeth, who stated, "My name has nine letters. Chrysanthemum's name has four more letters."

When everyone had a chance to compare his or her name to Chrysanthemum's, Lynne asked the class, "What if I asked, how many people have zero letters in their first names?"

"It can't be," Gabi said.

"Why not?" Lynne teased.

"They'd have no name," Gabi responded.

"What about a one-letter name?" Lynne continued.

"No way," several children called out.

"What about a two-letter name?" she asked next.

"I know someone named JJ," Jeffrey said.

Several children nodded in agreement and began calling out other two-letter names they knew.

"Stand up if you have three letters in your name," Lynne directed.

No one stood up.

"It looks like there are no people in our class with three letters in their names," Lynne commented, then continued, "Stand up if you have four letters in your name."

Eight children stood up while the class counted.

"Stand up if you have five letters in your name," Lynne said.

Six children were in this group.

"Ms. Zolli, you should stand up," Christine said, knowing that her teacher's first name was Lynne.

"That makes seven people with five letters," Dana said, correcting the original count.

"Stand up if you have six letters in your name," Lynne said next.

Six people had six letters in their names.

Lynne continued asking students to stand if they had seven, eight, nine, or ten letters in their last names. No one stood after Christine, who had nine letters.

"Nine is the most," Eric said when it became evident that no one had more.

"We have an idea about the number of letters in the names in this class, but now we want to make a record of the information," Lynne said. "Each of you will write your name like this," she told them as she wrote her first name on a sticky note. "Write it large enough for everyone to see it and be sure to put the sticky part on top. When you've written your name, return to the floor in the front of the room."

Lynne had the children return to their seats one table at a time, giving the sticky note to one of the group members to distribute.

In a few minutes the children had reassembled in front with sticky notes in hand.

Once Lynne had their attention, she asked Rory, Christine, Brian, Nelson, and Luis to place their sticky notes on the chalkboard. She wanted to select children whose names had varied lengths.

"How can we organize this information?" she asked.

"You could arrange them alphabetically," Eric called out.

"Look at the five names on the board," Lynne directed, "and think for yourself which name would come first and which would be last if you organized them alphabetically as Eric suggested."

After giving the class a minute to participate in alphabetizing, Lynne called on Eric to arrange the names in the way he recommended.

"Can anyone else think of a different way to organize these five names?" Lynne asked.

Several hands went up and she called on Christine.

"We could put them by the smallest name to the longest name," she offered.

Christine arranged them using her idea:

Rory

Luis

Brian

Nelson

Christine

Luis suggested that his name and Rory's name be put together, and he arranged them like this:

Rory   Luis

Brian

Nelson

Christine

Lynne then wrote the numbers 1–12 on the chalkboard and told the students that they should place their notes in rows next to the number of letters in their names. She called on clusters of children at a time to bring up their notes and added her name to the graph as well.

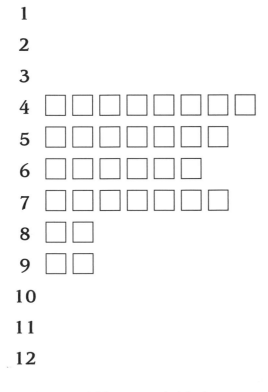

"What would be a good title for our chart?" Lynne asked the class.

"Letters in Our Names," Elizabeth suggested.

"You mean Letters in Our *First* Names," Dana added.

"What do you notice about our first names?" Lynne prompted.

"Four was the winner," Rory said.

"We have a lot of short names in our class," Collin added.

"They aren't that short," Dylan said. "No one has one, two, or three letters."

"What else?" Lynne asked.

"There are no names with one, two, three, ten, eleven, or twelve," Luis suggested.

"What is the least number of letters in our names?" Lynne asked.

"Four," the class responded.

"The greatest number of letters?"

"Elizabeth and I both had nine," Christine called out.

"Does anyone remember what mathematicians call it when you find the difference between the least and the greatest number on your graph?" Lynne probed. She had discussed this idea with the class several times previously in the year.

Eric, a very verbal student with an excellent vocabulary and a great interest in mathematics, responded, "It's called the range. The range of letters in our first names is five, and it goes from four to nine."

Lynne then told the class that tomorrow they would use this information to find out more about their names.

DAY 2

Lynne asked the children to gather at the front of the room so they could see the Letters in Our First Names chart. Once they were settled, she asked, "Who remembers what we found out about our names yesterday?"

"We found out how many letters were in our first names," Brian said.

"Your problem now is to figure out how many letters are in all of our first names.

What are some ways you could find out how many letters we have altogether?" Lynne asked.

"We could count all the letters on the sticky notes," Kelly suggested.

"Add them up," Dana offered.

"Use a calculator," Brendan stated.

"I think I'll use tallies," Jordan said.

"When you return to your seat, you will work with a partner. For this problem, your partner will be the person sitting next to you. This is what your paper will look like," Lynne said as she began to write on the board.

```
Name _____ Date _____
Partner's Name _____

Estimate: Letters in Our First Names
There are _____ letters in all our names
This is how we figured it out:
```

"What if you just write ninety-seven on your paper?" Lynne asked, wanting to emphasize the need to explain how they found the answer.

"You wouldn't know how we figured it out," Elizabeth said.

"That's right. I'm interested in how you think about this problem and I want to see all the different ways children use to find out how many letters are in all of our names. Your paper may have words, numbers, and pictures, and whatever else helps you explain your thinking. Also, you should write an estimate before you figure the total."

The children got busy preparing their papers and talking about how they would figure out the total. Lynne checked in with each table to see if partners were finding a way to work together compatibly. Once students had their papers ready, several moved to work on the floor in front of the name graph.

At the end of the period, Lynne collected their work. She sorted the papers,

grouping those with similar strategies and noting which ones might need additional information.

DAY 3

"Yesterday, you worked with a partner to figure out how many letters are in all of our first names," Lynne began. "Now I am interested in how you figured out the total number of letters in all of our names. Who would like to share how they did the problem?"

"Dana and I added," Jennifer said.

"Did anyone else use addition?" asked Lynne.

Several children raised their hands.

"Did anyone have a different way?" Lynne continued.

"We used the calculator," Brendan said.

"Did you use addition to find your answer with the calculator?" Lynne probed.

"I guess so," Brendan said. "We used the plus sign."

Other students still had their hands raised.

"We used tallies," Kelly said.

"We used tallies, too," Jordan said.

"We had a different way," Christine said. "We counted."

"Josh and I counted, too," Eric said, "but it didn't seem right, so we decided to count by fours, fives, sixes, sevens, eights, and nines and it came out better."

"That's what we did," Gabi said. "It was easier to check our work."

"Why is that?" Lynne wondered aloud.

"Well, when you count by ones, you get confused," Gabi continued. "There aren't as many numbers when you count by bigger numbers."

"Did anyone use a different way?" Lynne continued.

Brian timidly raised his hand. "We multiplied."

Lynne wrote a list on the board of all the methods the children had shared: *addition, tallies, counting, multiplication*, and *calculator*.

"Did I miss anybody's way of solving this problem?" Lynne asked.

Thomas and Valerie raised their hands.

"We counted, but we didn't use the chart," Valerie said. "We used a class list that had everyone's name on it and then we used the calculator."

Lynne added Thomas and Valerie's method to the list.

"As I was looking at your papers last night, it was interesting to see all the different ways you solved this problem," Lynne told them. "When I read a paper I want to understand what you are thinking. There are three things that help me understand your thinking. These are words, numbers, and sometimes an illustration or a chart. I'd like you to share some of your solutions with the class. While partners are reading, see if you can understand how they solved the problem."

Lynne called on Sonja and Gabi to share first (see Figure 7–1).

Then Brian and Jeffrey shared their paper (see Figure 7–2).

"I got the same total, but how did you get the sixty-seven?" Eric asked, pointing to the first sum on Brian's paper.

Jeffrey showed the class how four eights on the calculator makes thirty-two and how five sevens makes thirty-five. Then he explained how they added the two numbers to get sixty-seven.

"There are many ways to write a good math paper," Lynne said. "Words are very important and so are numbers. If you use a calculator, you need to explain how you got the answer. If you draw pictures, you need to label them. If you use numbers, you need to explain why you chose those numbers. Even the title is important. Think for a minute what you and your partner can add to your paper to help others understand what you are thinking."

The children returned to their seats as Lynne handed back the papers. She wanted students to talk to their partners for a few minutes about what they could do to

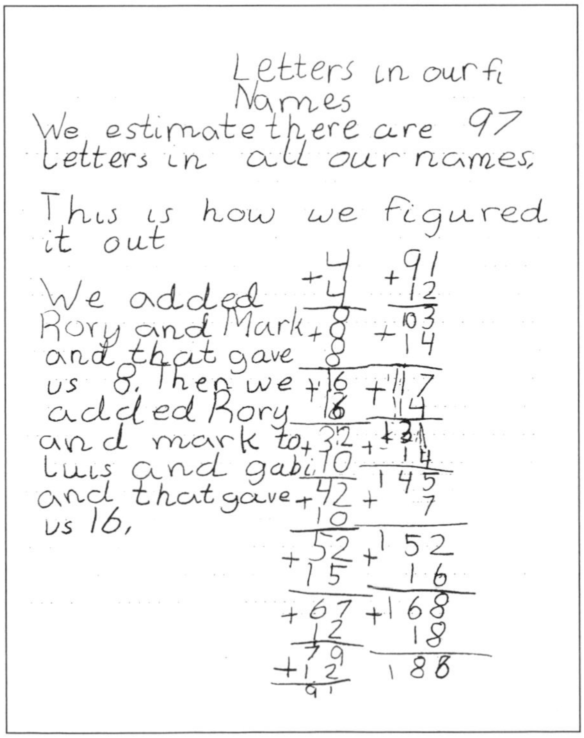

▲▲▲▲▲▲Figure 7–1 *Sonja and Gabi explained how they used subtotals to figure out their answer.*

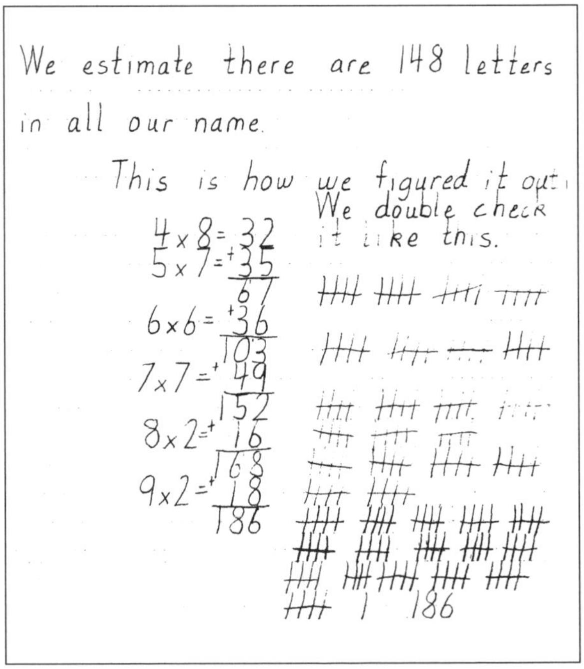

▲▲▲▲▲▲Figure 7–2 *Brian and Jeffrey used multiplication and addition and then checked their work with tallies.*

strengthen their work. Helping students learn how to communicate their ideas both verbally and in writing is a major goal to work on all year long.

When students finished revising their papers, Lynne gave them each a 2-by-12-inch strip of one-inch squares. She demonstrated how to write their first names on one row and their last names on the next row. She used her own name and the name of a child who was absent that day.

L	Y	N	N	E
Z	O	L	L	I

J	E	N	N	I	F	E	R
W	O	N	G

After students printed their names, they trimmed off the extra squares and Lynne instructed them to post their name strips in the correct place on a three-column chart she had prepared on large paper (see below).

"Where would I post Jennifer's name?" Lynne asked.

"Put it in the last box," Kenneth said.

When the chart was complete, Lynne had the students look at the chart and predict if there would be more letters in their last names or their first names. The math period was about over and Lynne ended by saying, "Think about how you could find out for sure if we have more letters in our last or first names. We'll work on this problem tomorrow."

DAY 4

Lynne began class by asking the students to write their last names on sticky notes and make a chart similar to the one they had made for the letters in their first names (see page 54). Briefly they discussed the data and compared it to the results of the investigation of first names. Lynne reviewed the different methods students used to find the total number of letters in their first names, again writing their methods on the board. Lynne then asked each student to select one of the methods on the board to find the total number of letters in their last names.

"Can we work with partners?" Jordan asked.

"For this problem, you will work on your own," Lynne told them. Lynne was using this assignment to assess each child's ability to work independently. "Remember to label the numbers you use, tell what you did to find the answer, and be sure the answer is clearly shown."

Once students figured out the total number of letters in their last names, Lynne called for their attention.

"Now that you have found the number of letters in all of our last names, you can compare that number to the number of letters in all of our first names. Be sure to tell which has more and how many more," Lynne directed. "Remember, you also have to explain how you figured it out." Figure 7–3 shows how one student compared the totals.

First name is shorter than last name	First name is same length as last name	First name is longer than last name

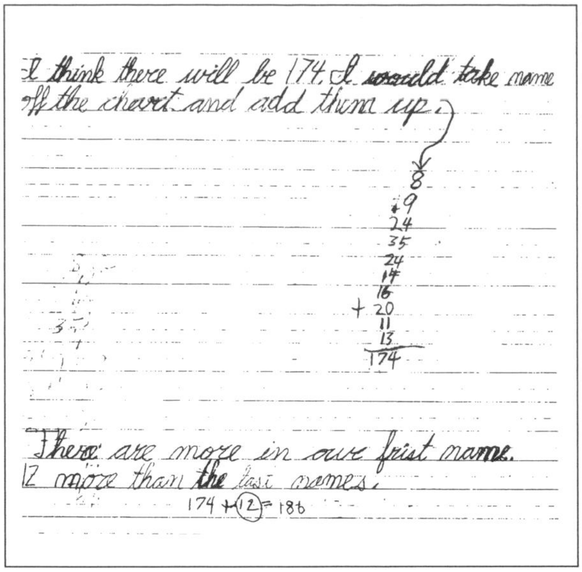

I think there will be 174. I would take name off the chart and add them up.

```
        8
        9
       24
       35
       24
       14
       16
     + 20
       11
       13
      ⎯⎯⎯
      174
```

There are more in our frist name.
12 more than the last names.
174 + (12) = 186

▲▲▲▲▲▲**Figure 7–3** *Josh found there were 12 more letters in the first names of the class than in the last names.*

EXTENSIONS

1. Have students find the total number of letters in the first names of Chrysanthemum's class and compare this total with your class total.

2. Give students a class list from another class in the school. Have them find the total number of letters and compare it to their own class total.

3. Have each student find the total number of letters in his or her family's first names. Use this information to write comparing problems for students to figure out. For example: *Kelly's family has 15 letters in their first names and Rory's family has 23 letters. Which family has more letters? How many more?*

Questions and Discussion

▲▲

▲ *Is it important to let every student share his or her solutions?*

Having everyone share his or her solution at one sitting can become tedious for young children. As children are working, it is important to observe and make note of their strategies so that you can direct the later discussion. It is helpful to have students with simpler solutions share first, followed by students with more complex solutions. After a solution is presented, ask if anyone did the problem in a similar way. All the students' work does not have to be presented at the same discussion time.

▲ *Do students always work with partners?*

In our classrooms, students often work with partners. One of the messages students get from the first day of school is that one of our goals this year is to learn how to work together and to have an opportunity to learn from one another. The goal is for each student to have the chance to work with each of the other students. For this reason, they need to change partners regularly. However, we also have children work alone at times, which is essential for being able to assess each child's understanding or skill.

CHAPTER EIGHT
PENNIES IN A JAR

Overview

In this lesson, students collect pennies to fill a quart mason jar. They first estimate how many pennies they think will fill the jar. Then, each day for a week they bring in extra pennies from home and put them in the jar. At the end of the week, they figure out how many pennies they have so far and use this information to predict how many pennies will fill the jar.

From this investigation, students have an opportunity to estimate, add two-digit numbers, predict the number of pennies that will fill a jar based on the number in a partially filled jar, and gain familiarity with our decimal system of numbers by figuring out how many dimes and dollars a collection of pennies is worth.

Materials

▲ a quart mason jar with lid
▲ pennies

Time

▲ thirty minutes for the introduction
▲ five to ten minutes each day for a week for collecting pennies
▲ one class period finding the total so far and predicting how many will fill the jar
▲ one class period finding how many dimes and dollars the penny collection is worth

Teaching Directions

1. On Monday show students an empty quart mason jar and ask how many pennies they think will fill the jar.

2. Give each child a note to take home requesting parents to contribute pennies for the investigation. Ask a student to read the note aloud to the class to be sure all the children understand.

3. Ask the students how many pennies they would have if each child brought ten pennies. Have the class count by tens to figure it out.

4. Collect pennies each day for the rest of the week. At the end of the week, give small groups of children a share of the pennies to count. Ask the groups to record their totals and be prepared to explain how they counted their pennies.

5. When the groups are ready, record their totals on the board and have children explain the methods they used. Have children put the pennies they counted back in the jar.

6. Have children work individually to find the total number of pennies collected so far.

7. With this new information, ask students in pairs to write new predictions of how many pennies will fill the jar. Make sure the jar is available for them to examine.

8. Have students share their ideas with the class.

9. On another day, discuss how many dimes and dollars the penny collection is worth and have students write about how they figured it out.

Teaching Notes

Finding the number of pennies collected over a one-week period gives students experience adding several two-digit numbers. Some students use strategies that may seem cumbersome to us but make sense to them. Others may choose to use a calculator. Each time students experience addition, they have the opportunity to learn something new and gain greater facility with combining numbers.

This activity can be done with any collection of small objects that may interest the class. The idea for this activity came about when one class got into a discussion about how pennies are not worth much these days. This is something they may have heard from their parents. The discussion had provoked so much interest that it seemed natural to start collecting pennies and see where it took us. In one classroom, we collected pennies in one jar and buttons in another so we could compare which had more each day. After a few days, the button collection slowed down and it was clear that pennies held a greater interest.

The Lesson

▲▲

INTRODUCTION

Near the end of math class one day, Bonnie introduced a new investigation. "Today we will begin a math investigation that involves collecting pennies, estimating, adding, and comparing," Bonnie told the class, holding up a quart mason jar. "If everyone in the class brings one penny, do you think this jar will be full?"

"No way!" Julian said. "That would only be twenty-seven pennies. They'd hardly fill the bottom."

"How many pennies do you think it would take to fill this jar?" Bonnie questioned.

The students started to call out numbers. Bonnie called for their attention and asked, "What would be a reasonable estimate? Would fifty be a good guess?"

"No, that's too small," Eric said. "If we each put in another penny, it would only be about fifty-nine or sixty. I think at least two hundred."

Bonnie had the students give their estimates as she wrote them on the board. Their guesses ranged from 84 to 585.

Next Bonnie told them that they could bring in any extra pennies they had at home each day for a week. At the end of the week they would count how many they had so far and make a new prediction. She gave each of them a note to take home to help explain the investigation to their parents. Bonnie had one of the students read the note aloud to the class.

Dear Parents,

We are starting a mathematics investigation that involves collecting pennies to fill a quart mason jar. This investigation will give students an opportunity to estimate, add, and compare numbers. Through their work with this penny investigation, students will develop their number sense, practice mental arithmetic, and learn more about the relationship between pennies, dimes, and dollars.

We would like each student to bring some pennies from home. These should be pennies you do not need back. When we finish with this investigation, the class will help decide how to spend the pennies they collected. We hope to collect at least ten pennies from each student.

Thank you for your help.

"If each child in the class brought in ten pennies, how many would we have?" Bonnie asked.

"If ten people brought ten pennies, we would have one hundred," Francesca offered.

"We have almost thirty people; that would be three hundred," Kevin told us.

"I think we'd have two hundred eighty," Kenneth said.

"How could we prove it?" Bonnie asked.

"We could count everyone's fingers," Mary said with a giggle.

"We could just go ten, twenty, thirty, like that," Mark suggested.

Bonnie had the class count by tens.

COLLECTING THE PENNIES

The next day, about half the class remembered to bring in pennies. Some students had baggies with about thirty pennies and others brought in one or two pennies. Several students assured us that they would bring in pennies the next day. The students continued to bring pennies in throughout the week. Instead of counting them each day, Bonnie decided to just place the pennies in the jar and do the count at the end of the week. On Friday, the jar was about one-third full.

Note: We have done this activity with several classes and each time the jar was about one-third full on Friday. If you have a group that gets extremely motivated and brings in large quantities of pennies, stop collecting whenever the jar gets about one-third full and do the following estimation activity.

FINDING THE TOTAL AND PREDICTING

"We've collected a lot of pennies in five days," Bonnie told the class on Friday. "I'm going to give each group part of our collection to count so everyone can help."

Bonnie took eight small containers and divided the pennies up so that each table would get about the same amount.

"As a group, count the pennies, and have someone record how many pennies you have and be prepared to tell us how you counted them," Bonnie instructed.

The class was eager to know how many pennies there were and went to work quickly. Many made piles of ten and grouped them on their desks. Before long, each group was ready to report. Bonnie called for their attention and asked each table to give their total and describe how they counted their pennies. Bonnie recorded the totals on the board and had the children put the pennies they had counted back into the jar (see below).

Almost before Bonnie could give further directions, many of the children were busily recording the totals on paper. They were eager to know how many pennies they had collected so far. Bonnie asked that each student find the total on his or her own. This would be a good opportunity for Bonnie to see if each student could find the sum of the eight numbers.

As Bonnie walked around the classroom observing students, she noticed who was able to attack this problem with independence and confidence and who seemed unsure. She also noticed the variety of strategies children used. Ronald was adding the

numbers in the ones place in pairs so that the eight numbers became four numbers—nine, fifteen, eleven, and thirteen. Next Ronald added the tens in his head and remembered to include the four tens from the forty-eight. (See Figure 8–1.)

Victor started by adding the tens and then the ones, recording his procedure carefully in fifteen steps. Carissa added the

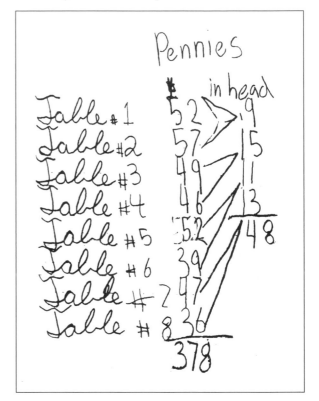

▲▲▲▲▲▲Figure 8–1 *Ronald added the ones in pairs to get 48. He added the tens in his head and remembered to include the four tens from the 48.*

Table 1:	52	"We made five groups of ten and had two more."
Table 2:	57	"Our group did the same. We had five groups of ten and seven extras."
Table 3:	49	"If we had one more we could have made five groups of ten. We had nine left over and four tens."
Table 4:	46	"We put ours in twos and counted by twos."
Table 5:	52	"We made two groups of twenty-five and had two more."
Table 6:	39	"We only had three tens and nine."
Table 7:	47	"We each took one at a time and we each got eleven and three remainder."
Table 8:	36	"We put them in tens first but then we decided on six groups of six."

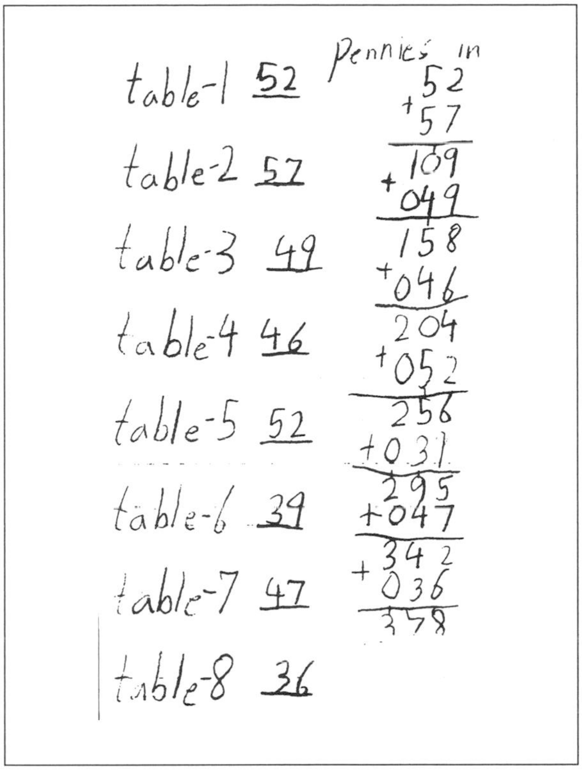
Pennies in
table-1 52
table-2 57
table-3 49
table-4 46
table-5 52
table-6 39
table-7 47
table-8 36
52
+57
109
+049
158
+046
204
+052
256
+031
295
+047
342
+036
378

Figure 8–2 *Kyle added the first two numbers and then continued adding on.*

ones by pairing all the doubles first—2 + 2, 7 + 7, and 9 + 9—and then combining those plus the extra six. She added the tens in the same way. Kyle added the first two numbers, found the total, then added the next number to that total and continued with the rest of the numbers (see Figure 8–2).

When each student had a total, Bonnie called for their attention. She selected three students to come to the board one at a time and share their strategies. She purposely chose students who she noticed had used their strategies successfully to arrive at the correct answer. This way, students who were less confident had the opportunity to hear different strategies for adding a column of numbers. After the three explanations, the children were convinced that they had collected 378 pennies so far.

"Now that we know how many pennies we've collected so far, I wonder if you have a new idea about how many pennies it will take to fill the jar?" Bonnie asked. "With your partner, try to calculate how many you think. Be sure to write how you figured out your estimate. A picture may help you communicate your thinking."

To review the question, Bonnie wrote on the chalkboard:

Pennies in the Jar

Our jar has 378 pennies. How many pennies do you think will be in the jar when it's full?

(Show how you figured it out.)

Bonnie passed out lined paper, checking to be sure each student had a partner. She observed as each pair began working. Partners seemed to have no trouble preparing their papers with their names, the title, and the question. They were clearly interested in figuring out how many pennies might fill the jar. Some students were dealing with three-digit numbers for the first time and seemed to enjoy the challenge.

The jar was available at the front of the room for partners to have a closer look. Some used their fingers to eyeball how many more layers of pennies the jar would hold (see Figure 8–3). Others brought paper to hold up to the side of jar and marked off layers. Eventually, someone thought of using a ruler to measure how high 378 pennies went on the jar and attempted to use that information to make a more accurate prediction (see Figure 8–4).

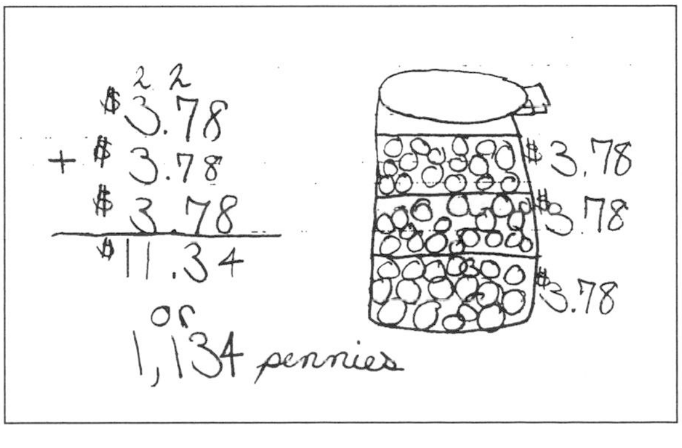
$3.78
+ $3.78
$3.78
$11.34
or
1,134 pennies
$3.78
$3.78
$3.78

Figure 8–3 *Mary used her fingers to mark off layers.*

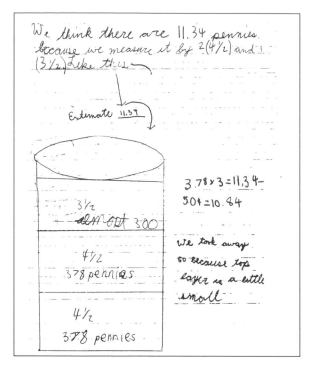

We think there are 11.34 pennies because we measure it by 2(4½) and 1 (3½). Like this →

Estimate 11.34

$3.78 \times 3 = 11.34$
$50¢ = 10.84$

We took away 50 because top layer is a little small

3½
almost 300

4½
378 pennies

4½
378 pennies

▲▲▲▲▲▲Figure 8–4   *Kevin and Mark used a ruler as a way to measure layers. They found two $4\frac{1}{2}$-inch layers and one $3\frac{1}{2}$-inch layer.*

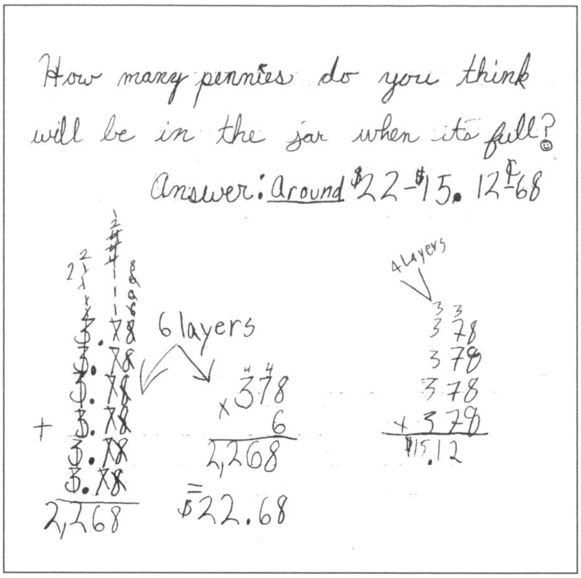

How many pennies do you think will be in the jar when its full?
Answer: Around $22–$15. 12–68

6 layers

$\times 378$

2,268

$= $22.68

4 layers

378
378
378
$\times 378$
$15.12

▲▲▲▲▲▲Figure 8–5   *These partners could not agree on one answer so they reported their prediction as a range.*

HOW MANY DIMES ARE THE PENNIES WORTH?

All of the students thought of the jar as being filled with layers of 378 pennies each. Their ideas about how many layers varied from three layers to as many as eight layers. In one case, partners could not agree, so they figured out the answer for both four layers and six layers, then reported their prediction as a range (see Figure 8–5). After finding an initial answer, some students decided to measure the height of the pennies in the jar again and use this new information to revise their prediction.

As the students finished their predictions and explanations, Bonnie collected their papers. She planned to review them and ask the children to share their results the next day.

The following day, the children gathered at the front of the room to discuss their ideas about how many pennies the jar would hold. After they shared their ideas, Bonnie initiated the following discussion to talk about trading pennies for dimes and dollars.

"Suppose your mother wanted to give you a dollar, but all she had were dimes," Bonnie began. "How many dimes would she need to give you?"

"Ten," Alan called out, unable to hold back.

"What if she decided to give you two dollars to spend, but all she had were dimes?" Bonnie asked. "Whisper to the person next to you what you think," she instructed, wanting to get more students involved.

Bonnie heard a chorus of "twenties" and continued this line of questioning with other amounts.

"What about a dollar fifty?" After a moment, children answered that there would be fifteen dimes.

"If you bought something for sixty-three cents, how many dimes would you need to give the clerk?" Bonnie asked.

Some said six, others said seven. A brief discussion resolved that six dimes and three pennies would work, and with seven dimes, there would be change.

Most of the class seemed to respond to these questions easily, but Bonnie wondered if each student had an understanding of how pennies, dimes, and dollars related and could explain what he or she was thinking. She posed the following question to find out: "What if we traded all of the pennies in our jar for dimes?" Then she added, "Each of you will explain what you think on paper."

Bonnie wrote on the chalkboard:

Dimes for Pennies

The jar has 378 pennies. If we traded them in for dimes, how many would we have? How would you convince someone that you're right?

Bonnie made sure that each student had lined paper and soon they were busy working on the problem. As they got into the problem, some students seemed to know easily that it would take thirty-seven dimes with eight pennies left over. For those students, the challenge was to explain clearly in words why this was right and to figure out how many dollars the dimes and the pennies would be worth. (See Figure 8–6.)

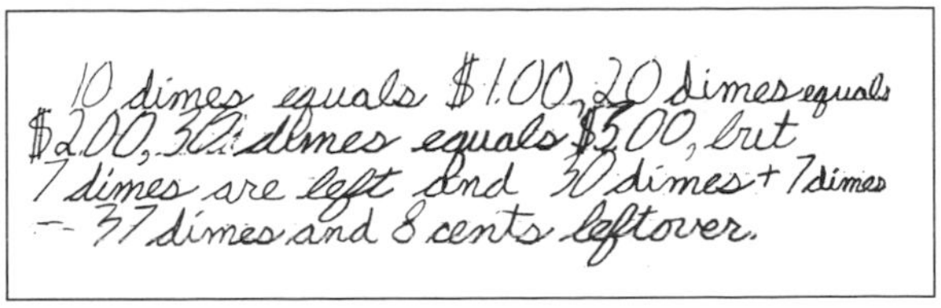
10 dimes equals $1.00, 20 dimes equals $2.00, 30 dimes equals $3.00, but 7 dimes are left and 30 dimes + 7 dimes = 37 dimes and 8 cents leftover.

Figure 8–6 *Eric clearly stated how he knew how many dimes could be traded for 378 pennies.*

For other students the answer was not immediately obvious, but they had a way to figure out how many dimes there would be. A few of these used some form of repeated subtraction, with some keeping track of how many dimes they would have with tallies. Others broke the 378 into 300 + 70 + 8 and figured each part separately. The children enjoyed the struggle and were persistent.

A few students managed to get their papers ready with the question copied but then seemed unable to proceed. Bonnie sat with these individuals, asking questions to find out what they knew and helping them think about how they could use what they knew to find a reasonable solution. Figures 8–7 through 8–9 show three students' strategies for solving this problem.

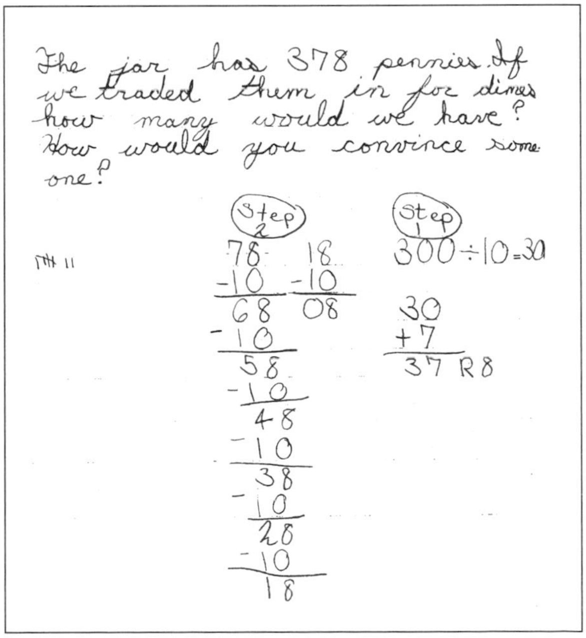

Figure 8–7 *Francesca used a combination of repeated subtraction and division to find her answer.*

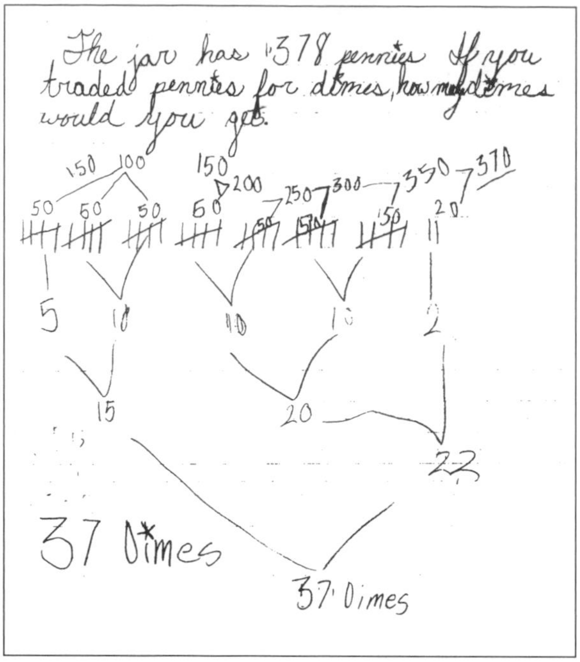

▲▲▲▲▲▲Figure 8–8 *With each tally representing a dime, Julian presented a convincing explanation of his thinking.*

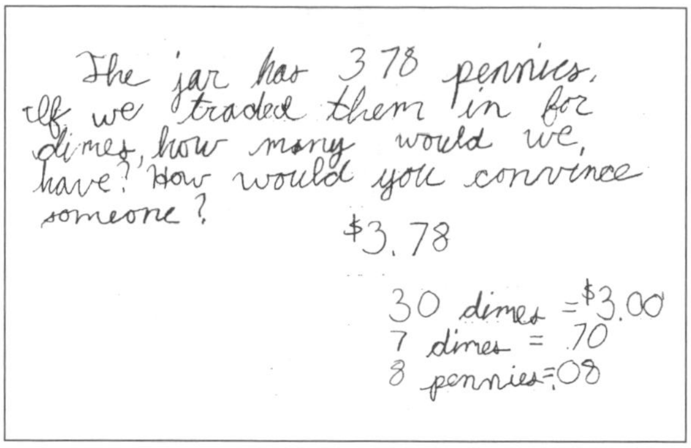

▲▲▲▲▲▲Figure 8–9 *Carissa used her knowledge of place value to solve the problem.*

Questions and Discussion

▲▲

▲ *How can you be sure that each student gets enough practice with numbers to gain facility with addition and subtraction?*

We think of facility with numbers as a continuum. Students in the second and third grades will always need more practice and will have new things to learn about large numbers and about one another's thinking. We definitely would like children in second grade to learn their basic facts for both addition and subtraction. This is our goal, but we may not get there with every student. We often find that when students come into third grade they need review and practice to have easy access to the basic facts.

In second grade, we want students to begin thinking about two-digit addition and subtraction and to develop a variety of methods for finding the answer in ways that make sense to them. By third grade we want students to compare methods for putting numbers together and taking them apart and consider methods that are more efficient. We have had the most success when students' experiences with computing are contextual and when they have many opportunities for reflection.

▲ *When do you allow students to use a calculator and what do you tell parents about calculator use?*

Calculators are available at all times in our classrooms. The calculator is one of a variety of methods and tools students can use to compute. We want students to make decisions about when a calculator can be helpful. We encourage our students to use the calculator as a tool to check their work, or as a second way to find an answer.

From the beginning of the year, we also give the message that mental arithmetic and estimation are important for them to learn. It is through their thinking about numbers and through classroom discussions that children develop number sense and skills.

▲ *How do you decide whether students should work with partners or work individually?*

We choose to have students do many of the activities with partners. When children work in pairs, it guarantees that each student has an opportunity to talk about his or her ideas. Talking increases a student's chance of making sense of the problems he or she is working on. When first starting a problem, we often hear one of the partners say to the other, "What are we supposed to do?" This question is useful as it encourages students to restate a problem in their own words. It provides a starting point for their work. We often model how we want partners to work together so that they learn how to ask questions and talk to each other. If we always worked as a whole class or as individuals, some students, often the shy ones, would never be heard.

Even though we have a strong rationale for having students work together, we know that each student also needs to learn to work independently. We ask ourselves before each activity if this recording should be done with partners or by individuals. We are constantly checking for balance. Having students do their work with partners gives us a sense of what the class can do. Having students work individually gives us a sense of what each child can do independently.

CHAPTER NINE
NAME VALUES

Overview

In this lesson, each letter of the alphabet is assigned a dollar amount. A = $1, B = $2, C = $3, and so on. The students find the values of their first names by adding the dollar values of the individual letters. They then compare the values of names, figure out how close each is to one hundred dollars, and find number pairs that add to one hundred dollars. Since the name values are most often two-digit numbers, this activity is an excellent way to develop and practice addition and subtraction strategies for numbers less than one hundred and to become more proficient in mental computation.

Materials

▲ *Letter Values* (see Blackline Masters)
▲ sentence strips cut into 8-inch lengths, 1 per student
▲ *How Close to $100?* worksheets, with students' names listed in the first column, 1 per student (see Blackline Masters)

Time

▲ four to five class periods

Teaching Directions

Day 1

1. Write the letter values of the alphabet on the chalkboard:

A = $1, B = $2, C = $3 . . . Z = $26

2. Explain how to add the individual letter values to find the value of a word.

C A T
3 + 1 + 20 = $24

M E
13 + 5 = $18

3. Have students practice adding two- and three-letter words mentally using the letter values on the chalkboard.

4. Pose the question: "Which is worth more, *cat* or *dog*?"

5. Present the class with pairs of words that have opposite meanings and ask children to guess which word in each pair they think is worth more. Then have the students find the values of each word to see if their guesses are correct.

H O T
8 + 15 + 20 = $43

C O L D
3 + 15 + 12 + 4 = $34

6. Ask students to compare the value of words and figure out how much more or how much less.

HOT is worth $9 more than COLD

As students share their strategies for finding the differences, represent them mathematically on the chalkboard. For example:

I added 6 to make 40, and then I added 3 more to make $43.

34 + 6 = 40

40 + 3 = 43

6 + 3 = 9

I took 10 away from 43 and got 33. Then I added one back to get 34.

43 − 10 = 33

33 + 1 = 34

10 − 1 = 9

7. Have the students continue working individually or in partners to compare the values of words with opposite meanings.

Day 2

1. Put up a chart with the letter values from A to Z.

2. Select two students with short first names. Have the class find the value of each name.

3. Ask the class to compare the values of the two names. Have students share the strategies they used to find the difference.

4. Have each student find the value of his or her own first name. As they finish, have each student compute the value of one classmate's name as a double check for accuracy.

5. Have a class discussion so students can share the strategies they used for adding.

S A N D Y
19 1 14 4 25

Sandy's Strategy	James' Strategy to Double-Check
19 + 1 = 20	1 + 14 + 4 = 19
20 + 25 = 45	19 + 19 = 38
45 + 14 = 59	38 + 25 = 50 +13 = 63
59 + 4 = 63	

6. Have the students write their names and name values on sentence strips. Collect them.

Day 3

1. Pass out the sentence strips from the day before.

2. Have the children arrange themselves in a semicircle starting with whoever has the name with the least value and ending with whoever has the name with the most value.

3. Ask children to examine the name values and see what they notice. Discuss the range, why some names are short but have more value, if any two names have the same value, where most of the values occur, if there is a relationship between gender and name value, and any other interesting observations about the numbers.

4. Have the students first compare their name values to those in their table groups. Then have them compare with other students in the class if time allows. Ask students to record how they found the differences. If they compute mentally, they should still record the thought processes they use. Give examples to model the procedure.

Mark $43 – Carolyn $93

Count by 10s from 43 to 93

Five 10s is 50.

The difference is 50.

Martha $61 — Christina $101

Take away 1 from each number.

Add 40 to 60.

The difference is 40.

Day 4

1. Put the name value sentence strips in a pocket chart. Have the students help you order them according to value.

2. Have the students decide which name values are closest to one hundred dollars and which are farthest away from one hundred dollars and determine exactly how far away they are from one hundred dollars.

3. Explain the importance of one hundred as a landmark number and the need to be able to take any number less than one hundred and determine how many more must be added to reach one hundred.

4. Ask the class for pairs of numbers that equal one hundred. Start with ninety-nine and one. Then do ninety and ten, eighty and twenty, and so on. Record:

    90 80 70 60 50 40 30 20 10 0

    10 20 30 40 50 60 70 80 90 100

5. Talk about other examples of number pairs that equal one hundred.

6. Distribute the *How Close to $100?* worksheet to the class. Direct students to fill in the values of students' names and find how close each student's name value is to one hundred dollars.

7. Correct the worksheets together as a group. If there is disagreement, have the children demonstrate their methods of computation.

8. Find any pairs of students whose name values equal one hundred dollars. For example:

Nancy $57 and Mark $43

Lydia $51 and Aaron $49

Teaching Notes

The value of words is an activity that has been used for many years by classroom teachers, but usually the value of each letter is given in cents (A = $.01, B = $.02, and so on). Often, students search for words that equal one dollar. Here, this activity is adapted to using whole numbers rather than decimals to give students practice in adding and subtracting one- and two-digit numbers. The focus of this lesson is on building computational proficiency with numbers less than one hundred and developing flexibility with numbers by providing students practice with taking numbers apart and putting them back together again. Being able to work with numbers mentally is an essential math skill and gives the student an advantage when faced with pencil-and-paper tasks and real-life mathematical problems.

Building the lesson around the students' names is a particularly effective way to engage their interest. Also, the names suggest a variety of conjectures for children to consider: Are shorter names always worth less? Is the longest name in the class also the most valuable? The lesson as described can keep a class meaningfully involved with adding and subtracting two-digit numbers for about a week, even longer with the extensions.

The Lesson

▲▲

DAY 1

"How many letters are there in the alphabet?" Bonnie asked after gathering the students at the chalkboard.

"Twenty-six," chorused the class.

"That's correct," Bonnie continued. "Today I am going to assign a dollar value to each letter."

Bonnie began writing on the board:

$A = \$1$

$B = \$2$

$C = \$3$

She stopped and asked the class if they knew how much Z would be worth.

"Twenty-six dollars," the class said.

"You're correct again," Bonnie answered.

She continued to write the letters of the alphabet on the board, but did not put in the dollar amounts. When she finished, she wrote $Z = \$26$.

"Can you tell me what any other letter is worth?" she asked.

"Of course," Carolyn said. "It's just one more each time."

"What if I asked you to skip a letter?"

"You'd count by twos," Carolyn answered.

Bonnie had the students fill in the rest of the values on the board and then continued by asking, "If I want to find the value of a word, what should I do?"

Franklin raised his hand. "I think you would just add up all the letters."

"Can you give me an example using the word *cat*?"

"Sure. The C is three dollars, the A is one dollar, and the T is twenty dollars. If I add those together I get twenty-four dollars," Franklin answered.

Bonnie continued having the class add up two- and three-letter words such as *go*, *me*, *fun*, and *zoo*.

"Which word do you think is worth more, *cat* or *dog*?" she asked.

"*Dog* has to be less than *cat*," Mark answered with confidence.

"Why?" Bonnie probed.

"Because it doesn't have that T worth twenty dollars."

"Let's add it up to be sure," Bonnie said.

Many of the students, including Mark, were surprised when the value of dog added up to twenty-six dollars. "They were actually pretty close in value," Bonnie remarked. "I was surprised, too."

The class then became interested in exploring the values of words with opposite meanings—*hot/cold, right/wrong, up/down*. Bonnie hadn't planned to focus on opposites. Her plan had been to have the students compare values of all kinds of words. The opposites worked fine for this, and the students were excited about finding their values. For each pair of words, the children guessed which word would be worth more and then found the values using paper and pencil. After they worked for a while, Bonnie stopped them and put some of their findings on the board:

HOT = $43   COLD = $34

UP = $36   DOWN = $56

RIGHT = $62   WRONG = $77

BIG = $18   SMALL = $57

"Let's make some comparisons with these numbers," she suggested.

"*Down* is worth twenty dollars more than *up*," Sandy offered.

"How did you figure that out?" Bonnie asked.

"I added ten two times."

Vincent raised his hand. "I did the same thing with *big* and *small*."

Bonnie asked Vincent to explain his thinking.

"Well, almost the same, except I added ten four times, twenty-eight, thirty-eight, forty-eight, fifty-eight, but I knew it was too much so I took away one and that was thirty-nine."

"*Small* and *down* are only one away from each other," Martha offered.

"What is the difference between the word with the most value and the word with the least value?" Bonnie continued.

The students thought awhile about the difference between eighteen and seventy-seven and when Bonnie asked them to explain their thinking, they came up with several strategies for computing the problem mentally. Bonnie recorded the methods

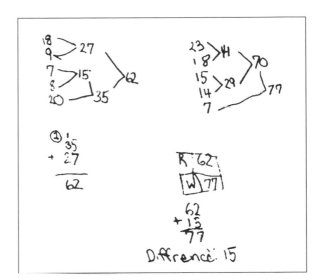

▲▲▲▲▲▲Figure 9–1 *Sandy found the value of the words* **right** *and* **wrong** *with subtotals and found the difference by adding up.*

on the board in order to keep a record of each student's thinking and also to model for the children how to represent their thinking mathematically (see below). Figures 9–1 and 9–2 show how two students compared opposite words.

DAY 2

Bonnie continued the lesson the following day. "Yesterday, you found the value of some words." She put up a chart with the letter values from A to Z on the chalkboard.

"Today we are going to work with the values

Sandy's Strategy	Greg's Strategy	Melissa's Strategy
18 + 10 = 28	18 + 60 = 78	77 − 20 = 57
28 + 10 = 38	60 − 1 = 59	57 + 2 = 59
38 + 10 = 48		
48 + 10 = 58	Greg knew to add the 60	Melissa took away 20 and
58 + 10 = 68	right away and then	added back the 2 extra.
68 + 10 = 78	subtracted the 1.	
60 − 1 = 59		

Sandy kept track on her fingers by tens. When she got to 78 (six tens), she realized she had to go back one to 77, and got 59.

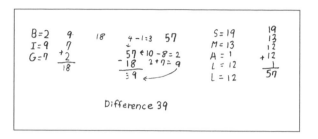

B = 2   9.   18   4 - 1 : 3   57   S = 19   19
I = 9   9   M = 13   13
G = 7 +2   57 ← 10 - 8 = 2   A = 1   12
       ___   - 18   2 + 7 = 9   L = 12   +12
       18   ___   L = 12   ___
                        39 ←   57

                  Difference 39

▲▲▲▲▲▲**Figure 9–2** *Hannah added with column addition but subtracted in a unique way, recording each step of her thinking.*

of our first names. Who has the longest first name in the class?"

"My name has nine letters," Elizabeth said.

"So does mine," Christina added.

"Who has the shortest first name?" Bonnie continued.

"Sam and I both have three letters," Ada said.

"If we compare Sam's and Ada's name values, whose name do you think will be worth more?" Bonnie asked.

"Sam, for sure," Mark said, "and this time I know I'm right because Ada's name is only worth six dollars and Sam is worth more just by looking at it."

"What is Sam's name worth?" Bonnie asked.

"Thirty-three dollars," Sam called out. "nineteen plus one equals twenty and twenty plus thirteen equals thirty-three." Sam had anticipated that Bonnie would ask him to prove his answer. Bonnie wrote on the board:

Ada $6   Sam $33

"How much more is Sam's name worth than Ada's name?" Bonnie continued. She asked the students to figure out the answer and be ready to explain their thinking. The students all came up with twenty-seven dollars, but how they arrived at that answer differed. Some counted up from six by ones, others counted back from thirty-three by ones. Some added four to six to make ten, then added twenty-three more to make thirty-three, and added four and twenty-

three to get twenty-seven. By explaining their thinking as part of every math lesson, students understand their own thinking better and are able to communicate it to others with greater facility.

"Today, we are going to find out the values of everyone's first name in this class. For practice, let's start with my name," Bonnie said.

She wrote her name across the board and asked the students to use the chart to find the value of each letter, which she then wrote under each letter.

B   O   N   N   I   E

2   15   14   14   9   5

"How can we add these numbers?" Bonnie asked.

She called on Greg.

"First add the fourteen and fourteen because doubles are easier," Greg said.

Bonnie showed this on the board: *14 + 14 = 28*.

"Then add two to the twenty-eight to make thirty. Then add the fifteen and the five to make twenty. Then it's easy; you just add the twenty and thirty to make fifty and add nine and you have fifty-nine," Greg said with a smile. Bonnie recorded each step:

14 + 14 = 28

28 + 2 = 30

15 + 5 = 20

20 + 30 = 50

50 + 9 = 59

"Did anyone think about this in a different way?" Bonnie asked. She called on Sandy.

"I added the first three numbers in my head and then the last three numbers and added them together."

"Can you tell me what you did?" Bonnie inquired.

Sandy explained, "Fourteen plus fifteen equals twenty-nine and twenty-nine plus two equals thirty-one and five plus nine equals fourteen and fourteen plus fourteen equals twenty-eight. Then I added the thirty-one and the twenty-eight together and got fifty-nine." As Sandy explained, Bonnie recorded on the chalkboard:

$$14 + 15 = 29$$
$$29 + 2 = 31$$
$$5 + 9 = 14$$
$$14 + 14 = 28$$
$$31 + 28 = 59$$

"Once you find the value of your own name, I want you to double-check each other's work just in case there is a mistake. When your name has been checked, show it to me." (Bonnie had already figured out the values of all their first names so she could easily see if they were done correctly.)

"Since Sam and Ada already know the value of their names, they can start double-checking other names," Bonnie added.

The class went to work, adding their values and checking with each other (see Figure 9–3). By the end of the math period they had all found the values of their first names. The children were very excited as they compared their values with one another.

"Christina's name is worth a lot. It's over one hundred dollars," Vincent said. "Mine is only worth eight-seven dollars." (See Figure 9–4.)

"How do you think I feel?" Ada remarked. "Mine is only worth six dollars."

Bonnie brought the class back together. "Now I want you to write your name and its value on a sentence strip." Bonnie had cut the sentence strips to 8-inch lengths. Now she modeled how she wanted the students to record on them.

Bonnie collected the sentence strips when they were finished and told the students they would continue the lesson the following day.

DAY 3

The children gathered at the front of the room and Bonnie passed out the sentence strips they had done the day before.

"I'm going to ask you to arrange yourselves in a semicircle according to the values of your names. Ada will start on this end, and Christina will be at the other end."

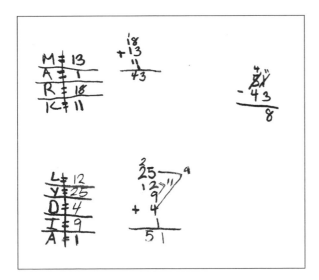

▲▲▲▲▲**Figure 9–3** *Mark and Lydia checked each other.*

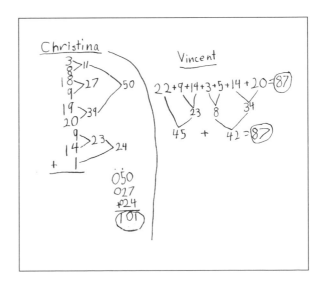

▲▲▲▲▲**Figure 9–4** *Christina found the value of her name and then checked Vincent's name value.*

There was some confusion as the students started, but in a short time they had themselves in order.

"What do you notice?" Bonnie asked.

"Elizabeth is only eight-eight dollars and I am one hundred and one dollars," Christina said, "and we both have nine letters in our names."

"And I have a Z in my name," Elizabeth remarked.

"Vincent and Elizabeth are only one dollar different," Stanley said.

"Nancy is exactly twenty dollars more than Greg," Sandy offered.

"Kevin and Martha are the same amount," Melissa commented.

"What is the range of the values of our names?" Bonnie asked.

"They go from six dollars to one hundred and one dollars," Kevin answered.

"I see a pattern," Ada called out. "Franklin is eighty-five dollars, Johnny is eight-six dollars, Vincent is eight-seven dollars, and Elizabeth is eight-eight dollars."

After a few more comments from the students, Bonnie had the class sit down once again and she explained what they were going to do next.

"Today we're going to take our name value cards and make comparisons with other people in the class," Bonnie explained. "We're going to start by comparing ourselves with the other three people at our table. Then we can compare ourselves with other students in the class if we have time. I want you to record how you find the difference between the value of your name and the value of someone else's name. If you can do it in your head, write on the paper what your brain was doing to get the answer."

"Let me give you an example," Bonnie continued. " If I were comparing myself with Elizabeth, I would write down Bonnie fifty-nine dollars and Elizabeth eight-eight dollars. I can do the problem in my head, but here is how I thought about it. I added thirty

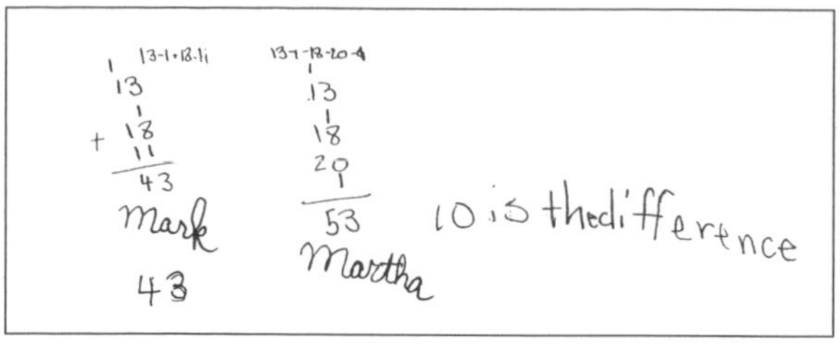

▲▲▲▲▲Figure 9–5 *Martha found the difference easily because she recognized the numbers were exactly 10 apart.*

to the fifty-nine and got eighty-nine. That was one too many, so I took one away from the thirty and got twenty-nine. Here is how I would write it."

Bonnie $59   Elizabeth $88

59 + 30 = 89

89 − 1 = 88

30 − 1 = 29

The difference is 29.

"You might do it a different way. Just make sure you show me how you figured out the answers on your paper."

The students worked on this activity for the rest of math class. They solved the problems in a variety of ways, depending upon the numbers. (See Figures 9–5 and 9–6.) At the end of class, Bonnie again collected their name value strips.

DAY 4

Bonnie put the name value strips in a pocket chart and had the class help her arrange them in order of value. "I notice how close Christina's name is to one hundred dollars," Bonnie commented. "It's just one away. Is anyone else's name close to one hundred dollars?"

"I'm only twelve dollars away," Carolyn said.

"I'm closer than that," Stanley said.

"I'm the farthest away," said Ada, the only member of the class with a one-digit value.

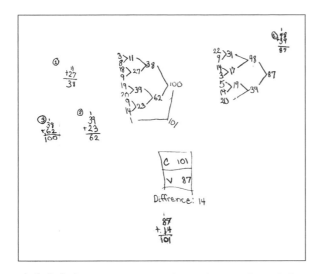

▲▲▲▲▲▲Figure 9–6 *When Vincent found the difference between his and Christina's name values, he added up.*

"The number one hundred is important in our number system, just like the number ten," Bonnie continued. "With practice, you should be able to take any number less than one hundred and know what number added to that number will make one hundred. If you are able to do that, mental math will be much easier for you."

"Let's start with ninety-nine. What number added to ninety-nine will make one hundred?" Bonnie asked.

"That's easy," Carolyn said. "Just add one."

"What if I turn it around and start with one? What number added to one makes one hundred?"

"It's the same thing just turned around," Carolyn said.

"What if I gave you the number ninety?"

"It's ten," the class answered.

"What about eighty?" Bonnie continued.

"Twenty," they replied.

Bonnie continued with seventy, sixty, fifty, and so on until she got to zero. As she asked the questions, she wrote on the board:

90 80 70 60 50 40 30 20 10 0

10 20 30 40 50 60 70 80 90 100

"Do you notice anything about these numbers?" Bonnie asked.

"They have partners," Melissa noticed. She came to the board and pointed to the 90, 10 combination and the 10, 90 combination as an example.

"Do you think other numbers less than one hundred have partners?" Bonnie queried.

"You could do it by fives," James offered and explained how ninety-five and five are partners.

"I think every number has a partner," Mark suggested. "If one and ninety-nine are partners, then two and ninety-eight are partners, and three and ninety-seven are partners. It's a pattern."

"How many partners are there?" Bonnie probed.

"One hundred," Mark replied quickly.

"Are you sure about that?" she asked. Bonnie knew that Mark liked to think about mathematics and got excited about mathematical patterns.

"I see what you mean," Mark said. "If I count ninety-nine and one as partners, then I can't count one and ninety-nine, can I?"

"I want you to keep thinking about that Mark," Bonnie said. "We'll come back to that problem."

Mark didn't want to let it go.

"I think it's fifty partners. It's half of one hundred. Can I prove it?"

"Sure," Bonnie said. "Why don't you work on that problem while I explain the activity I had planned for the class?"

Mark smiled, went to get paper, and set off to work.

Bonnie then passed out the *How Close to $100?* worksheets she had prepared with the students' first names listed in the first column.

"This is your task. In the first column are your names. In the second column I want you to write the name value of each student next to his or her name. If you all put your sentence strips on your desks, everyone will be able to walk around and fill in the chart.

In the third column I want you to record how close each person's name value is to one hundred dollars. When you have finished, we'll see if there are any hundred partners in our class."

The students set to work. Some copied all the name values before finding the differences between the names and one hundred dollars. Others worked on the differences as they went along. As they worked Bonnie circulated through the class asking students how they figured out the differences. She could see which students had facility with mental computation and which students needed tools such as the hundreds chart, a number line, or pencil and paper to help them. (See Figures 9–7 and 9–8.) She also kept her eye on Mark's progress in finding the number of pairs of numbers that add to one hundred.

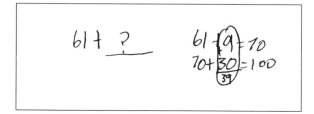

▲▲▲▲▲▲Figure 9–7 *When figuring how close Martha's name was to 100, Nancy added to the nearest 10 and then proceeded to add a multiple of 10 to 100.*

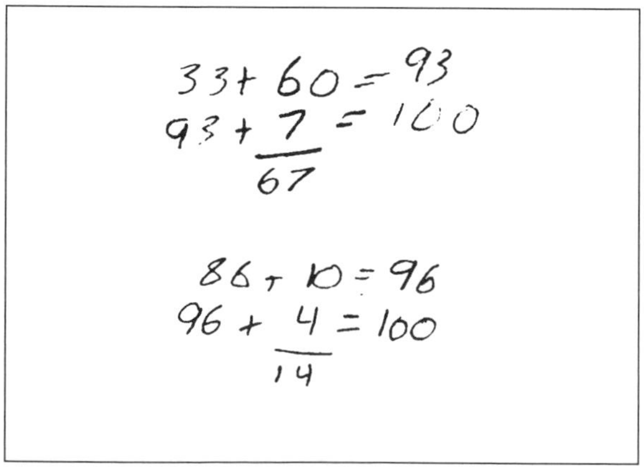

$$33 + 60 = 93$$
$$93 + 7 = 100$$
$$\overline{67}$$

$$86 + 10 = 96$$
$$96 + 4 = 100$$
$$\overline{14}$$

▲▲▲▲▲▲Figure 9–8 *Kevin added a multiple of 10 to get as close as possible to 100 and then added ones.*

As the students were finishing their worksheets, Bonnie asked for their attention. "We're going to be checking our charts to see if they are correct," she explained, "but first let's look at what Mark has found out about partners."

Mark came up to the front with a list of all the possible partners to make one hundred.

"I was right when I said fifty, but it's really fifty-one if you count zero and one hundred," Mark admitted.

Bonnie then had each child report how close to one hundred dollars his or her name was. If someone disagreed, Bonnie had students come to the front and explain how they had arrived at their answers.

When everyone's chart was complete and correct, Bonnie asked the class to look for hundred partners.

"I'm a partner with Greg," Sandy said.

"Why is that?" Bonnie asked.

"Because sixty-three plus thirty-seven equals one hundred."

"That's correct," Mark confirmed.

The students studied their papers and came up with two other pairs. Mark's and Nancy's names were worth forty-three and fifty-seven dollars, and Lydia's and Aaron's names were worth fifty-one and forty-nine dollars.

"I wish I had a partner," Carolyn moaned. "If only Ada were worth twice as much instead of six dollars."

"I'll never find a partner," Stanley said, laughing. "No one can be worth four dollars."

"You did a great job today," Bonnie complimented, "and by the way, Stanley, it's possible for you to have a partner. How about BB?"

"That's cool," Stanley said as the class lined up for recess.

EXTENSIONS

1. Ask children at each table to add up the name values of their group and post the data for comparisons. This gives practice with three-digit addition and subtraction.

2. Ask each child to figure out the individual name values and total value of his or her family members. This is a good homework assignment. Graph the results as a class and make comparisons between families.

3. Have children compare the values of other related words: opposites, synonyms, homonyms, animals, days of the week, months of the year, and so on.

4. Have children design problems for others to solve. For example, *Which is worth more, Wednesday or Friday? How much more?*

5. Reverse the letter values (A = $26, B = $25, C = $24, and so on) and ask children to figure out the values of their names again and compare them to the original values. Find out which names in the class change the most and the least.

Questions and Discussion

▲▲

▲ *What if a lesson takes a different direction than planned?*

In reality, most lessons do not turn out exactly as they were planned. A teacher can never be prepared for the questions or comments students will offer. What is important is that the teacher decides whether a question or an idea can possibly enrich the lesson or whether it will detract from the lesson. This is often a hard call to make. Many factors are involved. In this lesson, Bonnie chose to use the exploration of the values of opposites because of the students' interest and because she could continue with her plan of comparing values. When Mark wanted to find how many pairs of numbers make one hundred, Bonnie chose to let him research his question independently while she went on with the lesson as she had planned for the others. At the end of the math period, Bonnie was able to acknowledge Mark's efforts and incorporate his findings into the class discussion. These kinds of decisions must be made quickly, are largely intuitive, and are easier to make with experience.

▲ *Why is it important to write down each step of the students' mental computation if they are explaining it orally?*

It is often quite difficult to follow a person's thinking. By writing down each step, it is easier to understand that individual's thought process. Mathematics is a way of thinking and it is important to be able to communicate that thinking in ways that can be understood by others. Students can benefit from not only listening to a strategy different from their own but also seeing a representation of that strategy.

▲ *Why is mental computation important?*

Being able to compute mentally is vital for the development of estimation skills and number sense. Being able to know if an answer is reasonable comes from practice with mental arithmetic. When students look at a problem such as $100 - 54$, we want them to know that the answer must be less than fifty. This kind of fluency with numbers can be obtained by spending a great deal of time with the basic number facts and landmark numbers such as ten, twenty-five, fifty, and one hundred. Too often, students are pushed into working with multidigit numbers before they are fluent with smaller numbers. If students have a good understanding of numbers less than one hundred, their knowledge can be applied to the larger numbers. To obtain this understanding, daily opportunities for mental computation must be available for students.

CHAPTER TEN
LITTLE BOXES

Overview

This lesson combines the art of origami with measurement, estimation, data collection, and comparison. Students learn how to make an origami box out of a 6-inch square of paper. They estimate how many lima beans will fill their boxes and write about their reasoning. After discussing their estimates, students find the actual number of beans that fill their boxes. Data is collected from each pair and students reflect on the results.

Materials

▲ 3-by-3-inch sticky notes, 1 per student
▲ 6-inch squares of origami paper (colored Xerox paper or Astro Brite paper works well), 1 per student
▲ 5 to 8 1-quart ziptop bags, each filled with about 1 cup of large lima beans
▲ *Directions for Making Little Boxes* (see Blackline Masters)

Time

▲ two class periods

Teaching Directions

1. As you model and give directions, have students each make a box from a 6-by-6-inch square of origami paper. Remind them to fold carefully and make firm creases.

2. After the students have successfully made boxes, show a lima bean and ask for estimates for how many beans will fill a box.

3. Explain to the students that, working in pairs and using just one of their boxes, they should talk about how many lima beans they think will fill the box. Clarify that filling the box means that the beans are level with the top and the box is not bulging.

Then they put ten beans in the box and talk again. Finally, they record and explain their estimate.

Write the directions on the board and review them:

1. Use one box.

2. Look at one lima bean and talk with your partner about how many beans will fill the box.

3. Put 10 beans in your box and talk about how many beans you now think will fill the box. Record your estimate.

4. Explain your thinking in writing.

4. To help the children with writing, ask them for words they might need. Write these on the board for their reference.

5. When students have completed writing, have them share their ideas with the whole class.

6. On Day 2, model for the children how to fill a box with lima beans, reminding them that a box is full when the beans are level with the top and the box is not bulging. Give students directions for what they are to do with their partners. Write the directions on the board:

1. Fill the box you chose yesterday and count the beans.

2. Write that number on your paper and on a sticky note.

3. Fill the other box, count the beans, and write it on another sticky note.

4. Place both sticky notes on the front board.

7. With the class, organize the sticky notes so that the children can more easily discuss the data.

8. Lead a class discussion by asking the following questions:

What can you say about the number of beans it took to fill your boxes?

We all made the same origami box, so why did we get different numbers of lima beans?

9. Explain to the students that working in pairs, they will compare the estimates they made yesterday with the actual counts for their box. To help prepare the students for this activity, pose a specific question: "What if you estimated thirty-eight and your actual count was fifty? How would you compare these numbers?" Have several children respond.

10. Then direct each pair to find the difference between their estimate and the actual count for their box. Have them explain how they figured the difference on the paper they wrote the day before.

11. In a class discussion, have students explain how they figured the difference between their estimates and their counts. You may want to initiate the discussion with an example: "If you know the count and the estimate, you can find the difference. If you had a count of fifty-three and an estimate of forty, what would the difference be?" Record on the board.

Count	Estimate	Difference
53	40	?

Teaching Notes

Although this lesson involves estimation, measuring volume, and looking at data, the primary purpose for the lesson is to give students an opportunity to compare numbers. It also sets the stage for later work in comparing several sizes of origami boxes. We have chosen to stress comparing numbers in this lesson since it is one of the areas where students become easily confused if they have not had enough experience. The language that is involved with comparing is varied and sometimes not familiar to children. What's the difference? Who has more? How many more? What do you need to have the same number as I do? How do these two numbers compare? This is the type of mathematical language that children need to hear and make sense of in order to develop strategies that are meaningful to them.

Prior to this lesson, students had experiences with making simple origami shapes. When cutting their own squares for projects, they learned the importance of squares having equal and straight sides. While folding squares they had opportunities to see different shapes that could be made. Experience with origami can add to children's understanding of geometric concepts.

Each step of the following lesson requires students to work with partners. In our classrooms, each student does a great deal of work in collaboration with others. We regularly discuss the qualities of a good partner. We model how to share and how to decide who goes first. For these lessons to go smoothly, time must be spent on regularly reinforcing the expectations for partner work. The lesson involves at least two class periods. A follow-up extension may be introduced as a whole-class lesson or as an independent or choice activity.

In our experience, once students know how to make the origami boxes, they are eager to make more. Some students enjoy using different-size squares to make sets of graduated boxes, some make lids for their boxes so they can store their treasures, and others ask their parents to buy them origami paper.

The Lesson

▲▲▲

"Today we're going to make a little origami box and see how many lima beans it will hold," Lynne told the class. There was an audible sound of interest from the children.

Holding up a piece of origami paper, Lynne asked, "How would you describe this piece of paper?"

Several hands went up.

"It's a square," Brendan offered.

"All sides are the same length," Diana added.

"If we measure this square, how many inches do you think it is on each side?"

There were guesses of 3, 5, and 7. Lynne held a ruler up to the square to show it was just about 6 inches on a side.

"Six," the children sang out in chorus.

"We call this a six-inch-by-six-inch square," Lynne instructed.

Lynne flipped the ruler over to show that it was also 15 cm by 15 cm and showed them the origami paper package that read "150 mm by 150 mm."

"If I fold it on the diagonal, like this, what does it make?" she asked the class as she did the folding.

Fold on diagonal and crease.

"A triangle," the class called out.

"Next, fold the other diagonal," Lynne directed as she demonstrated, opening the square and folding the other diagonal.

Fold on other diagonal and crease.

Lynne unfolded the square and showed it to the class.

"It looks like a four-square court," Jeffrey noted.

"You mean a four-triangle court," Patricia corrected.

Lynne distributed the origami paper squares and told the students to fold their squares on both diagonals as she had just modeled. She reminded them to fold carefully and to make firm creases.

When everyone had folded the two diagonals, Lynne continued with the directions. "Fold each corner up to the center point, like this," she told them, "and then fold again."

Fold up one corner to meet the center point, then fold over again so that the fold edge meets the center point. Don't let the first fold slip.

Unfold and repeat with each corner.

Lynne opened the square and repeated the two folds for each of the other three corners. She then directed the children to fold their squares as she had, holding up her square as a model.

When you are finished, your square will have folds on all dotted lines.

Cut as shown.

After all of the children had folded their squares as Lynne had directed, she showed how to cut the square to prepare for making the box.

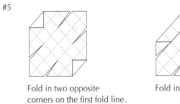

Fold in two opposite corners on the first fold line.

Fold in each of these edges.

Once students had their papers ready, she asked them to gather on the rug so that they could more easily see how to fold a square into a box.

Fold up each of the four flaps as shown.

The flaps you have just folded are the sides. Stand them up.

Fold each of the long flaps over and inside the box.

If you like, put a drop of glue under each point for added strength.

"It comes out smaller than I thought," Brian noted.

Lynne directed the students to return to their seats and complete their own boxes. Children worked together to help one another. When each had successfully made a box, she asked them to leave their boxes on their tables and gather at the front of the room.

First Lynne commented on how well they had helped each other and how well they all made the boxes. Then she held up her box and one lima bean. "How many lima beans like this one will fit in this box?" she asked.

"Seventy," Jeffrey responded.

"I think it's less than seventy," Susan commented. Several other students also gave estimates.

Lynne gave directions. "For the next part of the lesson, you and your partner will use just one of your boxes. You'll put the other box aside for now. First you will talk about how many beans you think it will take to fill the box so that it is full. Next, you will put ten beans in your box and see if your thinking has changed about how many beans it will take. Keep in mind that a box is full when the beans are level with the top and the box is not bulging. With this new information, you and your partner will write about how many beans you think will fill the box."

To review the directions, Lynne wrote on the board:

1. Use one box.

2. Look at one lima bean and talk with your partner about how many beans will fill the box.

3. Put 10 beans in your box and talk about how many beans you now think will fill the box. Record your estimate.

4. Explain your thinking in writing.

"What are some words you might need to write about this?" she asked. As students offered words, Lynne wrote them on the board as references:

lima beans

estimate

box

After starting the activity, children offered other words and Lynne added them to the list.

bottom

thought

layers

"Words are important, but what else will help you explain your thinking?" Lynne asked. Students were used to writing assignments such as this one and suggested numbers, pictures, and tallies.

Before the children got to work, Lynne asked Diana to read the directions on the board. She asked for questions and then sent partners off to their seats, each with ten lima beans and a piece of lined paper.

While students were discussing their estimates using one bean, Lynne circulated to make sure each pair had the needed supplies. One pair had trouble agreeing on which box to use and a few had trouble agreeing on their estimates, but soon everyone was busy writing.

As students finished writing about their estimates, Lynne directed them to sit with their partners on the rug and quietly practice reading aloud what they wrote on their papers. This would prepare them for sharing their ideas with the class.

A class discussion revealed that the children's estimates for filling the box ranged from thirty to fifty-seven lima beans. Most reasoned that ten beans filled the bottom of a box and that it would take four or five layers of ten to fill the box. Some thought only eight or nine beans filled the bottom. Others imagined how clumps of ten beans would fit into the box. Several partners made estimates and then adjusted them, increasing or decreasing them by a few beans. (See Figures 10–1 through 10–3.)

Lynne collected their papers and told them to put their names on each of their boxes since they would need them tomorrow for the next part of the lesson.

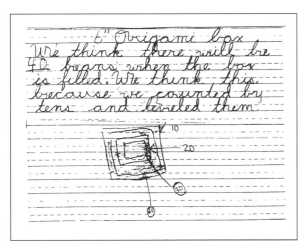

▲▲▲▲▲▲**Figure 10–1** *Diana and Albert made a three-dimensional drawing to show their thinking.*

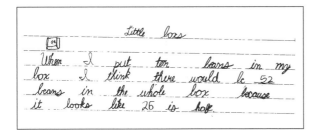

▲▲▲▲▲▲**Figure 10–2** *Eric and Rory attempted to show their beans in layers of 10.*

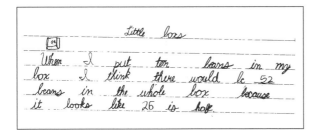

▲▲▲▲▲▲**Figure 10–3** *Ben and Brian looked at filling half the box.*

DAY 2

The next day, Lynne placed on each table a ziptop bag with about 1 cup of lima beans and then gathered the children at the front of the room to give them directions for filling their origami boxes.

"First of all, with your partner, take the box you used yesterday and fill it with lima beans," Lynne told them while filling her box. "Gently tap down the beans, make sure the beans are level on top, and make sure the box is not bulging on the sides. After you fill your box, you have several jobs to do. First, count the beans and record the number in two places—on the paper you wrote yesterday and on a sticky note. Next, so that we have more data to look at, fill your other box, count the beans, and write that number on another sticky note."

Lynne wrote the directions on the board:

1. Fill the box you chose yesterday and count beans.

2. Write that number on your paper and on a sticky note.

3. Fill the other box, count the beans, and write it on another sticky note.

4. Place both notes on the front board.

The students returned to their seats and began to fill their boxes. Lynne circulated, returning their papers from the day before and observing the students working. Patricia and Susan were busy grouping their beans by fives. Dylan and Collin were meticulously counting by tens. Kelly and Gabi were counting by ones. Everyone was busy and soon all the sticky notes were on the board.

Lynne asked for the children's attention to begin a class discussion.

"Why don't we put them in order?" Albert suggested before Lynne had a chance to give any instructions.

"That's exactly what we need to do so we can make sense of all of this data," Lynne responded. "We need to arrange them so we can easily find the lowest and the highest numbers."

By scanning the sticky notes, the students determined that the lowest count was forty-seven and the highest was seventy-six. Lynne asked Rory and Brian to come to the board and put the sixties in order in a row. Albert and Diana arranged the fifties. Lynne put the remaining numbers in order to complete the sticky note chart.

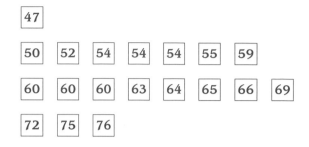

"What can you say about how many beans it took to fill our origami boxes?" Lynne asked the class.

"Most are in the fifties and sixties," Nelson suggested.

"Three people got sixty and three got fifty-four," Maria noted.

"The range is forty-seven to seventy-six," Collin added.

"We all made the same origami box, so why did we get different numbers of lima beans?" Lynne asked.

"The beans are different," Ben offered.

"Some boxes turned out bigger and some were littler," Dylan called out.

"Some people stuffed their boxes," Jennifer observed.

"You've pointed out some reasons for the differences in the number of lima beans it took to fill the boxes," Lynne acknowledged. "Now that you have your actual counts, your task is to compare the estimate you made yesterday for one of your boxes with the actual count for that box."

Lynne then posed a specific problem to help prepare the class. She asked, "What if you estimated thirty-eight and your actual count was fifty? How would you compare these numbers?"

Ben explained what he would do. He said, "Add two to thirty-eight and that would be forty. Then add ten and that would be fifty. So that's twelve."

"Add ten to thirty-eight to get forty-eight, add two more and get fifty," Diana offered. "You had to add ten and two, so that's twelve."

"I took fifty minus thirty and got twenty. Then take away eight from twenty and that makes twelve," Patricia added.

"You've just heard some ways to explain how to compare two numbers. Working with your partner, find the difference between your estimate and the actual count for your box. Write a sentence to explain how you figured the difference. As soon as you finish, come back to the front to share your strategies," Lynne directed.

As Lynne walked around the room checking to see how the class was doing, she saw that Nelson and Jeffrey didn't seem to know what to do.

"The difference is twenty-five," Nelson said.

"What numbers are you comparing?" Lynne probed.

When the boys looked blank, she asked, "What was your estimate?"

"Forty-one," Jeffrey said.

"How many beans filled your box?" Lynne continued.

"Sixty-six," Nelson said.

"Tell me in words what you did with those two numbers to get twenty-five," Lynne directed.

Once Nelson and Jeffrey explained their strategy in words, Lynne said, "Now write what you just told me. That's your strategy." They got right to work.

After everyone had finished, Lynne began a class discussion.

"How many of you used the word *difference* in your writing?" she asked. Most hands went up.

"Read how you used it," she told them.

"'The difference between fifty and sixty-three is thirteen,'" Patricia read (see Figure 10–4).

"'We had a twenty-bean difference,'" Eric read.

"'The difference between our estimate and our answer was thirteen,'" Kim read.

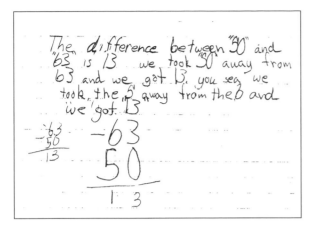

The difference between "50" and "63" is 13 we took 50 away from 63 and we got 13. you see we took the 5 away from the 6 and we got 13

$$
\begin{array}{r}
-63 \\
-50 \\
\hline 13
\end{array}
\qquad
\begin{array}{r}
-63 \\
50 \\
\hline 13
\end{array}
$$

▲▲▲▲▲▲**Figure 10–4** *Patricia and her partner explained their thinking.*

"So, if you know the count and the estimate, you can find the difference," Lynne said and then asked, "If you had a count of fifty-three and an estimate of forty, what would the difference be?" Lynne wrote on the board:

Count	Estimate	Difference
53	40	?

Several students offered thirteen as the answer and explained their thinking.

"If you knew the estimate and the difference, could you determine the actual count?" she asked, adding to what she had written on the board.

Count	Estimate	Difference
53	40	?
?	37	17

"Twenty," Luis suggested.

"No one had twenty beans," Rory reminded us.

"So it must be, let's see, thirty plus ten is forty and seven plus seven is fourteen, and fourteen and forty is fifty-four," Eric thought out loud.

There was time for three pairs to read their papers to the class; other students would report the next day. (See Figures 10–5 and 10–6 for two pairs' work on this problem.) Lynne ended the lesson by telling the students that later on they would have a

6 by 6 box
Our estement for the 6 by 6 box is 80.
Are real anwer was 66.
The diffrence is 14

How we figured it out:

This is the diffrence

We counted all the tens and added six and got 66 there were ten and six left over. We counted them and got 66 that means the diffrince is 14

▲▲▲▲▲▲**Figure 10–5** *Jennifer and Gina grouped tens and ones to make 66 and then counted up to 80.*

When we counted there were 55 beans in the box. The difference between 30 and 55 is 25. We got 25 by making the 55 change into a 50 and we minused 20 from the 50 and added 5 and 20 plus 5 equals 25.

▲▲▲▲▲▲**Figure 10–6** *Collin and Brendan found it easier to subtract from 50 to find the difference.*

chance to make different-size boxes, find the volume of each, and compare the results.

EXTENSION

For a follow-up lesson, or as an independent task or a choice activity, have students estimate how many beans will fill boxes made from 5-by-5-inch squares and 7-by-7-inch squares. As they did with the 6-by-6-inch squares, they should fill the boxes to get the actual count. Once they have this information, have students compare how many beans filled the boxes made from the 5-inch squares with the number of beans that filled the boxes made from the 6- and 7-inch squares. (See Figures 10–7 and 10–8.)

Students can repeat the activity using centimeter cubes or different-size beans. When recording all of this information, some students find ways to organize their papers, others don't. For those that need help, show them how a table might be useful:

Box size	lima beans	cm cubes	navy beans
5 inch			
6 inch			
7 inch			

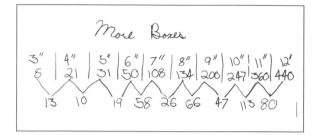

▲▲▲▲▲▲Figure 10–8 *Maria created her own investigation making 3-inch to 12-inch boxes and finding differences.*

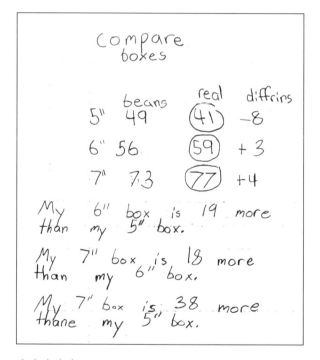

▲▲▲▲▲▲Figure 10–7 *Susan and Kim organized their information and made comparison statements.*

Questions and Discussion

▲▲

▲ How do you encourage students to explain their thinking?

From the beginning of the year, students learn that explaining their thinking is something that we do daily as part of our mathematics lessons. If students communicate regularly about their thinking beginning in kindergarten and first grade, by the time they reach second grade they have some idea about what it means to describe their strategies and reasoning processes. If not, they can learn how to do so as third graders.

From the first day of the school year, we have students doing mental arithmetic and we ask them to explain their thinking. Typically, at first only a few hands go up. However, once they have some models of what this means, more and more hands go up, and after a few weeks, most students are volunteering their thinking.

When we encounter a class that doesn't seem to know what explaining one's thinking means, we become the models. To give the children an idea of how to describe their reasoning, we think out loud. For example, for the problem 26 + 26, we might say, "When I see these numbers, I think about quarters. I know that twenty-five cents and twenty-five cents is fifty cents, so twenty-six plus twenty-six must be two more than fifty, or fifty-two. What's another way you could think about this problem?"

When we ask students to write about their thinking, we try to be very explicit about what we expect to see on their papers. At the beginning of the year we often provide a frame for students to copy and complete. For example, in the origami box problem, we might write:

We think that ___ lima beans will fill our origami box.

We think this because_____.

When asking for verbal explanations we sometimes do the same thing. We provide the beginning of sentences for each student to complete. For example, we might write the following on the board prior to having students orally share their findings for the origami box:

Our estimate was _____.

Our actual count was _____.

The difference was _____.

We figured it out by _____.

We have also found it helpful to have partners practice their presentations before coming up to the front to share. This also provides a time for students to decide who will read and who will hold the paper. The sharing time goes more smoothly when we provide this preparation time.

▲ When the students were making their boxes, what did you do for children who had difficulty or made an error when cutting on the required folds?

The first time students make origami boxes, we tell them the boxes might not be perfect since they have never made one before. We also encourage students to help each other. As students follow each step of the directions, we check to see if everyone is on the right track. If one student seems to be struggling, we stand close by to assist. Often when students get to the step where they need to cut, we ask them to draw a line with a pencil to show where they will cut, and then after checking, we give them scissors. Also, we have plenty of extra squares ready if needed.

▲ *When students find the difference between two numbers, shouldn't they be taught to use subtraction and take the smaller number from the larger number?*

As adults, we have figured out or been taught that subtraction is one way to find the difference between two numbers. But when doing mental arithmetic, we often rely on our number sense to make the problem meaningful. First of all, what we do to figure out the difference depends on the numbers we're dealing with, what we know about those numbers, and their relationship to each other.

Whether students subtract, add up, count backward, use counters, or do some combination of these actions depends on how they see the problem and what strategies they have to make sense of the numbers they're comparing. What is important is that students have systematic strategies that they understand. If a strategy works, and the child can explain it, then it is appropriate.

▲ *When students share their strategies with the class, how do you get other students to pay attention?*

From the beginning of the year, we work on how to verbalize one's thinking and how to listen to others while they share their ideas. It's not always easy to ensure total engagement, but we have learned some tips from our experience. First of all, we rarely have every student share during the same discussion period. We limit the sharing time to no more than ten minutes, especially with younger children. Also, we have found it more effective not to squeeze in the sharing time at the end of the math period. It is more helpful to collect the students' work, have a brief review of what they did, and have them share at the beginning of the math period the next day.

Another strategy we have tried is to give students a job to do while listening. For example, "Your job is to listen to Kim's report and see if her strategy is like yours," or, "Listen to Brian's strategy so that you can describe it in your own words," or, "Collin's strategy is similar to one we've already heard; see if you can figure out who's strategy it's like."

CHAPTER ELEVEN
BODY MEASUREMENTS

Overview

This lesson gives children experience with comparing quantities in the context of measuring a variety of lengths. The story *How Big Is a Foot?*, by Rolf Myller, provides a way to introduce to children the importance of standard units for measurement. After learning how to use a measuring tape, partners measure, record, and compare their body measurements in both inches and centimeters. The students then take their teacher's measurements and compare them to their own, again in both inches and centimeters.

Materials

▲ *How Big Is a Foot?*, by Rolf Myller (New York: Young Yearling, 1991)

▲ measurement tools for length: rulers, tape measures, meter sticks, and yard-sticks, several of each

▲ tape measure with inches on one side and centimeters on the other, 1 per pair of students

▲ directions for *Body Measurements* (see Blackline Masters)

▲ record sheets, 1 each per student: *Measuring Ourselves in Inches*, *Measuring Ourselves in Centimeters*, *Teacher/Student Comparisons* (see Blackline Masters)

Time

▲ two to three class periods

Teaching Directions

1. Read *How Big Is a Foot?* to the class. Discuss the need for a standard unit of measurement.

2. Show rulers, tape measures, and meter sticks and/or yardsticks to the class. (Optional: show other measuring tools such as scales, thermometers, and timepieces.) Ask the students what these tools measure and what unit or units of measurement each tool uses.

3. Review the meanings of *length, width,* and *height.*

4. With a tape measure, find the height of the chalkboard in inches and in centimeters.

5. Use the tape measure to demonstrate the size of an inch and the size of a centimeter.

6. Remeasure the chalkboard in both inches and centimeters.

7. Have each table group find things that are 1 inch long and something that is 1 centimeter long.

8. Measure an object in the room, such as a chalkboard eraser, in inches, centimeters, and interlocking cubes.

9. Explain the activity *Body Measurements* and how to record in both inches and centimeters.

10. Have students help measure you in both inches and centimeters.

11. Ask students to record both your measurements and their own measurements in centimeters and in inches on their *Teacher/Student Comparisons* record sheets and make comparisons.

Teaching Notes

Measuring involves attaching a number to a quantity. The numbers we assign depend upon the property of measurement we want to describe. Properties of measurement include length, area, weight, capacity, volume, elapsed time, and temperature.

The history of measurement tells us that throughout the years various measures have been used to calculate and communicate quantities. The metric system was developed in France at the time of the French Revolution and is the standard system currently used in most parts of the world. In this decimal system, the unit of length is the meter, the unit of weight or mass is the gram, the unit of volume is the liter, and the unit of temperature is the Celsius scale. The United States is slowly converting to the metric system of measurement, but it still uses the foot as the unit of length, the pound as the unit of weight, the gallon as the unit of volume, and the Fahrenheit scale for temperature. Since the United States uses two systems, it is important that students have experiences with both.

This lesson focuses on the property of length and uses the book *How Big Is a Foot?* to present children with the rationale for using standard units when measuring. This book tells the story of a king who is struggling to think of a present to give his queen for her birthday. What could he give someone who already has everything? He finally thinks of having a bed made for her. Beds haven't yet been invented, so the queen certainly doesn't already have one. To figure out how big the bed should be, the king asks the queen to put on her new pajamas and lie down on the floor. Using his paces, he measures and finds that the bed must be six feet long and three feet wide. The carpenter's apprentice who makes the bed, however, is a good deal smaller than the king. Although he carefully builds a bed that is six of *his* feet long and three of *his* feet wide, the bed is far too small. The king gets so angry that he has the apprentice thrown in jail. While in jail, with lots of time to think, the apprentice realizes what the problem was. He explains his solution to the king and is able to make a new bed in time for the queen's birthday. The king is so pleased that he releases the apprentice from jail and makes him a royal prince.

The story introduces children both to the need for standard units and, therefore, the need for standard measuring tools. While children use tape measures for this specific activity, it's valuable to introduce them to a variety of measuring tools as well as to both systems of measurement we use when measuring how long things are.

The Lesson

▲▲

Lynne began the math period by reading aloud to the class *How Big Is a Foot?*, by Rolf Myller. When she got to the part in the story where the apprentice goes to jail, she talked with the children about the apprentice's problem and asked what advice they would offer him.

"What is the problem?" Lynne asked.

"The bed was too small," Gabi answered.

"But why was it too small?"

"The king's feet are much bigger. The apprentice has tiny feet, and he used his little feet to make the bed," Gabi explained.

"He measured wrong," Thomas offered. "He measured it wrong because the apprentice and the king don't have the same foot size."

Lynne could see that the students were beginning to understand the need for standardized measurement.

"What could the apprentice do if he were given one more chance?" Lynne asked the class.

The students talked to one another for a few minutes and came up with a variety of solutions.

"He could have the king step in paint and make a rectangle."

"The apprentice could mark where the king walked with chalk."

"Cut out a piece of paper the right size and then build the bed."

Brendan suggested making a ruler. "Make a ruler. Cut a stick the size of the king's foot. Actually, you'll need eighteen sticks. Make eighteen rulers. Put six on one side, three on the top, six on the other side, and three on the bottom. Then it will be the right size bed for the queen."

"Your ideas are great," Lynne said. "Now let's see how the problem was solved in the book." She then continued reading the story.

After talking with the children about the importance of having a standard unit of length that everyone uses, Lynne showed the class a collection of tools for measuring length—several rulers, cloth and metal tape measures, a meter stick, and a yardstick.

"What do these things measure?" she asked.

"How tall we are," Thomas said.

"How long something is," Gabi replied.

"How much we've grown," Collin said.

"We measured length with cubes," Albert remembered.

"What's the difference between the cubes and these tools?" Lynne asked.

"We had to count the cubes," Kelly said, "but these things already have numbers on them so it's easier."

Lynne picked up a cloth tape measure and said, "If I measure the height of the chalkboard, I get thirty. But, if I turn the tape over and measure again, I get seventy-five. What do these numbers mean?"

The students weren't sure, so Lynne showed them the tape measure again. "This side shows inches," she explained. "An inch is a measure of length that is about this big." Lynne held her thumb and index finger apart to show them the length of an inch. She measured the chalkboard again to show 30 inches.

Lynne then turned the tape measure over. "This side measures centimeters," she said. "A centimeter is a much smaller unit of measure." Lynne showed the class the length of a centimeter, using her thumb and index finger again. She measured the chalkboard again to show 75 centimeters.

"Wow, there's a lot more centimeters than inches," Brendan exclaimed.

"But centimeters are smaller," Patricia commented.

Lynne said, "Inches and centimeters are two different units for measuring length. If I want to compare my height with your height, I can use either inches or centimeters, but I need to measure both of us with the same unit."

Although these measurement concepts were confusing, Lynne knew that with practice the students would build their understanding.

"When you use a tape measure, how will you know if you are using inches or centimeters?" Lynne asked.

"Centimeters are the tiny ones," Kim said.

"About how big is one centimeter?" Lynne asked.

"Not very big," Patricia offered with a smile.

"We need to be a little more exact," Lynne said with a laugh.

"About the size of that little piece of chalk," Brian said.

Lynne took a tape measure and confirmed Brian's suggestion that the width of the chalk measured about 1 centimeter. She then gave each table group a tape measure and said, "Let's find some things in the room that are about one centimeter in length."

The students began measuring and came up with a number of suggestions including the top of a pen, the width of a finger, and the length of a staple.

"Now let's look at the side of the tape that shows inches," Lynne instructed. She asked them to show her how long one inch was using their thumbs and index fingers.

"Which one is bigger, an inch or a centimeter?" Lynne asked.

"An inch," responded the class.

"It's much bigger," Sonja added.

"Show me a centimeter with your thumb and index finger on one hand, and an inch with your other hand," Lynne asked. She scanned the room to be sure students were doing this correctly.

"Now I'm going to measure something in two different ways," Lynne continued. She picked up a chalkboard eraser and measured its length in inches and in centimeters. "This eraser is six inches long, and it's also fifteen centimeters long."

"It was eight cubes long when I measured it," Albert said.

Lynne concluded by saying, "The more you measure things in inches and in centimeters, the more familiar you will become using these different units of measurement and the better able you will be to make reasonable estimates of how long something is. Today, you will work with a partner and take measurements, first in inches, and then in centimeters. You will each have your own record sheets." Lynne showed them the two record sheets they would use, one for the inch measurements and one for the centimeter measurements.

"First you measure in inches," Lynne said, demonstrating how to use the tape measure on the correct side for inches. "After you measure each other in inches, you will compare your measurements." Lynne showed the centimeter side of the measuring tape and continued, "Then you will measure each other in centimeters and make comparisons."

Lynne distributed the tape measures and the record sheets for inches. "When you finish this sheet, come up and get the one for measuring in centimeters," she said.

The students enjoyed the activity and worked carefully to be as accurate as possible. As they measured, Lynne checked to make sure they were using the measuring tapes correctly. Figure 11–1 shows how one pair of students worked on this activity. When the students finished both record sheets she asked them to write if they preferred measuring in inches or centimeters. (See Figure 11–2.)

DAY 2

"Yesterday you compared each other's measurements in inches and in centimeters. Today you are going to compare your body measurements to mine," Lynne explained.

	Me	my Partner	Difference
Length of head	19	18	1
Around neck	29	28	1
Around waist	66	56	10
Waist to floor	75	77	2
Height	121	118	3
Length of foot	16	16	0
Around ankle	19	17	.2
Length of arm	56	58	2
Length of hand	13	14	1
Around knee	36	29	7
Length of thumb	5½	5	½

What do you notice about you and your partner's measurements? The diffrence is that the numbers were almost the same.

▲▲▲▲▲▲Figure 11–1 *These students measured each other in centimeters and recorded their findings.*

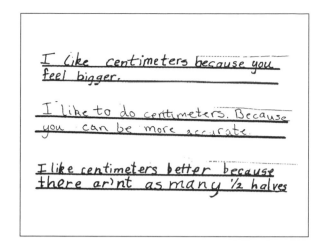

I like centimeters because you feel bigger.

I like to do centimeters. Because you can be more accurate.

I like centimeters better because there ar)nt as many ½ halves

▲▲▲▲▲▲Figure 11–2 *Students often prefer measuring in centimeters.*

"Who's going to measure you?" Linda asked.

"I'm going to ask all of you to help me," Lynne answered as she distributed a *Teacher/Student Comparisons* worksheet to each student.

Lynne had different students help take her measurements in both inches and centimeters. All of the students recorded them on their worksheets. For her height, she laid down on the floor.

"One hundred and seventy centimeters!" Ben gasped. "You're really tall."

"But I'm only sixty-eight inches," Lynne said as she got up.

"That's still big for inches," Jane commented.

"Your job now," Lynne continued, "is to write your measurements on the sheet and then compare them. Use the record sheets you completed yesterday so you don't have to measure all over again."

Lynne returned their completed worksheets. While the students were working, Lynne observed to make sure the students knew what to do and to see how each student was computing the measurement differences. She made notes about the students' strategies and computational skills as she circulated around the room.

Body Measurements 95

EXTENSIONS

1. Do other measurement investigations in this book:

▲ Chapter 10, *Little Boxes* (capacity)

▲ Chapter 12, *In One Minute* (time)

▲ Chapter 13, *Weather Report* (temperature)

2. Have students do similar comparisons with other areas of measurement.

▲ Have them compare weights using a bathroom scale for pounds or a balance scale for grams.

▲ Have students work with thermometers to compare temperatures at different times of the day or in different parts of the school.

▲ Have them compare the capacity of two containers using small beakers or graduated cylinders.

Questions and Discussion

▲▲▲

▲ *Won't students get confused if you teach two systems of measurement at one time?*

We live in a world where we encounter both the English and the metric systems. We have gallons of milk and 2-liter bottles of soda. We use rulers and tape measures that show both centimeters and inches. Grocery labels are written in both ounces and grams. Students need familiarity with both systems so they can establish referents for the various units of measure and thus be able to select a suitable unit for a specific measurement. It is important that the purpose of teaching both systems is for students to become comfortable working within each system, not making mathematical conversions between systems.

▲ *How can parents get involved?*

Measurement is an ideal topic for continued practice at home. Students can work with parents to find the heights of their family members. They can also look at labels to find the weights of various food and household items, measure the lengths and the widths of household objects, time household chores, or record the inside and outside temperatures.

▲ *Why do you do activities that seem similar?*

Students need to make many comparisons in order to gain understanding. It is important to provide students with many experiences for practice. By presenting a number of similar tasks that address the same concept, it is possible to provide both repetition and variety.

CHAPTER TWELVE
IN ONE MINUTE

Overview

Clocks are part of all our daily lives so it's beneficial to provide children experiences with time in school. This lesson provides children experiences with one minute. Working in pairs, children time each other to see how many letters and then numerals they can write in one minute. They then analyze their data to make comparisons.

Materials

▲ wall clock with second hand or other timepieces
▲ instructions for *In One Minute* (see Blackline Masters)

Time

▲ one to two class periods

Teaching Directions

1. Ask the children to close their eyes and raise their hands when they think one minute has elapsed. Tell them to keep their eyes closed until you ask them to open them, which you'll do when everyone has raised a hand.

2. Time one minute again, but this time ask the children to sit quietly with their eyes open. Call out ten-second intervals.

3. Discuss with the children things that they think they can do in one minute.

4. Invite a student to come to the board and write the letters of the alphabet for one minute, starting over at A after reaching Z. Count the letters in several ways.

5. Explain the activity to the class. (See instructions below and in Blackline Masters.) You may want to post the directions or duplicate and distribute them to the students.

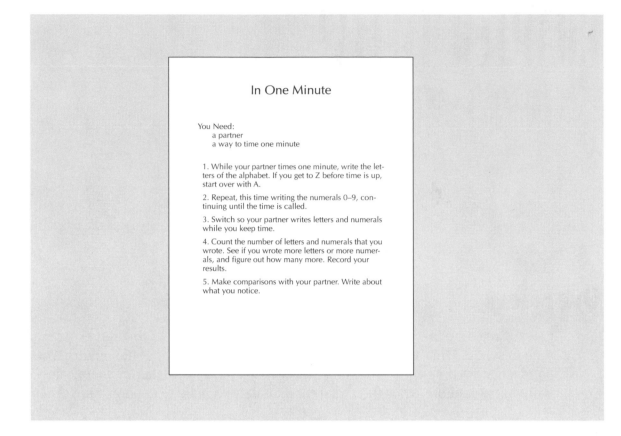

In One Minute

You Need:
   a partner
   a way to time one minute

1. While your partner times one minute, write the letters of the alphabet. If you get to Z before time is up, start over with A.

2. Repeat, this time writing the numerals 0–9, continuing until the time is called.

3. Switch so your partner writes letters and numerals while you keep time.

4. Count the number of letters and numerals that you wrote. See if you wrote more letters or more numerals, and figure out how many more. Record your results.

5. Make comparisons with your partner. Write about what you notice.

Teaching Notes

Time is divided into seconds, minutes, hours, days, weeks, months, and years and depends upon a uniform system of worldwide time measurement. Accurate and reliable tools for keeping track of time or measuring elapsed or expected time are also necessary.

The division of time into the twenty-four-hour day, the sixty-minute hour, and the sixty-second minute had its origins in ancient civilizations but has been in general use since about 1600 A.D.

Accurate watches and clocks are a result of an observation made in 1880 by Pierre Curie, a French scientist. Curie noticed that when quartz crystals are under pressure, they vibrate at a constant frequency. Later investigations showed that exposing crystals to an alternating electric current also caused them to vibrate. The first use of these discoveries was in the design of radios and the ability to provide a broadcast wave of constant frequency. In 1928, Bell Laboratories built the first quartz-crystal clock, which used quartz instead of a pendulum or the other mechanical devices used in ealier timepieces. The quartz clock was so accurate and reliable that by 1939 it replaced the mechanically regulated clocks at the Royalty Observatory in Greenwich, England.

It is important for this activity that the children all have some way to time one minute. A class clock with a second hand is ideal. If your classroom doesn't have one, bring one from home or provide students with some other timepieces such as stopwatches.

The Lesson

▲▲▲

DAY 1

To begin the lesson, Lynne gathered the students together and told them they were each going to time one minute. The students looked up at the classroom clock.

"You're going to try to time one minute without looking at the clock," Lynne said. "When I say go, I want you to close your eyes. Raise your hand when you think one minute has gone by. Keep your eyes closed. I will ask you to open them after everyone's hand is up."

The students closed their eyes and Lynne began timing. Some students raised a hand after only fifteen seconds. The last hand went up after two minutes.

"You may open your eyes now," Lynne said. She told the class the range of responses.

"Do you know how many seconds are in a minute?" she asked.

Many students knew that the answer was sixty.

"Yes, there are sixty seconds in one minute. Let's sit quietly for one minute," she continued, "but this time you may keep your eyes open and I will count the seconds by tens."

"Start," Lynne said and then counted off, "Ten seconds . . . twenty seconds . . . thirty seconds . . . forty seconds . . . fifty seconds . . . one minute.

"Think about things you could do in about one minute. Could you eat your lunch?"

"I could," Robby announced. "I eat my lunch really fast so I have more time to play."

"Could you finish your homework?"

"I wish I could," Jane lamented.

"Could you write the alphabet in one minute?"

"I think so," Greg said.

"Why don't you try?" Lynne suggested. "Come up to the board and write the alphabet from A to Z. If you finish, start writing the letters again. We'll see how many letters you are able to write in one minute."

The students used the classroom clock. They waited for the second hand to reach the 12 and then said, "Go." Greg began writing. After exactly one minute they yelled, "Stop!"

"I wrote a lot of letters," Greg said.

"How can you count them?" Lynne asked.

"I'll count them by twos." Greg counted off by twos and found that he had written eighty-one letters.

"Can anyone think of another way?" Lynne asked.

"Just count them in twenty-sixes," Christina said.

"Why?" Greg wondered.

"It's easy; the alphabet has twenty-six letters, so just find out how many times you did A to Z," Christina explained.

"What if he missed a letter?" Robby asked skeptically.

"He knows his alphabet," Christina retorted.

Greg found that he had written A to Z three times and had three letters left over. He calculated the three twenty-sixes in his head and added the three. He smiled when he got the same answer of eighty-one again.

"See, Robby, I didn't miss a letter."

The class then wanted Greg to count by fives to be absolutely sure. He circled every group of five, adding as he went, and came out to eighty with one left over.

"Today we're going to do an activity called *In One Minute*," Lynne explained.

She then explained the task to the class.

"In this activity, you need a partner, a piece of paper, and a way to keep track of one minute. You can use the clock, a watch, or a stopwatch. Your partner will time you for one minute. While he or she is timing, you will write the letters of the alphabet from A to Z. If you get to Z before the time is up, start over again as Greg did. Next, your partner will write the alphabet as you do the timing. When you have both finished writing letters, each of you will count the number of letters you wrote. Be sure to show how you did the counting and record the results on your paper. Then compare your results. Who had more? How many more?"

Lynne continued, "When you finish with letters, you are going to do the same thing for numerals. You will each write the numerals zero to nine as many times as you can. You will each count how many numerals you wrote and compare your results."

"When you have finished comparing, write about what you notice," Lynne added.

Lynne interacted with the students as they worked, asking questions and making suggestions. Some students needed help organizing their data. Others didn't know what to write about at the end. Lynne made a note to discuss the activity again using some actual data from one set of partners.

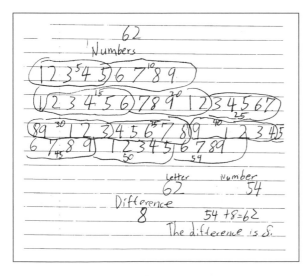

▲▲▲▲▲▲**Figure 12–1** *Dylan grouped and counted his numerals by fives and then found the difference between his numbers and letters by adding up.*

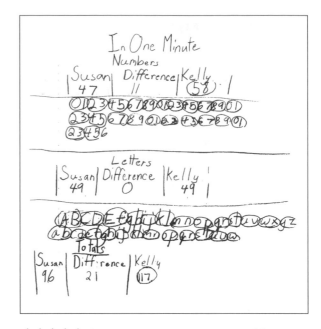

▲▲▲▲▲▲**Figure 12–2** *Susan counted her numerals and letters by twos and then compared her totals with Kelly's results.*

Figures 12–1 and 12–2 show how two students recorded for this activity.

DAY 2

When Lynne brought the class together the following day, she had Dana's and Jordan's papers from *In One Minute* to share with the class. She showed the papers to the students.

"Notice how neatly both Dana and Jordan wrote their numerals and letters. By writing neatly, they were able to count them easily."

"Look how they circled their groups," Lynne continued. "Jordan counted by fives and Dana counted by tens. Then they wrote down their totals. Jordan had fifty-nine letters and seventy-four numerals. Dana had fifty-six letters and ninety-two numerals.

"It was easy for Dana and Jordan to examine their data because they made a chart," Lynne explained.

She then asked the two students to make their chart on the chalkboard and to fill in their results.

	Dana	Jordan
Letters	56	59
Numbers	92	74

"What do you notice about their results?" Lynne asked. The class studied the chart for a moment and began noticing several things.

"Dana has more numbers."

"Jordan has more letters."

"Jordan has three more letters than Dana."

"They both have almost the same number of letters, but Dana has a lot more numbers," Jane observed.

"How many more?" Lynne asked.

"Eighteen more," Jane answered.

"How did you figure that out?" Lynne probed.

"I added twenty to the seventy-four, which made ninety-four, and took off two to get to ninety-two," Jane explained.

"Did anyone do it a different way?"

James raised his hand. "I started with seventy-four and added six to make eighty. Then I added twelve more and it was eighteen."

Lynne often stops to ask children how they make comparisons mentally. She finds that they usually start with tens and add up to the larger number, or they add up to a ten first before continuing. By articulating their methods, they clarify their own thinking processes and also offer alternative strategies for others.

Lynne then directed the students' attention back to the chart. "This time I want to compare Dana's numerals and letters. Did Dana write more letters or more? How many more?" The students figured out that Dana had written thirty-six more numerals.

Lynne then had the class compare Jordan's numerals with his letters and they

found that Jordan had written fifteen more numerals.

Next, Lynne had the students figure out the totals for Dana's and Jordan's work. They figured out the total amount of letters and numerals each one had written. They also figured out some differences. Dana and Jordan added more information to their chart.

	Dana	Jordan	Difference
Letters	56	59	3
Numbers	92	74	18
Totals	**148**	**133**	**15**

"What do you notice?" Lynne asked.

"They wrote more numbers than letters," Robby said.

"Dana has more altogether," Ben remarked.

"How many more does she have?" Lynne asked.

"She has fifteen more," Ben answered.

"These are the kinds of ideas you should record for this assignment," Lynne explained. "Be sure to write down your data for how many letters and how many numerals you each did in one minute. Then add up your totals and make some comparisons."

The students went back to work. Some of the students decided to do the activity over again. Others reorganized the data they had already collected so that it would be clearer and easier to read. Several students used a chart like Jordan and Dana's for their own work. Jordan and Dana decided to time themselves again and see if they could beat their previous results. Figures 12–3 and 12–4 show how two students improved their work.

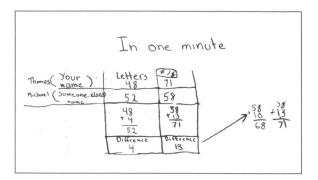

▲▲▲▲▲▲Figure 12–3 *Thomas organized his results on a chart and showed how he found the differences.*

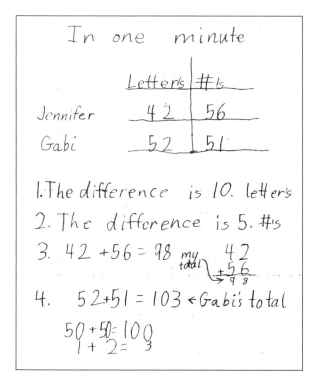

▲▲▲▲▲▲Figure 12–4 *Jennifer clearly described her findings in words, showing both differences and totals.*

EXTENSIONS

1. Have students predict how many letters and numerals they think could be written in half a minute. Partners time each other to test their estimates, then compare their results with their one-minute data.

2. Instead of writing letters and numerals, have the students time each other to see how many stars or dollar signs they can write in one minute.

3. Have pairs of students who have names with the same number of letters time each other on how many times they can write their names in one minute.

4. Use this activity as an introductory lesson on time measurement. Explore elapsed time problems using clocks or do time conversions such as calculating minutes, hours, days, and weeks given smaller units of time.

Questions and Discussion

▲▲

▲ *Why do students have difficulty with time measurement, and what can be done to develop time concepts?*

Time concepts are abstract and often difficult for students. Learning to tell time on an analog timepiece calls for the understanding that there are two, sometimes three, hands on the clock, each representing a different unit of time measurement. Also, while the numbers on a clock go from 1 to 12, the intervals between two numbers are five minutes long. If the minute hand is on the 4, it is twenty minutes past the hour. In addition, children have to equate "half hour" with thirty minutes or "a quarter past the hour" with fifteen minutes. There is much for children to learn. To help them, it's valuable to incorporate time into informal conversations, pointing out special times of the day such as recess, lunch, and dismissal. Using toy clocks with moveable hands can be helpful to show elapsed time. Schedules for classroom activities can be written on the chalkboard using standard time notation. An activity like *In One Minute* will not teach students to tell time but will give them experience in using a timepiece and developing measurement and mathematical language.

▲ *Why didn't you give the students record sheets instead of having them record their own way?*

It is important for students to have opportunities to organize data in their own ways in order to make sense of information for themselves. A problem often arises when students try to communicate this information to their teacher or to their classmates. It may make sense to them, but it is not always clear to others. Teachers can help students by offering models for organization or giving students prepared worksheets, but a worksheet offers only one possibility for demonstrating mathematical thinking and organization. Whenever possible, give students the chance to organize information on their own. Using actual student work that comes from their peers, as Lynne did in this lesson, can be an effective method for teaching students how to communicate mathematical thinking, the value of neatness, and the importance of clarity.

CHAPTER THIRTEEN
WEATHER REPORT

Overview

In this lesson, students use a thermometer to measure temperature in both Fahrenheit and Celsius. They compare the temperature in the room to the predicted outside high temperature for the day. They become familiar with the newspaper weather page and read the high and low temperatures of different cities. They choose cities to investigate, recording and comparing the high and low temperatures for the day. They reflect on whether finding the difference between two temperatures is an addition or a subtraction problem.

Materials

▲ copies of the weather page from a major newspaper, 1 per student
▲ 1 large classroom thermometer
▲ optional: small thermometers, 1 per pair of students

Time

▲ two class periods

Teaching Directions

1. Show the class a thermometer large enough for all the students to see and ask if they know what it is used to measure. Discuss the difference between Celsius and Fahrenheit.

2. Find the temperature in the room using the Fahrenheit scale. Have students find the difference between the room temperature and one hundred degrees. Ask students to explain how they figured out the difference.

3. Show the class the weather page from the newspaper. Give each student a copy of the part that shows the highs and the lows for the day.

4. Have students locate Chicago to find the low and high temperatures. Ask if anyone can find a city that has a higher temperature. Ask the children to find the highest and lowest temperatures in the nation. Practice locating cities and comparing the high and low temperatures until you're sure all of the children are comfortable doing this.

5. Have the class look at Oklahoma City. Write the name of the city on the board and list the high and low temperatures using the degree sign. Ask children to compare the temperatures and describe their methods. Model how to record.

6. Give students directions for an individual assignment. Have them each title a piece of paper *Weather Report* and fold it in half horizontally. On the top half of the paper, they should record the temperatures they are comparing and explain how they figured out the difference. They should do another problem on the bottom half of their papers.

7. The next day, discuss with the students some of the methods they used to figure out the differences between two temperatures. Then pose a problem for all of the students to solve, asking them to find the difference between two temperatures from the weather page and to decide if it is an addition or a subtraction problem. Write the problem on the board. For example:

Addition or Subtraction?

In Hawaii it is 80 °. In San Francisco it is 63 °. What is the difference?

Is this an addition problem or a subtraction problem?

8. After all the students have solved the problem, lead a discussion about their methods and how the problem can be thought of as addition and as subtraction.

Teaching Notes

We are continually searching for ways to encourage students to look at number relationships in real-world contexts. Radio and television newscasts always include reports about the temperatures around the area and the nation. They often predict the highs and the lows, touting record-breaking temperatures. Children hear these numbers often. We hope that when they see or hear these numbers, they think about them and do some mental comparing. This lesson encourages them to do so.

Becoming familiar with the tools and the language of measurement is important for students. They need to hear and use words such as *Fahrenheit, Celsius, thermometer, degrees, difference, highest, lowest,* and *forecast.* Experience with different thermometers is also useful.

In this lesson students are asked to compare temperatures and find the differences. One way to find the difference between two numbers is to subtract, but students often find the difference by adding up. What students do to figure out the difference depends on the numbers they are dealing with, what they know about those numbers, and the relationship between the numbers.

Whether students subtract, add up, count backward, use counters, or do some combination of these actions depends on how they see the problem and what strategies they have to make sense of the numbers they are comparing. What is important is that students have systematic strategies that they understand and can explain.

The Lesson

▲▲

DAY 1

"What are we talking about when we work with centimeters and inches?" Bonnie asked the class to begin the lesson.

"Measurement," several students responded.

"That's right," Bonnie acknowledged. "Centimeters and inches are the units we use to measure how long things are. You used them when you measured your height, the length of the chalkboard, and lots of other things in the classroom."

Bonnie then held up a large thermometer. "What do you think we can measure with this?" she asked.

"Weather," Randy called out.

"Degrees," Eric added.

"We use this to measure temperature," Bonnie told the class and then commented, "It's been really hot the past few days."

"I wish I was swimming instead of going to school," Weslie said.

"Me too," Bonnie agreed. "It's usually around sixty-five degrees this time of year, but I heard on the radio that it was going to be a scorcher today. It may even get to one hundred degrees. Right now the temperature in the class is eighty-two degrees according to this thermometer. How many more degrees to get to one hundred?"

"Eighteen, because I started from eighty-two and counted on to one hundred," Mary said, telling how she had figured it out without being asked.

"I thought eighteen, too," Victoria offered, "but I did it a different way. I know that if you add eight to eighty-two, you get ninety, and ten more is one hundred."

"Who got it in a different way?" Bonnie asked.

Jenny answered, "I got eighteen. First I thought if it was eighty, it would need twenty, but it's two less."

"What does the other temperature mean?" Carissa asked, pointing to the Celsius side of the thermometer.

"The C on this side of the thermometer stands for Celsius," Bonnie explained. "The F on this other side stands for Fahrenheit. We will learn more about these two scales for measuring temperature, but today we're going to focus only on the Fahrenheit side of the thermometer." Bonnie wrote the two new words on the chalkboard.

"Let's keep an eye on the temperature and see just how hot it gets today," Bonnie suggested.

"Can we see what the temperature is outside?" Alvin asked.

"Certainly," Bonnie told him. "Remind me just before recess."

Next, Bonnie showed the class the weather page from a newspaper. "This is one of my favorite pages because it has lots of numbers, maps, and interesting information about the moon and the tides," Bonnie explained. "I made copies of the temperature part of the page so you can each look at it. We're going to use this information to make some comparisons."

Bonnie then had the class form a circle on the rug and she distributed the copies she had made.

"Oh, they put it in alphabetical order," Jason announced.

"Let's look at Chicago," Bonnie suggested. "What was the low temperature?"

"It was seventy-four," Kyle called out.

"Let's see if everyone can find the seventy-four degrees next to Chicago," Bonnie responded. "When you find Chicago, put your finger on it." Bonnie waited to give everyone time to find it. "Do you see the two numbers, seventy-four and ninety-two, after Chicago? The first one is yesterday's low temperature and the second one is yesterday's high temperature. The next two numbers are the possible low and high temperatures for today. If you keep looking across, you'll see the temperature prediction for tomorrow. What was the high temperature yesterday in Chicago?" Bonnie asked.

"Ninety-two," Mary reported.

"Can anyone find a higher temperature on the page?" Bonnie asked.

"Little Rock is higher. It's one hundred and one degrees," Julian offered.

"Yuma was one hundred and six degrees," Eric said.

"Where was the hottest place in the country?" Bonnie asked.

Several students called out, "Death Valley."

"I've been there!" several exclaimed.

"I wonder what the lowest temperature was yesterday," Alan commented.

"It says the highest and the lowest right here in the corner," Nichole offered as she pointed to the information.

"Wow, one hundred and twenty degrees in Death Valley and twenty-nine degrees in Stanley, Idaho," Bonnie said. "That's a big difference! Do you think it's more or less than a one hundred-degree difference?"

"It's less," Victoria said. "If it were one hundred degrees, the high would be one hundred and twenty-nine degrees.

"Can you figure out the exact difference?" Bonnie asked.

"I think it's one hundred minus nine," Kyle said.

"I agree," Bonnie said. "Does anyone know what one hundred minus nine is?"

"That's easy," Jenny said. "It's ninety-one. It's almost like minus ten."

Bonnie felt that the children seemed comfortable locating information on the chart and introduced an individual assignment. "What you will do today is use your copy of the weather report to write some comparison problems," she instructed. Bonnie did an example for the class. She asked the students to find the high and low temperatures for Oklahoma City. While they did this, she wrote the name of the city on the board and then showed the children how to write the temperatures using the degree sign. She asked several children to explain how they would compare the temperatures and modeled how to record.

Bonnie then asked the students to return to their seats. Once the class was settled, she told the students they would use lined paper to do their work. "What should we call this paper?" Bonnie asked.

"Weather Report," several students suggested. Bonnie wrote *Weather Report* on the front chalkboard and instructed the students to fold their papers in half horizontally.

"On the top half of your paper, choose two temperatures to compare. Be sure to label the cities and the degrees. Find the difference between these two temperatures and tell how you figured it out. Do the same for two other temperatures on the bottom half of your paper. Remember, you can compare the high and low temperatures of one city, or the highs or the lows of two different cities. You can choose any cities you want," Bonnie instructed. She then distributed paper and the students got to work.

"Where's China?" Jennifer wondered, wanting to choose the place where her mother was born.

"There's a section at the bottom for cities outside the United States," Bonnie told her as she pointed to the section. "There are a few cities in China listed under Asia. Beijing is a city in China and so is Hong Kong." Jennifer seemed satisfied and decided to compare Hong Kong and San Francisco.

"I'm going to do Kansas City," Mary said. "I went there last summer and it was so hot."

The class had no trouble finding temperatures they wanted to compare. Many seemed to find a personal connection to one of the cities listed. Some seemed to select numbers because they were easy to compare, while others challenged themselves by finding numbers with the greatest difference. (See Figures 13–1 through 13–3.) After children had completed their papers, Bonnie collected them and ended the activity for the day.

DAY 2

"I was looking at your weather report papers from yesterday and noticed that you used some interesting strategies for finding the difference between two temperatures," Bonnie told the class. "Here's an example of how two different people figured out the difference between the temperatures sixty-two degrees and ninety-five degrees." Bonnie recorded the two methods on the board.

High Low
Honolulu

90   76

76 + 10 = 86 + 4 = 90

10 + 4 = 14

The difference is 14.

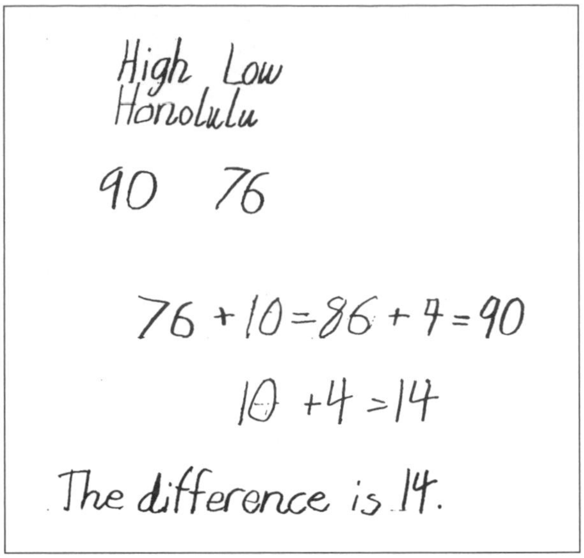

▲▲▲▲▲▲**Figure 13–2** *Kyle added 10 and then added the ones to find the difference.*

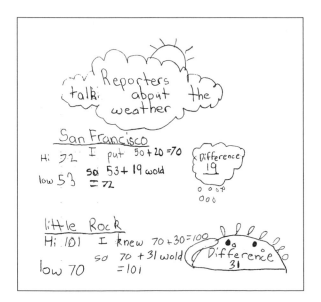

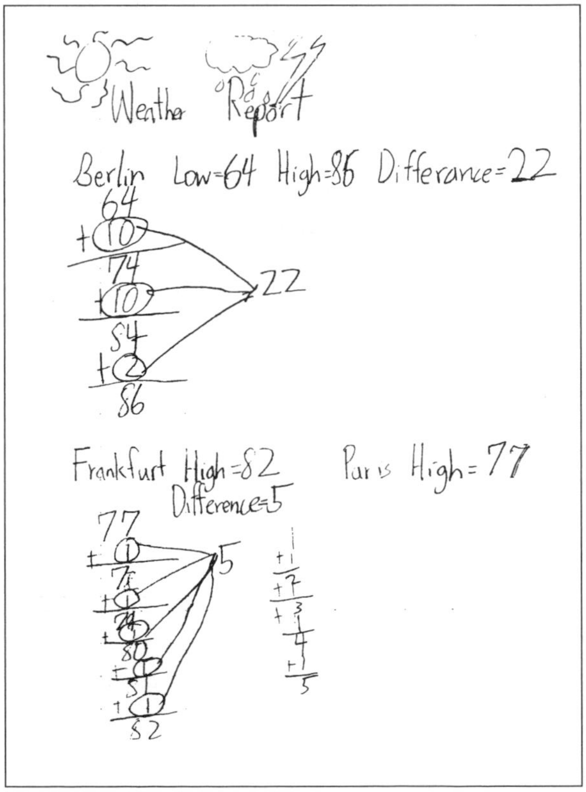

▲▲▲▲▲▲**Figure 13–1** *Jenny rounded off in one problem and added to 100 in her second comparison.*

▲▲▲▲▲▲**Figure 13–3** *Randy chose temperatures from Germany because it was his grandparents' home.*

method 1	method 2
95	95
−10	−30
85	65
−10	−3
75	62
−10	
65	
−3	
62	

"Look at these two methods and see if you can describe what's the same about them and what's different about them," Bonnie directed. "When you have an idea, tell the person sitting next to you one thing you noticed." The children began talking and seemed eager to offer their ideas to each other.

Bonnie called on Carissa to explain what she had noticed. "I noticed that both started with ninety-five and did take-away," she said.

"They both got sixty-two," Alvin pointed out.

"What is the difference between ninety-five and sixty-two?" Bonnie asked.

Alan raised his hand and said, "Thirty-three."

"How do you know that?" Bonnie asked for further clarification.

Alan went to the board and pointed to the numbers. "This method shows three tens, which makes thirty, and three more, which makes thirty-three," he said, pointing to the first method. "This other method shows thirty and three more, which makes thirty-three. So they both got thirty-three."

"Are there any other things that are different about the two methods?" Bonnie probed.

"Method two used fewer numbers," Nichole suggested.

"How do you think that person knew to take away thirty?" Bonnie asked.

"Maybe he thought that sixty to ninety is thirty," Alvin said.

Bonnie was always looking for opportunities for students to compare different methods and to begin thinking about being efficient.

"Now I want you to think about another problem. Yesterday, we looked at the weather page and you compared temperatures all over the country and even in Europe and Asia," Bonnie reminded the class. "Today, you will do one more problem and then tell whether you think the problem is an addition or a subtraction problem."

Bonnie had written the problem on a sheet of chart paper and now showed it to the class.

Addition or Subtraction?

In Hawaii it is 80°. In San Francisco it is 63°. What is the difference?

Is this an addition problem or a subtraction problem?

"First solve the problem, then tell if you think it's an addition or a subtraction problem," Bonnie told the class. "What sign do you use to show an addition problem?" Bonnie asked to further clarify the question.

"Plus," several students called out.

"What about subtraction?" Bonnie asked.

"Take away," a few suggested.

"What else do we call it?" Bonnie asked.

"Minus," Jennifer said.

"That's right, we use the plus sign when we add and the minus sign when we subtract," Bonnie reviewed, writing the signs on the board. "Spend some time thinking about this question. I'm interested in hearing your ideas."

Two students distributed paper and the class began to copy the title and the question.

As students considered this problem, Bonnie circulated to make sure everyone understood what he or she was to do. Bonnie was curious to see if those who usually chose to add up to find the difference also knew that they could subtract. Some students regularly showed both addition and subtraction as proof of their answers, using one operation to double-check the other. When all the students had completed their work, she collected the papers and asked students to come to the front of the room. (See Figures 13–4 through 13–7.)

"What if someone looked at this problem about the temperature and told you that to find out how much warmer Hawaii is than San Francisco, you have to subtract?" Bonnie began. "What would you say to that person? Would you agree or disagree?" Several hands went up. Bonnie called on Eric.

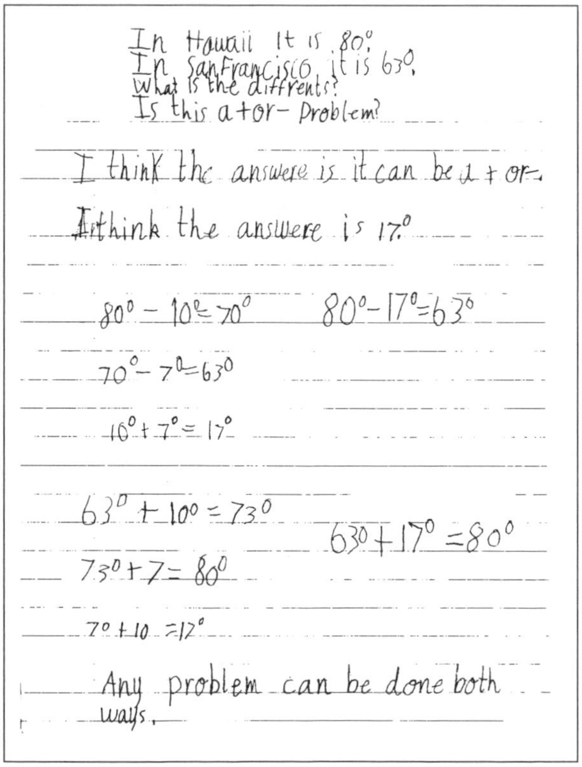

It can be a subtraction or addition problem because if you started like this 63+?=80, it would still equal 17. (63+17=80)

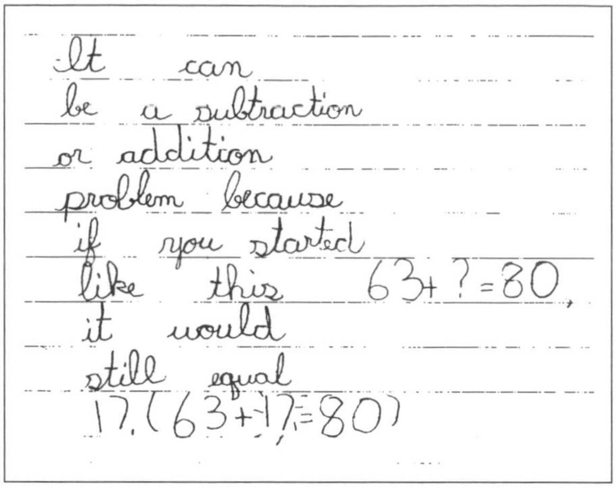

▲▲▲▲▲▲**Figure 13–5** *Louise showed how the missing addend related to subtraction.*

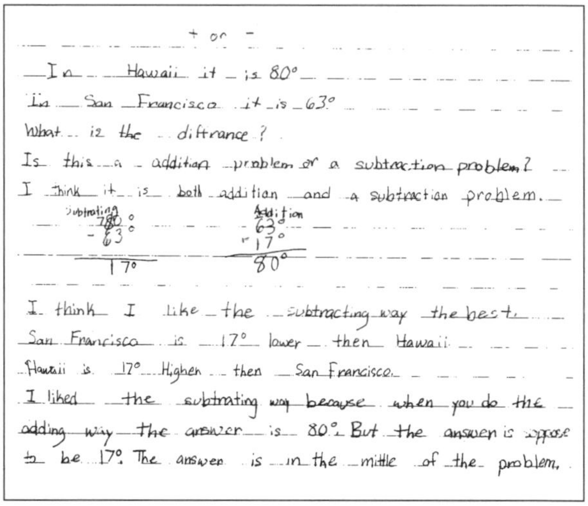

+ or –

In Hawaii it is 80°
In San Francisco it is 63°
What is the diffrance?
Is this a addition problem or a subtraction problem?
I think it is both addition and a subtraction problem.

Subtracting
$$80°$$
$$-63°$$
$$17°$$

Addition
$$63°$$
$$+17°$$
$$80°$$

I think I like the subtracting way the best.
San Francisco is 17° lower then Hawaii.
Hawaii is 17° higher then San Francisco.
I liked the subtrating way because when you do the adding way the answer is 80°. But the answer is spose to be 17°. The answer is in the mittle of the problem.

▲▲▲▲▲▲**Figure 13–6** *Eric knew the problem could be done both ways, but he offered a rationale for choosing subtraction.*

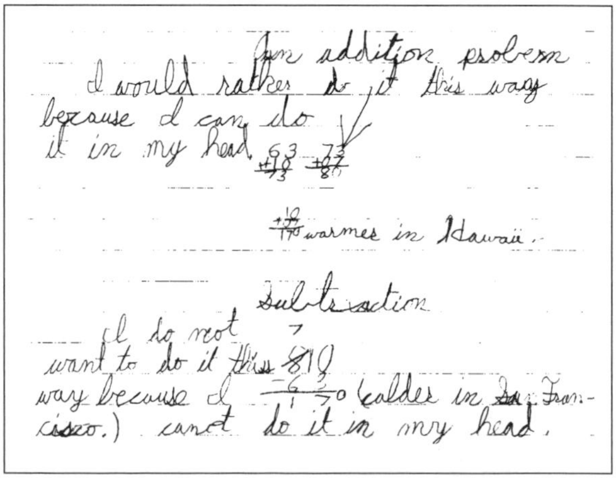

In Hawaii it is 80°
In SanFrancisio it is 63°
What is the diffrents?
Is this a + or – Problem?

I think the answere is it can be + or –.
I think the answere is 17°

$$80° - 10° = 70° \quad 80° - 17° = 63°$$
$$70° - 7° = 63°$$
$$10° + 7° = 17°$$

$$63° + 10° = 73°$$
$$73° + 7 = 80° \quad 63° + 17° = 80°$$
$$7° + 10 = 12°$$

Any problem can be done both ways.

▲▲▲▲▲▲**Figure 13–4** *Weslie proved that the answer could be found by using both addition and subtraction, and she made a generalization.*

An addition problem I would rather do it this way because I can do it in my head. 63 73
$$\frac{+17}{...}$$

17° warmer in Hawaii.

Subtraction
I do not want to do it this 810 way because I $\frac{-63}{...}$50 (calder in San Francisco.) canot do it in my head.

▲▲▲▲▲▲**Figure 13–7** *Julian liked using addition because he could do it mentally.*

"Well," he said, "I'd tell them you can subtract, but you could also add."

"Subtract is easier," Mary called out.

"I think add is better," Kyle said.

"So far, it sounds like you can figure out this problem using addition or subtraction," Bonnie summarized. "Who can explain how to find the difference between eighty degrees and sixty-three degrees using subtraction?" Bonnie asked Julian to come to the board. He wrote:

$$
\begin{array}{r}
80 \\
-60 \\
\hline
20 \\
-3 \\
\hline
17
\end{array}
$$

"Who can show how addition can be used to find out how much warmer it is in Hawaii?" Bonnie asked.

"I just count up from sixty-three," Jennifer explained.

"Show us on the board," Bonnie suggested. Jennifer wrote:

$$63 + 10 = 73$$

$$73 + 7 = 80$$

$$10 + 7 = 17$$

$$63 + 17 = 80$$

"I think you can do any problem both ways," Carissa declared.

The time for math was over. "We'll have to try some other problems to see if that's true," Bonnie said.

EXTENSIONS

1. Give each student or pair of students a small thermometer. Have them examine it closely to see what they notice. Remind them that the C means Celsius and the F stands for Fahrenheit. Help them read the temperature in the room in both Fahrenheit and Celsius. Ask them what happens to the temperature when they hold their thumb on the bulb of the thermometer.

2. Have students each select a city listed on the weather page in the newspaper and keep track of their adopted city for a week. Have them compare your own city with their chosen cities each day.

Questions and Discussion

▲▲▲

▲ *Is it your goal to have students do all addition and subtraction in their head? What about paper-and-pencil algorithms?*

When students begin having experience with two-digit addition and subtraction, we want them to develop a variety of methods for finding the answers in ways that make sense to them. We encourage them to do problems mentally and keep track of the steps they took with paper and pencil. We model for them how to record their methods so that someone else can follow their thinking. We ask them to share their procedures with one another and try the ideas of others. Often, a student presents the standard algorithm, which we treat as *one way* to find the solution. In third grade we talk with students about methods that are efficient. In general, we have had the most success when experiences with computing are contextual and when there are many opportunities for students to share their thinking both orally and in writing.

▲ *What about computing with numbers greater than one hundred?*

We often find that teachers, parents, and even students are eager to work with numbers larger than one hundred. Just as first and second graders need to spend a good deal of time with single-digit numbers, we believe that second and third graders need to spend a good deal of time with two-digit numbers. Once children become fluent with number relationships involving one- and two-digit numbers, they are more likely to transfer this understanding to three- and four-digit numbers.

Building a solid understanding of one- and two-digit numbers takes time. We have seen too many fourth graders who moved too quickly into working with large numbers without the foundation of the smaller numbers to build upon. They have a difficult time understanding relationships and are often forced to rely on someone else's structure for finding an answer. They often give up on trying to make sense of the numbers. Our goal is for students to find ways to build for themselves a strong sense of numbers, and they need repeated experiences to do so.

CHAPTER FOURTEEN
COMPARING STORYBOOKS

Overview

After students have had many experiences with mathematical comparisons, they write comparing story problems. Each story must end with a question that can be answered by comparing two quantities. Each student writes three problems and solves them, showing his or her work. Their story problems are then made into comparing storybooks. The solutions are put on a separate answer sheet. The students exchange their completed storybooks and solve one another's problems.

Materials

▲ chart paper (one piece)
▲ 12-by-18-inch drawing paper folded into storybooks, 1 per student (see instructions and diagram in "Teaching Directions")
▲ optional: *How to Make a Book* directions, 1 per student (see Blackline Masters)

Time

▲ two to three class periods

Teaching Directions

1. Review the idea of comparing using examples from previous lessons.

2. Write on a chart the comparing words from the examples.

3. Model the writing of a story problem that makes a comparison. Emphasize that the story must end with a question. For example: *Yesterday it was 92 degrees in New York City and 65 degrees in San Francisco. How much hotter was it in New York City?* Give a few examples, having children suggest the questions at the end.

4. Ask each student to write three story problems, each comparing two things, and show how each problem could be solved. After they've worked for about ten minutes, have several students read a problem aloud. Ask each what they are comparing.

5. Check stories and make editing suggestions as needed.

6. Hand out directions to students for making storybooks.

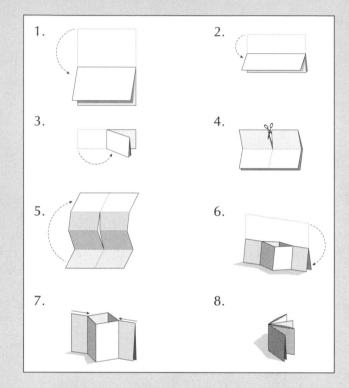

7. Have students copy and illustrate their problems in the storybooks.

8. Ask each student to make an answer sheet for his or her story problems on a separate piece of paper.

9. Have students exchange storybooks and write solutions to one another's problems.

10. Have them check their solutions with the answer sheets.

Teaching Notes

The learning of mathematics cannot be separated from language. Language connects mathematical ideas through verbal and symbolic representation. Students often have trouble with word problems because of their inability to understand mathematical language. Therefore, it is important to give students many opportunities to hear and use this language in contexts. Putting problems into words reveals whether students are able describe a mathematical situation and if they understand how mathematics relates to the world around them. As they write stories, students get practice in using mathematical vocabulary and connecting that language to mathematical concepts. Putting their thoughts into writing requires students to organize their thinking and communicate it to others.

The Lesson

▲▲

"We've done a lot of comparing with numbers," Bonnie commented. "Can you remember some of the things we've compared?"

"Our names," Lydia said.

"How did we do that?" Bonnie asked.

"We found out who had long names and who had short names and who had medium names."

"But how did we compare them?" Bonnie asked.

"We compared our own names to other people's names," Lydia continued. "Mine was four letters shorter than Christina's."

"Do you remember when we did the value of our names? How did your name value compare with someone else's value in our class?" Bonnie asked.

"Mine was worth four more dollars than Sam's," Greg said.

"Mine was one more than Kevin's," Robby said.

"Mine was the same as Kevin's," Martha added.

"Can you think of other things we have compared?" Bonnie asked.

Bonnie spent a few more minutes asking the students to think back on some of the comparison activities they had done together in class. They recalled comparing their body measurements, the temperature in different cities, and the number of beans in their origami boxes.

"When you make comparisons, I hear many of the same words over and over again," Bonnie said as she continued the lesson.

"I hear *more*, I hear *less*, and I hear *the same*." Bonnie wrote those words on a piece of chart paper.

"I also heard words like *longer* and *shorter*." She added these to the chart.

"Many words that we use for comparing things end in *er*," Bonnie told the class. "If I talk about the weather, I might say it was warmer than yesterday. Can you think of another way to compare the weather?"

"You could say how much colder it was yesterday," Melissa said.

"If I wanted to compare Johnny's height with Sam's height, what words might I use?" Bonnie asked.

"How much taller is Johnny," Hannah offered.

"You could also say how much shorter is Sam," Bonnie said. "Can you think of other words ending in *er* that can be used to compare things mathematically?"

As the students made suggestions, Bonnie added to the list. For each word, she asked for its opposite to show that the same two things could be compared in two ways. For example: Greg has more money than Stanley. Stanley has less money than Greg.

When the students could think of no more comparing words, Bonnie added a title to the chart.

Comparing Words

more	less
longer	wider
taller	shorter
thicker	thinner
hotter	colder
warmer	cooler
heavier	lighter
faster	slower

"These words are helpful in writing comparing stories," Bonnie said. "You are going to write some story problems that make comparisons. After you write them, you will copy your stories into a storybook."

"I will give you some examples of what I mean by a comparing story," Bonnie explained. "Remember when we found the values of our names? Kevin's name was worth sixty-one dollars, and James' name was worth forty-eight dollars. If I wrote a comparing story, I would write: *Kevin's name is worth sixty-one dollars. James' name is worth forty-eight dollars. How much more is Kevin's name worth?* Your story problem must end with a question."

"Let me give you one more example," Bonnie continued. "Yesterday, it was ninety-two degrees in New York City and sixty-five degrees in San Francisco. How much hotter was it in New York City?"

"Now I'll give you a story starter. You tell me what the question should be," Bonnie said. "Franklin read thirty-two pages of his library book last night. Martha had company, so she could read only six pages of her book. What question could I ask?"

"How much more did Franklin read?" Nancy said.

"How much less did I read?" Martha said.

"Can you say it in a different way?" Bonnie asked.

"How many more pages did Franklin read?" Christina offered.

"Those are all good questions," Bonnie said. "Now you try to think of a story problem of your own. Does any one have an idea?"

Jeffrey raised his hand. "Can I talk about baseball cards?"

"Sure," Bonnie said, "as long as you make a comparison."

"Mark has ninety baseball cards, and I have seventy-four baseball cards. How many more does Mark have than me?"

"You've got the idea," Bonnie said after hearing a few more stories from the class.

"I'll give you a piece of paper. You will write three different stories. The words on the chart may help you write your questions."

"Do the stories have to be real?" Mary asked.

"No, you can you use your imagination," Bonnie answered. "Just remember that you have to compare two things, and your story must end in a question."

The students set off to work. Bonnie helped individual students get started if they couldn't think of an idea. She also helped them with spelling.

After they had worked for about ten minutes, Bonnie asked some of the students to read their stories aloud to the class.

"'In Spain it was one hundred degrees,'" James began. "'In San Francisco it is seventy degrees. How much hotter is it in Spain?'" (See Figure 14–1.)

"What is James comparing?" Bonnie asked.

"He's comparing the weather in two places," Greg replied.

"That's a good comparison story," Bonnie said.

Martha read, "'Annie had forty pencils. Robby had one hundred and fifteen pencils. How many more pencils does Robby have?'" (See Figure 14–2.)

"What is Martha comparing?" Bonnie asked.

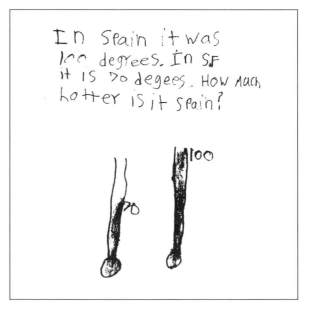

▲▲▲▲▲▲Figure 14–1 *James showed a comparison model of subtraction in his story and his illustration.*

▲▲▲▲▲ **Figure 14–2** *Martha wrote a clear question using comparison words.*

"She's comparing Annie's and Robby's pencils," Sam answered.

"That's correct," Bonnie confirmed.

"Let's hear one more story," Bonnie said. She called on Carolyn.

"'My mother gave me five dollars. I spent three dollars and ninety-six cents at the toy store. How much money do I have left?'" Carolyn read.

"What are you comparing?" Bonnie asked.

Carolyn wasn't sure, so Bonnie tried to clarify the difference between a comparing story and a take-away story. "When you have a take-away story, something is lost, something is given away, something leaves, or money gets spent. Read your story again and tell us what was taken away."

Carolyn reread her story. "The money was taken away at the store."

"Can you think of a way to rewrite your story so it compares two things? You can still use money if you like," Bonnie continued. "Using words from the chart may be helpful."

Carolyn went back to her desk. After looking at the chart for awhile, she came up with another story. Bonnie had her read it to the class.

"'My mother gave me five dollars,'" began Carolyn. "'She gave my brother three dollars and ninety-six cents. How much more money did I have?'"

"What are you comparing?" Bonnie asked.

"How much I have and how much my brother has," Carolyn replied.

"Now you've got it," Bonnie said.

By listening to the stories of their classmates, the students were able to get ideas for their own stories. Hearing the mathematical vocabulary of comparisons (how many more, how many inches taller, how many degrees hotter, how much more money, etc.) helped students formulate their own questions.

Bonnie asked the students to show her each story as they finished writing. This way she was better able to see if the class was on the right track rather than waiting until each student had finished all three stories. Not only did she check for spelling and punctuation, but she checked the solutions for accuracy and made sure the stories showed comparing. When students had each finished all three stories, Bonnie gave them a final proofreading. The students then made folded storybooks into which they began copying and illustrating their problems (see Figures 14–3 through 14–5).

The following day, Bonnie gathered the students together to give them their final task.

"The last thing you need to do is make an answer sheet," Bonnie said. "You'll need your storybook and the paper you used to write your stories." She showed the class Vincent's completed storybook and his original paper.

"On a new piece of paper, I want you to write this title: *Answer Sheet for Vincent's Comparing Stories.* Of course you'll use your own name, not Vincent's," Bonnie reminded. "Write the answer to each problem, and show how you got the answer."

Comparing Storybooks **117**

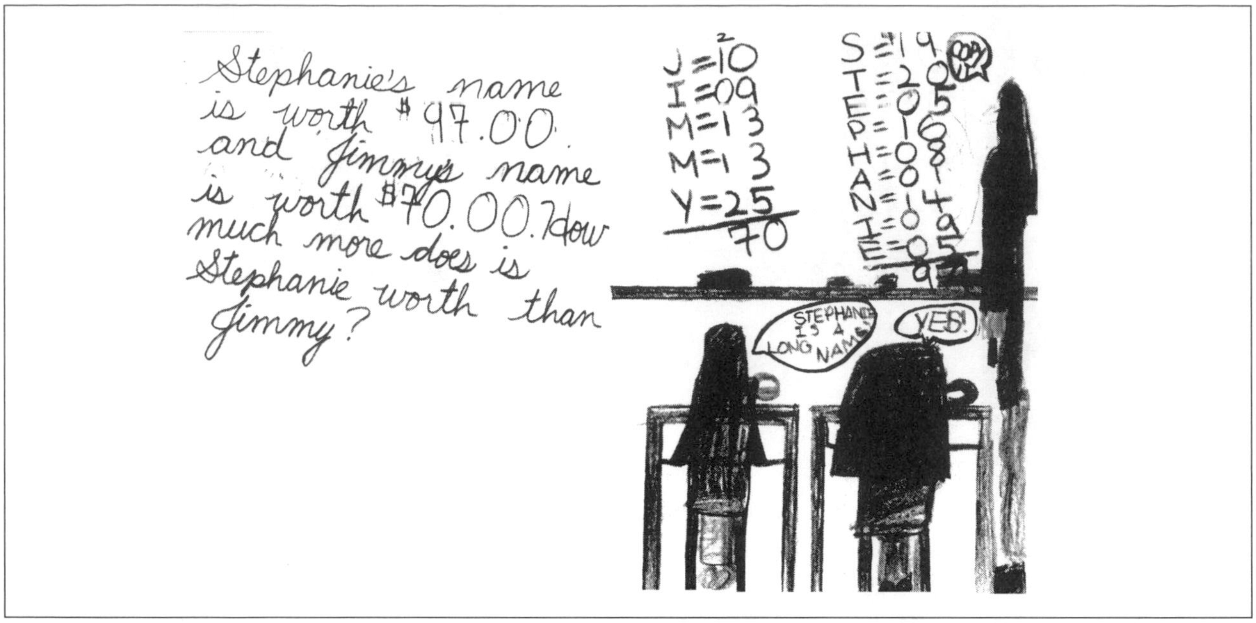

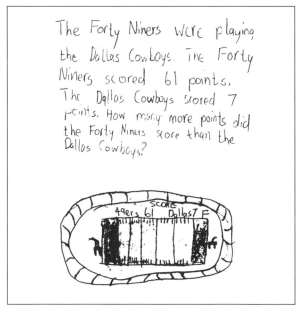

Stephanie's name
is worth $97.00.
and Jimmys name
is worth $70.00.How
much more does is
Stephanie worth than
Jimmy?
J=10
I=09
M=13
M=13
Y=25
70
S=19
T=20
E=05
P=16
H=08
A=01
N=14
I=09
E=05
YES!

Figure 14–3 *Nancy understood the mathematics of comparison stories but was still developing language skills.*

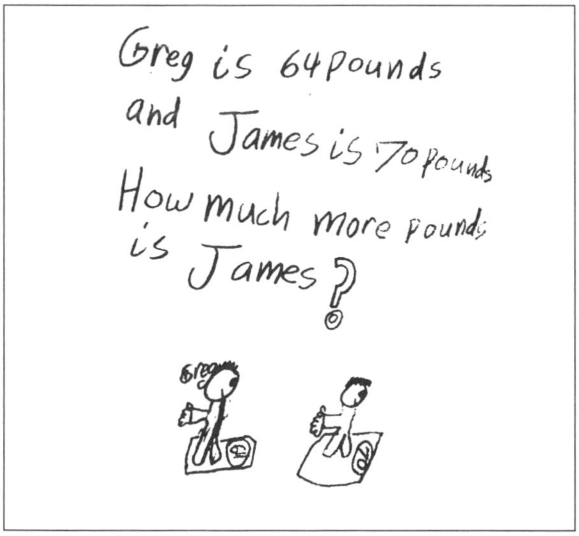

Greg is 64 Pounds
and James is 70 Pounds
How much more Pounds
is James?

Figure 14–4 *Franklin used real measurement data from his classmates to write his story.*

The Forty Niners were playing
the Dallas Cowboys. The Forty
Niners scored 61 points.
The Dallas Cowboys scored 7
points. How many more points did
the Forty Niners score than the
Dallas Cowboys?
SCORE
49ers 61 Dallas 7

Figure 14–5 *Vincent's story reflected his hopes for his favorite team.*

When all the storybooks were completed, the class exchanged books. Students wrote their answers and solution strategies on separate pieces of paper and then used the answer sheets to check their work.

EXTENSIONS

1. Have students make other types of storybooks. They can write problems using one operation, such as addition storybooks, or they can make storybooks for take-away subtraction problems.

2. If students need extra help in writing story problems, have them create story books for younger students to solve. This allows the students an opportunity to work with smaller numbers and/or simpler problems while still using mathematical language.

Questions and Discussion

▲▲

▲ *What implications do story problems have for communication of mathematical understanding?*

Language is a vital component in the learning of mathematics. Students need clear and correct words to communicate mathematics effectively. Using words correctly is not an easy task for children and can be extremely challenging for second language learners. Story problems serve as a link to connect abstract ideas to verbal and symbolic representations. When students listen to story problems presented by the teacher or by other students, they hear mathematical language in context. When students verbalize or write their own problems, they are communicating their understanding of mathematical ideas. Students need many opportunities to practice using the language of mathematics.

▲ *Why is context important?*

Context helps build comprehension and understanding. Although context is emphasized in language arts instruction, it is often overlooked in the teaching of mathematics. Too often the focus in mathematics is on computation in isolation with worksheets of arithmetic exercises. By not involving students in problem-solving situations, there is little opportunity to help them with the real-life uses of arithmetic. Students need to use the language of mathematics. When students work with numbers in context, they are better able to develop understanding of the abstract nature of mathematics. When students write and solve their own story problems, teachers can assess not only computational ability but also students' understanding and ability to communicate mathematically.

ADDITIONAL ACTIVITIES

Games and warm-up activities enrich mathematics instruction, increase communication and social interaction, and provide teachers with meaningful assessment information. This section contains a collection of eleven games, activities, and warm-ups that arc casy to usc and require a minimum of materials and preparation. Each game or activity helps reinforce or build understanding of one or more key mathematical ideas for addition and subtraction. Developing strategies through logical reasoning, practicing basic facts, and doing mental computation are additional benefits. A brief summary and the key mathematical ideas precede the teaching directions for each activity. All necessary game boards and record sheets appear in the Blackline Masters section of this book.

Teaching Notes

There are many reasons for using games in the classroom. It is important for teachers to not only be aware of the value of games but to develop a rationale for their use to articulate to parents, administrators, and themselves. Games can reinforce or provide repeated practice in basic computational skills and offer an alternative to traditional worksheets or flashcard drills. Knowing what skills and mathematical ideas can be gained from each game is important when making classroom selections.

When students are playing games, they have an opportunity to interact with their classmates while they talk about and do mathematics together. Games can promote cooperation and allow children to take risks in a nonthreatening situation. Many games offer opportunities to develop strategies and work with probability concepts. In other games, students can apply logical reasoning skills such as being systematic, eliminating possibilities, using prior knowledge, organizing ideas, and making inferences and predictions.

Teachers can gain insights into children's thinking and reasoning by observing them play or by playing games with them. Noticing their moves, listening to their comments, and asking them informal questions can be valuable assessments of mathematical understanding that can, in turn, guide instruction.

Starting the mathematics period with a daily warm-up or by playing a game together as a class ensures that addition and subtraction concepts are revisited throughout the year. Students need time and repeated practice to develop flexibility, efficiency, and accuracy with numbers. Warm-ups and games provide opportunities for children to revisit mathematical concepts and also provide opportunities to connect addition and subtraction to other mathematics topics. When students do *What Do You Notice?*, for example, they not only notice addition and subtraction relationships, but can also focus on odd and even numbers, multiples, and fractional relationships.

Students enjoy daily routines and look forward to repeating familiar activities. *Today's Number* can be done daily, incorporating variations. *X-Ray Vision*, *Roll Five Times*, and *Tile Riddles with 20* can be repeated many times by varying the numbers. Also, warm-ups and games help build a positive classroom climate. As students become comfortable they can lead activities such as *Too High, Too Low, Just Right* and *Four Strikes and You're Out*. Playing games together, working together on *Make 100* grids, or solving a student's *Tile Riddles with 20* problems are just a few ways children can work and learn together.

Before students play games on their own, they should be familiar with the rules and the recording procedures. Modeling games several times in a large-group setting can make game playing in pairs a positive and successful experience. The modeling of a game can be done as a warm-up activity. After students know how to play, games such as *Addition Tic-Tac-Toe*, *How Close to 0?*, *Roll Five Times*, and *Fifteen-Number Cross-Out* can be played with the teacher challenging the class or with the students divided into two teams.

X-Ray Vision

OVERVIEW

X-Ray Vision is a two-person game that gives students practice with basic subtraction facts and writing number sentences. In this game, students play in pairs and take turns rolling two dice to determine how many cubes to remove from a paper bag containing twelve cubes. Players try to "see" through the paper bag to determine how many cubes are left. Once they predict how many cubes are left in the bag, they look inside to check and then record the play with a subtraction sentence. Changing the number of cubes in the bag gives children practice with other combinations.

MATERIALS

▲ paper bags, 1 per pair of students

▲ 1-inch or 2-centimeter cubes, at least 12 per pair of students

▲ dice, 2 per pair of students

▲ *X-Ray Vision* record sheet (see Blackline Masters)

▲ optional: *X-Ray Vision* directions, 1 per pair of students (see Blackline Masters)

TEACHING DIRECTIONS

1. Distribute to each pair of students twelve cubes in a paper bag, two dice, and an *X-Ray Vision* record sheet.

2. Explain the rules for play. Either write the directions on the board or an overhead transparency or distribute a copy to each pair of students. Model a few rounds to be sure the children know how to play. Explain that they can play two games on the same record sheet.

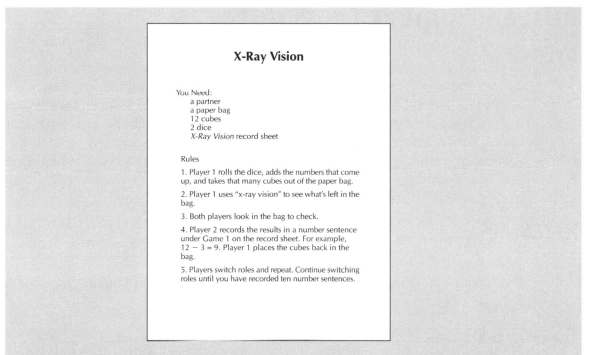

X-Ray Vision

You Need:
    a partner
    a paper bag
    12 cubes
    2 dice
    X-Ray Vision record sheet

Rules

1. Player 1 rolls the dice, adds the numbers that come up, and takes that many cubes out of the paper bag.

2. Player 1 uses "x-ray vision" to see what's left in the bag.

3. Both players look in the bag to check.

4. Player 2 records the results in a number sentence under Game 1 on the record sheet. For example, $12 - 3 = 9$. Player 1 places the cubes back in the bag.

5. Players switch roles and repeat. Continue switching roles until you have recorded ten number sentences.

3. After all of the students have completed at least one game, talk to the class about the subtraction sentences that are possible when playing this game. List them on the board. Have students describe patterns they notice.

$12 - 2 = 10$

$12 - 3 = 9$

$12 - 4 = 8$

$12 - 5 = 7$

$12 - 6 = 6$

$12 - 7 = 5$

$12 - 8 = 4$

$12 - 9 = 3$

$12 - 10 = 2$

$12 - 11 = 1$

$12 - 12 = 0$

4. After children have played several games, lead a discussion using their record sheets. Use the following questions:

Which subtraction sentences appeared most often?

Which subtraction sentences appeared least often?

Does your x-ray vision work better for some numbers than others?

Variation

For an easier version, children can play with six to eleven cubes in the bag and one die. For more difficult versions, they can play with thirteen to eighteen cubes in the bag and two dice or eighteen to twenty cubes and three dice. Giving students a choice of variations allows them to customize the game for themselves.

Fifteen-Number Cross-Out

OVERVIEW

This two-person game helps children learn to decompose numbers into two or more parts. *Fifteen-Number Cross-Out* also provides good addition practice for sums up to twelve. Using a list of fifteen numbers from one to nine, students cross out addends that make a sum rolled by two dice. Children choose their own numbers for their lists but must include exactly five fives. The winner is the first player to cross out all fifteen numbers. However, if both players are blocked, the winner is the player with the fewest numbers left on his or her list.

MATERIALS

▲ dice, 2 per pair of students
▲ optional: *Fifteen-Number Cross-Out* rules, 1 per pair of students (see Blackline Masters)

TEACHING DIRECTIONS

1. Distribute two dice to each pair of students.

2. Explain the rules for play. Either write the directions on the board or an overhead transparency or distribute a copy to each pair of students.

Fifteen-Number Cross-Out

You Need:
  a partner
  2 dice

Rules

1. Each player makes a list of fifteen numbers. Five numbers must be 5s; the other ten numbers can be any numbers from 1 to 9. You may repeat any of these numbers as many times as you like, and you don't have to include every number from 1 to 9.

2. Player 1 rolls the two dice; both players add the numbers and agree on the sum.

3. On his or her list, each player crosses out either the sum or a combination of numbers that makes that sum. For example, if the sum of the dice is seven, a player might cross out a 7, or a 3 and a 4, or a 5 and a 2, or a 3 and two 2s. For each roll of the dice, a player can make the sum only one way.

4. Player 2 rolls the dice and, again, both players add the numbers, agree on the sum, and cross out numbers from their lists.

5. If a player cannot make the sum that comes up with any numbers on his or her list, that player waits for the next roll of the dice to try again.

6. The game continues as long as one player is able to cross out numbers for the roll of the dice.

7. The game ends in one of two ways. If one player crosses out all of the numbers on his or list, the game is over and that player is the winner. Or, if both players are unable to make a play, the game is over and the winner is the player with the fewest numbers left on his or her list.

3. Have the children help you create two lists of numbers that follow the rules. For example:

Player 1	Player 2
5	5
5	5
5	5
5	5
5	5
1	1
2	1
3	2
4	2
5	2
6	3
7	3
8	4
9	4
1	6

4. Model how to play for a few rolls of the dice to be sure the children understand the rules. Also, carefully explain the two possible ways the game can end.

5. After children have played the game several times, initiate a class discussion about which numbers are best to put on their lists.

Variation: Twenty-Number Cross-Out

Have the children play using three dice instead of two. Five numbers must be 5s. The other fifteen numbers must be from 1 to 9.

Roll Five Times

OVERVIEW

Roll Five Times is a two-person game that gives students practice adding one, five, and ten to numbers less than fifty. Players roll a number die with faces marked with two 1s, two 5s, and two 10s. For each of five rolls, players take cubes representing the number that comes up and place them on squares on a 5-by-10 grid. After rolling five times, they record the number of covered and uncovered squares.

MATERIALS

▲ cubes the same size as the squares on the game board, 50 per pair of students
▲ number dice, each with two 10s, two 5s, and two 1s on its faces, 1 per pair of students
▲ *Roll Five Times* game boards, 1 per pair of students (see Blackline Masters)
▲ optional: *Roll Five Times* rules, 1 per pair of students (see Blackline Masters)

TEACHING DIRECTIONS

1. Distribute to each pair of students one number die, a game board, a record sheet, and fifty cubes. Talk with the class about how many squares are on the game board grids and what numbers are on the number dice. Point out that the other cubes they have fit exactly on the squares of the game board.

2. Explain the rules for play. Either write the directions on the board or an overhead transparency or distribute a copy to each pair of students.

Roll Five Times

You Need:
  a partner
  a number die with two 10s, two 5s, and two 1s
  50 Unifix cubes
  a *Roll Five Times* game board and record sheet

Rules

1. Player 1 rolls the number die and places that many cubes on the game board, starting at the upper left corner and covering the squares in order. You must complete a row before starting at the beginning of the next row.

2. Player 2 records the number rolled in the first blank on the *Roll Five Times* record sheet.

3. Player 2 rolls and places cubes on the game board, continuing in the next available space.

4. Player 1 records the number in the second blank on the record sheet.

5. Play continues for five rolls with players alternating jobs. After five rolls, record how many squares are covered and how many are uncovered.

		Covered	Uncovered
<u>1</u> +<u>10</u>+ <u>5</u> + <u>1</u> + <u>1</u> = 18		18	32

Roll Five Times
Game Board

Name_____   Name_____

							Covered	Uncovered
Game 1	____ + ____ + ____ + ____ + ____	=	____	____
Game 2	____ + ____ + ____ + ____ + ____	=	____	____
Game 3	____ + ____ + ____ + ____ + ____	=	____	____
Game 4	____ + ____ + ____ + ____ + ____	=	____	____
Game 5	____ + ____ + ____ + ____ + ____	=	____	____

3. Model a game for the students to be sure they understand how to record and how to figure out the number of covered and uncovered squares.

Variation

Players use individual game boards and record sheets. Each player rolls and records five times. The winner of a game is the player who has covered closest to fifty squares.

Addition Tic-Tac-Toe

OVERVIEW

Addition Tic-Tac-Toe is a two-person game that gives students practice combining two addends up to twenty-five. It also gives students practice taking apart numbers in various ways and working with missing addends. After students become familiar with the game, they can discuss and investigate possible winning strategies.

MATERIALS

▲ paper clips, 1 per student

▲ cubes or other game markers in two colors, 12 of each color per pair of students

▲ *Addition Tic-Tac-Toe* game board, 1 per pair of students (see Blackline Masters)

▲ optional: *Addition Tic-Tac-Toe* rules, 1 per pair of students (see Blackline Masters)

TEACHING DIRECTIONS

1. Project an overhead transparency of the game board or post a large version that all of the children can see.

2. Explain the rules for play.

Addition Tic-Tac-Toe

You Need:
a partner
2 paper clips
cubes or other game markers in two colors, 12 of each color
an *Addition Tic-Tac-Toe* game board

Rules

1. Each player uses a different color of cubes or game markers.

2. Player 1 chooses two numbers from those listed at the bottom of the game board, places a paper clip on each, and marks the sum of the numbers on the game board with a cube of his or her color.

3. Player 2 moves just one of the paper clips to another number, adds, and marks the sum with a different color cube. **Note:** It is legal to start the game with both paper clips on the same number and to move a paper clip to the same addend as the other paper clip. This allows for adding doubles, such as 6 + 6.

4. Play continues.

5. The winner is the player who places four cubes of his or her color on numbers in a row vertically, horizontally, or diagonally. If neither player has four in a row, and there are no more numbers on the board or it's impossible for a player to make any of the numbers left on the game board by moving just one paper clip, the game is a tie.

Players use cubes in two different colors. The first player chooses two addends (from 1–13 underneath the game board), places a paper clip on each, and marks the sum on the game board with a cube. The second player moves one of the paper clips to a new addend, finds the sum, and marks the sum with a different color cube. Play continues until one player has marked four sums in a row, a column, or a diagonal. Note: It is legal to move a paper clip to the same addend of the other paper clip to allow for doubles such as 6 + 6.

2	3	4	5	6
7	8	9	10	11
12	13	14	15	16
17	18	19	20	21
22	23	24	25	26

1   2   3   4   5   6   7   8   9   10   11   12   13

3. Play the game several times with you as one player and the whole class as the other.

4. When you feel the students understand how to play, have them play the game in pairs.

5. After the students have become familiar with the game, initiate a discussion about the strategies they use.

Variations

1. The students have the option to make a play by either adding or subtracting the two numbers.

2. Have students make new game boards by putting the numbers from 2 to 26 in different places.

How Close to 0?

OVERVIEW

This two-person game provides children practice with subtraction. Both players start with one hundred and try to get as close as possible to zero in seven rolls of the die. Players take turns rolling the die, deciding to use the number that comes up either as a ten or as a one, and subtracting the quantity first from one hundred and then from whatever number is remaining. The object is to get as close to zero as possible without going below zero. The game also gives children probability experience as they decide whether to subtract tens or ones.

MATERIALS

▲ dice, 1 per pair of students
▲ *How Close to 0?* record sheet (see Blackline Masters)

TEACHING DIRECTIONS

1. Distribute to each pair of students one die and one *How Close to 0?* record sheet.

2. Explain the rules for play. Either write the directions on the board or an overhead transparency or distribute a copy to each pair of students.

How Close to 0?

You Need:
　a partner
　a die
　How Close to 0? record sheet

Rules

1. Player 1 rolls the die, decides whether to use the number as a ten or as a one, and subtracts the number from 100. (Example: a 5 can be 50 or 5.) Player 1 records his or her calculation on the record sheet.

2. Player 2 does the same—rolls the die, decides whether to use the number as a ten or as a one, subtracts the number from 100, and records the play.

3. Play continues until each player has rolled seven times.

4. The player closer to zero after seven rounds is the winner and receives a score of whatever number is left for the opposing player.

5. If a player reaches zero before the seventh round, the game is over. The other player wins and scores the points left over from the opponent's previous round.

---

3. Model a game for the class to be sure the students understand how to play, record, and keep score. Following is a sample game in which Player 2 wins and scores 7 points from Player 1.

	Player 1	Player 2
Round 1	100 − 6 94	100 − 20 80
Round 2	94 − 60 34	80 − 40 40
Round 3	34 − 5 29	40 − 10 30
Round 4	29 − 10 19	30 − 3 27
Round 5	19 − 4 15	27 2 25
Round 6	15 − 6 9	25 − 3 22
Round 7	9 − 2 7	22 − 20 2

4. Explain that if a player reaches zero or below before the seventh round, the game is over. The other player scores the points left over from the opponent's previous round. In the following example, Player 1 will go below zero in Round 7 and, therefore, cannot play. Player 2 wins the game and gets 3 points from Player 1's previous round.

	Player 1	Player 2
Round 5	$\begin{array}{r} 29 \\ -\ 20 \\ \hline 9 \end{array}$	$\begin{array}{r} 30 \\ -\ 6 \\ \hline 24 \end{array}$
Round 6	$\begin{array}{r} 9 \\ -\ 6 \\ \hline 3 \end{array}$	$\begin{array}{r} 24 \\ -\ 4 \\ \hline 20 \end{array}$
Round 7	$\begin{array}{r} 3 \\ -\ 6 \\ \hline \end{array}$ can't play	

5. After the students have had a chance to play for awhile, lead a discussion about the strategies they used to decide whether to use numbers as tens or ones.

Tile Riddles with 20

OVERVIEW

Students put twenty color tiles in a bag in an assortment of four colors. They then write addition or subtraction problems for three of the four colors. Others then use these problems as clues to figure out how many tiles of each color there are. Using this information, they figure out how many tiles there are of the last color, which gives practice with missing addend problems. *Tile Riddles with 20* gives children practice with sums up to twenty, decomposing numbers, and working with missing addends.

MATERIALS

▲ paper bags, 1 per riddle
▲ paper clips, 1 per riddle
▲ color tiles (a combination of red, blue, yellow, and green tiles), 20 per riddle
▲ 3-by-5-inch index cards, 1 per riddle

TEACHING DIRECTIONS

1. Explain to the students that they are to select any combination of twenty color tiles so that there are some each of red, blue, yellow, and green tiles. Demonstrate with two red tiles, nine blue tiles, six yellow tiles, and three green tiles.

2. Tell the students that they will then write on an index card addition or subtraction problems for three of the four colors. Model this by writing sample clues on the board.

Sample Clues #1

I have 10 − 8 red tiles.

I have 6 + 3 blue tiles.

I have 2 + 4 yellow tiles.

How many green tiles are in the bag?

---

3. Talk with the children about how they would use the clues you wrote to figure out how many of each color are in the bag. Model how to record computation strategies for solving the riddles.

4. Write another set of clues for the same assortment of tiles and discuss with the class how to use them to solve the riddle.

Sample Clues #2

I have 3 + 2 + 1 yellow tiles.

I have 14 − 5 blue tiles.

I have 11 − 8 red tiles.

How many red tiles are in the bag?

---

5. Tell the children that after they write a set of clues on the index card, they are to put the twenty tiles in a paper bag and attach the card to the bag with a paper clip. Demonstrate this for the class.

6. Give the students time to create their own riddles.

7. After you've checked students' riddles for accuracy, have students solve one another's riddles, showing their computation strategies on paper. After a student solves a riddle, he or she may look in the bag to check.

Too High, Too Low, Just Right

OVERVIEW

In this whole-class activity, students apply mental computation and logical reasoning skills. One student acts as the leader and selects a number from the 1–100 chart. The other students guess what the number might be by giving an addition or a subtraction problem. The leader mentally computes the answer to the problem and places a marker on the chart to indicate if the answer is too high, too low, or just right. Play continues until someone guesses the correct number.

MATERIALS

▲ pocket chart filled with numbers from 1–100
▲ 3 colored paper markers to fit in pockets: 1 red, labeled *Too High*; 1 blue, labeled *Too Low*; and 1 yellow, labeled *Just Right*
Note: If you do not have a pocket chart, you can either project an overhead transparency of a 1–100 chart or make a 1–100 chart on chart paper. Use transparent markers cut from overhead transparency material colored with red, blue, and yellow permanent marking pens.

TEACHING DIRECTIONS

1. Model the activity by taking the role of the leader. Select a number from one to one hundred (for example, eighteen).

2. Ask someone in the class to guess the number by giving you an addition or a subtraction problem (for example, 12 + 13).

3. Say, "Too high," and put the red Too High marker into the 25 pocket.

4. Ask another student for a different problem (for example, 20 − 5).

5. Say, "Too low," and put the blue Too Low marker in the 15 pocket.

6. Continue until someone identifies the correct number. If 20 − 2 were offered, for example, you would say, "Just right," and put the yellow Just Right marker in the 18 pocket.

7. Then choose a child to be the leader and repeat the activity. Play the game from time to time whenever you have a few minutes.

Today's Number

OVERVIEW

This warm-up activity is appropriate as a daily classroom routine during calendar time or at the start of the math period. Use the day of the month, the day of the school year, or a number from one to one hundred chosen randomly as today's number. Children discuss the number and write addition and subtraction equations to represent it, thus helping build their number sense and providing computation practice. From the activity, children become aware of numerical relationships, the relative magnitude of numbers, and the importance of context for interpreting numbers and their uses.

MATERIALS

▲ none

TEACHING DIRECTIONS

1. Choose a number, write it on the board, and ask students to share what they know about it. Record their ideas. Examples include the following:

Today's Number—25
Can mean a quarter (25-cent coin)
An odd number
Easy to count by (25, 50, 75, 100 . . .)
Age of my uncle
More than two dozen, less than three dozen
My soccer team number
My street number

2. Next ask students to write addition and subtraction equations that represent the number. You may have them do so as an individual written assignment and then have them share their equations or collect equations in a whole-class discussion. Sample equations include the following:

50 − 25 = 25
17 + 8 = 25
25 − 0 = 25
100 − 75 = 25
(20 + 8) − 3 = 25

3. As students become comfortable writing equations, you may wish to impose some limitations. For example:

You must use the number one hundred in one of your equations.

You may not use one-digit numbers.

You must use both addition and subtraction in one of your equations.

What Do You Notice?

OVERVIEW

This warm-up activity provides opportunities for students to notice, discuss, and develop understanding of numerical relationships. Write ten to fifteen numbers on the board in ascending order. Then ask students to look for how these numbers go together or what number relationships they see. Students often find relationships that are not obvious, and listening to their responses is an excellent way to assess their number sense and their facility with mental computation.

MATERIALS

▲ optional: a paper bag with 50 slips of paper numbered from 1 to 50

TEACHING DIRECTIONS

1. Write ten to fifteen numbers on the chalkboard. You may select the numbers with relationships in mind or choose a random assortment from a paper bag with numbered slips of paper.

2. Ask students to look at the numbers to see how they relate to one another.

3. Have students share their findings.

Example 1

1 2 5 8 9 10

16 18 20 32 36 50

Possible Relationships

▲ Some numbers have doubles: 5 and 10, 8 and 16, 10 and 20, 16 and 32, 18 and 36.

▲ Some numbers can be put together in equations:

$8 + 2 = 10$

$18 - 2 = 16$

$(20 + 32) - 2 = 50$

$(50 - 16) + 2 = 36$

▲ All the two-digit numbers are even.

▲ All of the numbers are less than 51.

▲ The difference between the largest and smallest numbers is 49.

▲ Three of the numbers are consecutive: 8, 9, 10.

Example 2

The following twelve numbers were pulled from a bag that held all numbers from 1 to 50.

23 42 7 36 41 18

26 1 39 47 16 10

The students rearranged them in ascending order and then looked for relationships.

1 7 10 16 18 23

26 36 39 41 42 47

▲ $1 + 7 + 10 = 18$

▲ $26 - 10 = 16$

▲ $(42 - 7) + 1 = 36$

▲ If you double $1 + 7$, you get 16.

▲ Six out of the 12 numbers are odd.

▲ Half of the numbers are even, and half of them are odd.

▲ If you add the two largest numbers you get 89.

▲ If you add the two smallest numbers you get 8.

▲ The difference between the largest and smallest numbers is 46.

Four Strikes and You're Out

OVERVIEW

This activity doesn't require much time and can be repeated regularly throughout the year. The students work together and try to solve an equation before they receive four strikes. *Four Strikes and You're Out* reinforces mental arithmetic, working with missing addends, and understanding place value. It can be used as a warm-up activity or when you have an extra few minutes before recess or lunch. Also, students can work in pairs and alternate writing equations for their partners to solve.

MATERIALS

▲ none

TEACHING DIRECTIONS

1. Write the digits from 0 to 9 on the chalkboard.

2. Write an equation on a small piece of paper hidden from view; for example: 24 + 48 = 72. Then, using a blank for each digit, write a template for the equation on the chalkboard or overhead.

___ ___ + ___ ___ = ___ ___

3. Ask a student to suggest a digit from 0 to 9. Cross out the digit from your list. If that digit is in the equation, write it wherever it should appear in the blanks. For example, if a student selected 2, you would record it in two places.

_2_ ___ + ___ ___ = ___ _2_

4. The same student continues to guess as long as he or she selects a correct digit.

5. If the student selects a digit that doesn't appear in the equation (for example, 9), the class gets a strike. Choose another student to select a digit. Each time a student selects a number that doesn't appear in the equation, the class gets a strike. Write Xs on the board to keep track of the strikes.

6. If the new student selects a 4, write it in all places it appears. The equation would now look like this:

_2_ _4_ + _4_ ___ = ___ _2_

There is now information that students can use. By looking at the equation, students can reason that the number added to the ones place in 24 must equal a 2. To do that, the two numbers would total more than ten. They might also notice that adding the numbers in the tens place will produce a 6; however, if the ones add up to more than ten, they'll need a 7 in the tens place.

7. If the student selected a 6, there would be three strikes since there is no six in the equation.

8. If the next student selected an 8, the equation would look like this:

_2_ _4_ + _4_ _8_ = ___ _2_

9. If that same student selected a 7 for the next move, the equation would be complete, and the students would have won that round because they correctly completed the equation in fewer than four strikes.

_2_ _4_ + _4_ _8_ = _7_ _2_

Following are some possible equations to use with this activity:

7 + 3 = 10	6 + 6 = 12	13 − 4 = 9
16 + 9 = 25	27 + 35 = 62	90 − 42 = 48
100 − 36 = 64	(20 + 5) − 4 = 21	(10 − 6) + 30 = 34

Make 100

OVERVIEW

This activity offers practice identifying pairs of numbers that add to one hundred, giving students experience with this important landmark number. Being familiar with number pairs that add to one hundred builds important mathematical relationships for place value, our monetary system, missing addends, and the inverse relationship between addition and subtraction.

MATERIALS

▲ none

TEACHING DIRECTIONS

1. Draw a 4-by-4 grid on the board or an overhead transparency. Write numbers in each square so that there are number pairs that add to one hundred.

2. Ask students to circle the pairs that add to one hundred.

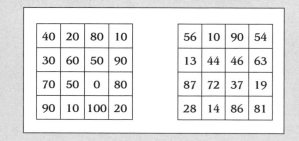

40	20	80	10
30	60	50	90
70	50	0	80
90	10	100	20

56	10	90	54
13	44	46	63
87	72	37	19
28	14	86	81

Variations

1. Use numbers that add to sums other than one hundred.

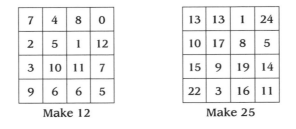

7	4	8	0
2	5	1	12
3	10	11	7
9	6	6	5

Make 12

13	13	1	24
10	17	8	5
15	9	19	14
22	3	16	11

Make 25

2. Ask students to create number puzzles for others to solve.

3. Give partially filled grids to students. Have them write numbers in the blank squares and circle pairs that add to one hundred.

ASSESSMENTS

Overview

The assessments in this section are designed to help teachers know what students are learning as they study addition and subtraction. Each assessment task is linked to one or more of the instructional goals listed in the introduction of this book.

The first assessment, *What Do You Know About Addition and Subtraction?*, is useful both before and after children have had experiences with addition and subtraction. *Why Is 9 + 5 = 5 + 9 and Why Is 10 − 4 ≠ 4 − 10?* provides insights into the children's understanding of the commutative and associative properties as they relate to addition and subtraction. *Spending $1.00* assesses students' strategies for computing combinations that make one hundred. *Can You Write an Addition Story Problem? Can You Write a Subtraction Story Problem?* tells whether students can connect addition and subtraction to real-world situations. *Is This a Take-Away or Comparing Story?* assesses whether students can solve, write, and categorize word problems. *The Penny Problem* assesses students' ability to apply addition and subtraction to a problem-solving situation. *Is This an Addition or a Subtraction Problem?* uses classroom data from the *How Many Pockets?* lesson to assess if students can find the difference between two-digit numbers and are aware of the inverse relationship between addition and subtraction.

Teaching Notes

Teachers can gain valuable information about their students by incorporating assessment into daily classroom mathematics instruction. As we teach, it's important to gather information about what students are learning in order to assess their mathematical skills and understanding. This information guides our classroom instructional choices throughout the year, helping us plan and select appropriate instructional tasks.

For a classroom teacher, standardized test data is probably the least useful in providing insights into children's mathematical understanding. That's because on these tests, students are not required to explain their thinking or show their reasoning strategies. Several years ago, a third-grade student in one of our classes solved all the addition and subtraction problems on a standardized test by making and counting tally marks. The student solved many of the problems correctly, but she spent so much time drawing and counting tallies that she was unable to complete the test in the allotted time. The following year, when the fourth-grade teacher looked at the test results, the data showed mastery of addition and subtraction and non-mastery of multiplication. Based on the test results alone, the teacher would not know that this student lacked efficient computational strategies for addition and subtraction and missed the multiplication items because she left them unanswered!

One way to gather useful information about students is to listen to them during class discussions. However, not all students participate actively in these discussions, so teachers must use other means of assessment to provide more complete pictures of children's learning. For example, keeping folders of each student's work over time is a way to collect valuable evidence about students that can show their strengths, weaknesses, and growth. Reading and reviewing this work helps chart a child's progress, and the folders provide concrete examples to refer to when holding pupil conferences or reporting to parents.

Observing students and talking to them as they work each day probably are the best sources of information to assess understanding. It's useful to take notes about individual students and add these to the information in the children's folders. Depending on the activity, we observe to answer one or more of the following questions:

Do the students have strategies for solving problems?

Do the students have a good sense of numbers? Can they estimate answers?

Do the students use landmark numbers as benchmarks?

Do the students have multiple strategies that vary depending upon the numbers involved?

Are the students' strategies accurate and/or efficient?

Can the student do mathematical calculations mentally?

Do the students use place value, or are they counting by ones to determine answers?

Can students communicate their thinking verbally and in writing?

When students are working, we also ask questions to probe and stimulate their mathematical thinking:

How did you get that answer?

What would happen if . . .?

Do you see a pattern?

Does that make sense?

Can you make this a simpler problem?

Can you show this problem in a different way?

The answers students give are valuable for assessing their learning. Asking the right question at just the right time isn't always possible, but with practice our questioning techniques improve.

It is also important to assess children throughout the year with short and specific assignments that they complete individually and in writing. The following seven assessments, used in conjunction with whole-class discussions, observations, informal conversations, written work, and individual conferences, help build a comprehensive picture of a student's mathematical understanding.

What Do You Know About Addition and Subtraction?

PROMPT

Write what you know about addition and subtraction. When do you use addition? When do you use subtraction?

Your students know the words *addition* and *subtraction*, but they have probably never been asked to write about what the words mean. If you are using this as a pre-assessment before beginning instruction, don't push too hard for long responses. You can shorten the prompt by asking for examples of addition and subtraction problems or asking children what happens when they add and subtract. Collecting information in this way can give you a general sense of the range of understanding and experience in the class.

When giving this task as a post-assessment, you might encourage students to tell what they've learned about addition and subtraction, which operation they use more often, or how they use addition and subtraction in their daily lives. Comparing pre- and post-assessments often reveals growth not only in mathematical thinking but in the students' ability to communicate mathematical ideas as well.

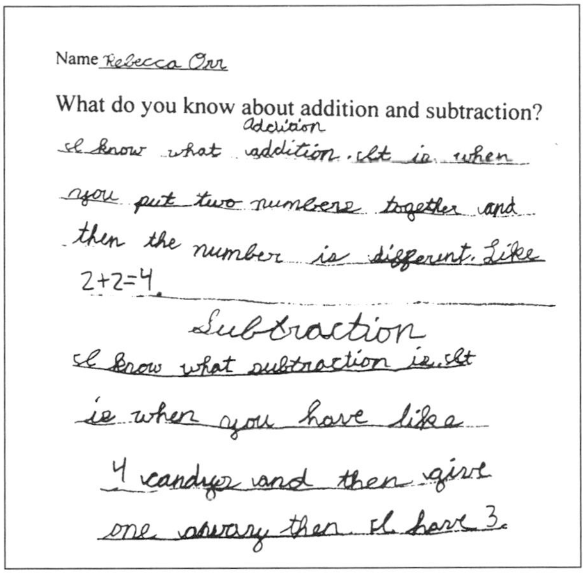

Name *Rebecca Orr*

What do you know about addition and subtraction?

addition

I know what addition. It is when you put two numbers together and then the number is different. Like 2+2=4.

Subtraction

I know what subtraction is. It is when you have like 4 candys and then give one away then I have 3.

▲▲▲▲▲▲**Figure 1** *Sandy showed basic understanding of the two operations.*

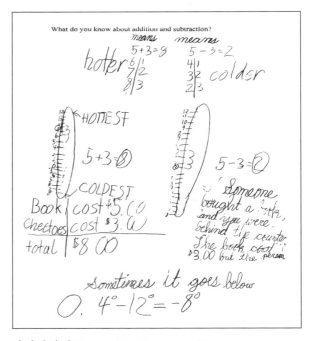

▲▲▲▲▲▲**Figure 2** *Greg used temperature and a chart to help explain the meaning of addition and subtraction.*

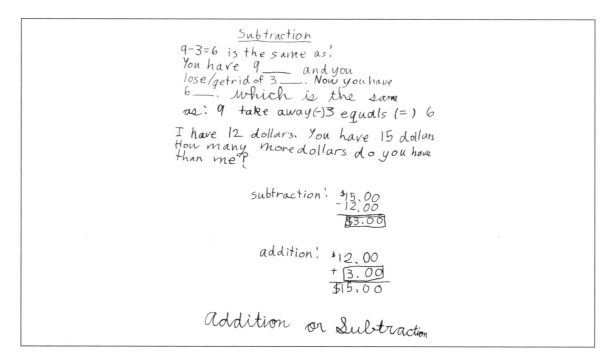

What do you know about addition and subtraction?

1. Addition means to add more to that number that your useing.
   like 5+3 means to add 3 more to the 5 and it will equar 8.

2. Subtraction means to take away the number that your useing equal 3.
   like 10-7 means to take away 7 from the 10 and it will equal 3.

example for Addition

10 + 8 = 18

ɪɪɪɪ ɪɪɪɪ + ɪɪɪ ɪɪɪ = 18

```
 10
+ 8
 18
```

example for subtraction

20 - 6 = 34

```
   1 2 3
  20
 - 6
  3 4
```

10 - 6 = 4
4 + 0 = 4

▲▲▲▲▲▲Figure 3   *In this pre-assessment, Hannah's example for subtraction showed that she confused the standard algorithms for addition and subtraction.*

Subtraction

9 - 3 = 6 is the same as!
You have 9 ____ and you
lose/get rid of 3 ____. Now you have
6 ____. Which is the same
as: 9 take away (-) 3 equals (=) 6

I have 12 dollars. You have 15 dollars.
How many more dollars do you have
than me?

subtraction:
```
 $15.00
-12.00
 $3.00
```

addition:
```
 $12.00
+ 3.00
 $15.00
```

Addition or Subtraction

▲▲▲▲▲▲Figure 4   *In her pre-assessment, Jennifer used only the take-away model for subtraction, but in this post-assessment she included both models.*

Why Is 9 + 5 = 5 + 9 and Why Is 10 − 4 ≠ 4 − 10?

PROMPT

Look at these equations: 9 + 5 = 5 + 9 and 10 − 4 ≠ 4 − 10. Do you agree? Use words, numbers, or pictures to help explain your thinking.

The commutative and associative properties of addition are important for children to learn, and this assessment asks students to think about and compare these properties as related to addition and subtraction. Being able to reverse addends is important for learning basic math facts or when computing mentally. When first encountering 3 + 8, for example, it's easier to reverse the digits and think of three more than eight, rather than eight more than three. When adding 25 + 18 + 25 mentally, adding the two twenty-fives first is more efficient for most people. Subtraction, however, doesn't have the commutative or associative properties.

When talking about why 10 − 4 isn't equal to 4 − 10, it's mathematically incorrect to tell students, "You can't take away a larger number from a smaller number." Although young children don't study negative numbers, it would be better to use a contextual situation, such as a change in temperature or borrowing money, to informally introduce the idea that 4 − 10 results in a quantity less than zero.

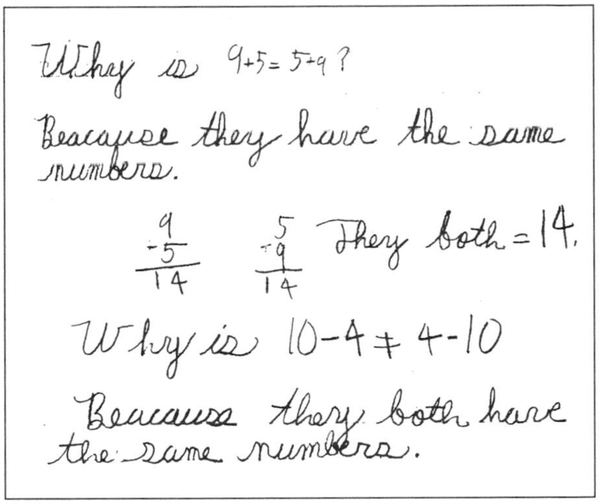

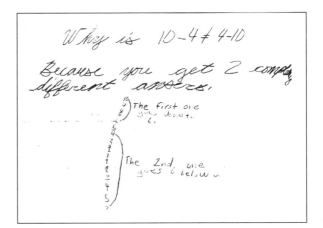

▲▲▲▲▲▲**Figure 5** *Kevin did not show understanding of the commutative property for addition or subtraction.*

▲▲▲▲▲▲**Figure 6** *Mary used a number line to explain her answer for subtraction.*

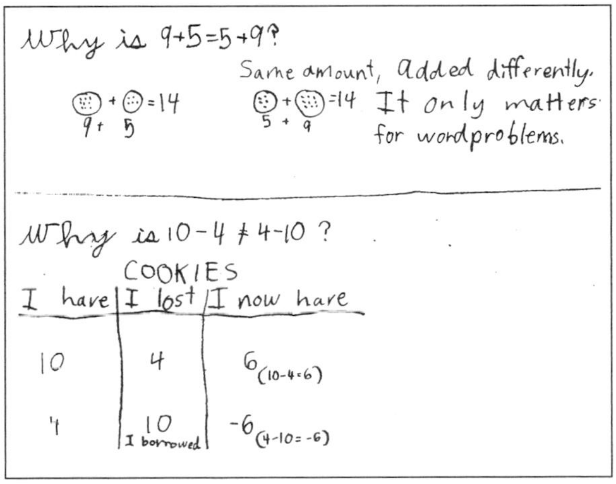

▲▲▲▲▲▲**Figure 7** *Jennifer showed good understanding of both operations.*

Spending $1.00

PROMPT

You have $1.00. I am going to ask you to show me how you spend that dollar in three different ways. Be sure to show how you solved each problem, even if you do it mentally.

> *Problem 1: How could you spend exactly $1.00 by buying two things that have different prices?*
>
> *Problem 2: How could you spend exactly $1.00 buying three things with different prices?*
>
> *Problem 3: How could you spend exactly $1.00 buying three things with different prices if one of the items cost $.39?*

This assessment can reveal the strategies students use when thinking about problems involving money. Children's work will also reveal their skill using correct monetary symbolism and their comfort level in working with combinations that make one hundred. We've found that when given this assessment, students rarely use subtraction to solve the problems. Also, when students have the opportunity to select their own numbers to add, we find it interesting to note the numbers they select.

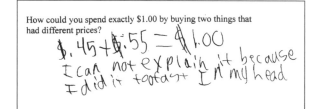

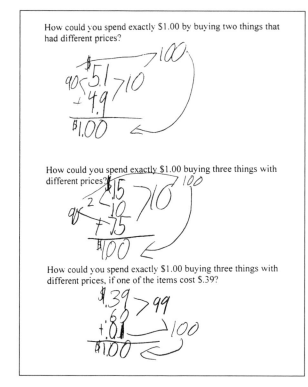

▲▲▲▲▲▲**Figure 8** *Sam explained how he did the computations mentally.*

▲▲▲▲▲▲**Figure 9** *James just "knew" the answer and couldn't explain it.*

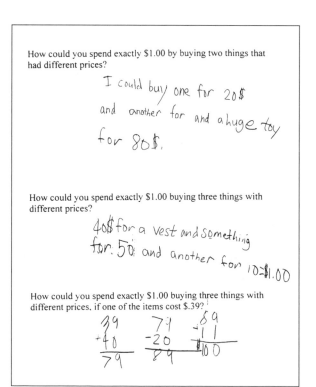

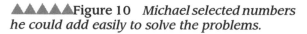

▲▲▲▲▲▲**Figure 10** *Michael selected numbers he could add easily to solve the problems.*

Can You Write an Addition Story Problem? Can You Write a Subtraction Story Problem?

PROMPT

Write two story problems. One must be an addition problem. The other must be a subtraction problem. Each story must end with a question.

This assessment shows if students are able to create contextual situations from the world around them that relate to addition and subtraction. Word problems help students connect mathematics with language, offer practice in written expression, and can also develop mathematical vocabulary. Students' stories reveal their ability to communicate effectively in writing. Children with limited proficiency in English need many opportunities to write word problems.

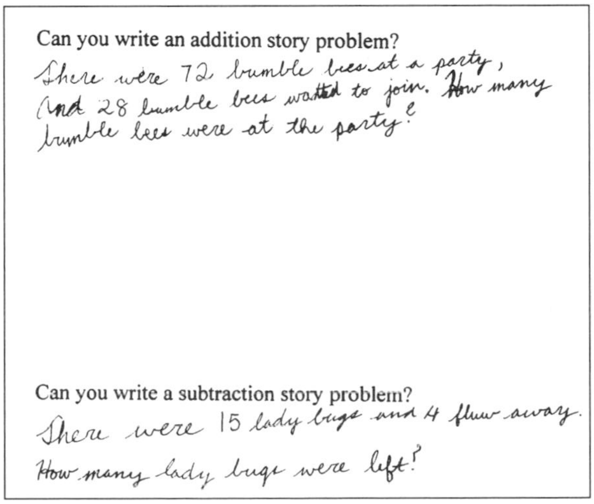

Can you write an addition story problem?
There were 72 bumble bees at a party, And 28 bumble bees wanted to join. How many bumble bees were at the party?

Can you write a subtraction story problem?
There were 15 lady bugs and 4 flew away. How many lady bugs were left?

▲▲▲▲▲▲**Figure 11** *Christina was able to write both addition and subtraction story problems.*

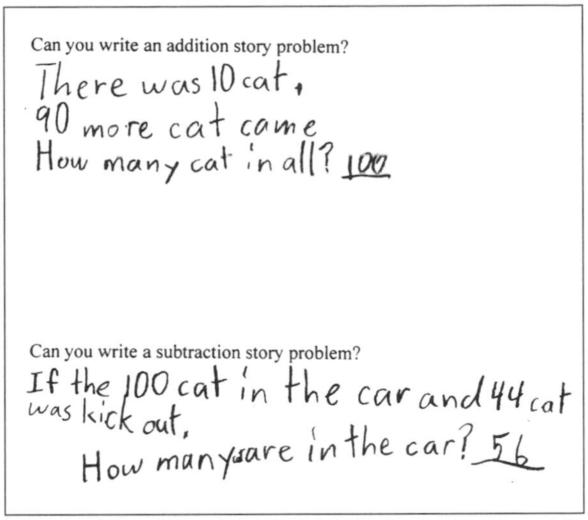

Can you write an addition story problem?
There was 10 cat, 90 more cat came How many cat in all? 100

Can you write a subtraction story problem?
If the 100 cat in the car and 44 cat was kick out, How many are in the car? 56

▲▲▲▲▲▲**Figure 12** *Franklin had limited English proficiency, but he understood the difference between addition and subtraction.*

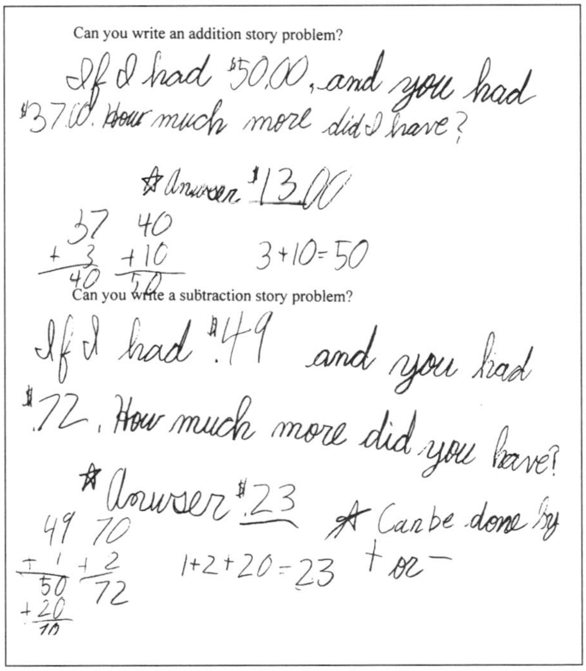

Can you write an addition story problem?
If I had $50.00, and you had $37.00. How much more did I have?

★Answer $13.00

37   40
+ 3   +10   3+10=50
40   50

Can you write a subtraction story problem?
If I had $.49 and you had $.72. How much more did you have?

★Answer $.23   ★ Can be done by

49   70
+ 1   +2   1+2+20=23   + or −
50   72
+20
70

▲▲▲▲▲▲**Figure 13** *Jeffrey understood that addition and subtraction can both be used to solve similar problems.*

Is This a Take-Away or Comparing Story?

PROMPT

Solve both story problems and tell whether each is a take-away or a comparing problem. Be sure to explain your thinking. Then write either a take-away story or a comparing story of your own and tell what type of story you wrote.

> *Problem 1: Brandon weighs 65 pounds. Stanley weighs 80 pounds. How much more does Stanley weigh?*
>
> *Problem 2: Maria had $3.50. She spent $1.75 at the toy store. How much money does she have left?*

This assessment shows whether students can solve two different models of subtraction. Also, it shows if they can identify the type of the problems and also explain how they are different. Being able to read and solve word problems is a different skill from writing them. In this assessment, students use both receptive and expressive language as well as demonstrating strategies for computation.

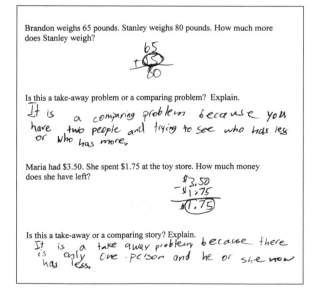

Brandon weighs 65 pounds. Stanley weighs 80 pounds. How much more does Stanley weigh?

65
+ ⑤
80

Is this a take-away problem or a comparing problem? Explain.

It is a comparing problem because you have two people and trying to see who has less or who has more.

Maria had $3.50. She spent $1.75 at the toy store. How much money does she have left?

$3,50
$1:75
$(1.75)

Is this a take-away or a comparing story? Explain.

It is a take away problem because there is only one person and he or she now has less.

▲▲▲▲▲▲**Figure 14** *Randy had a clear understanding of different types of subtraction.*

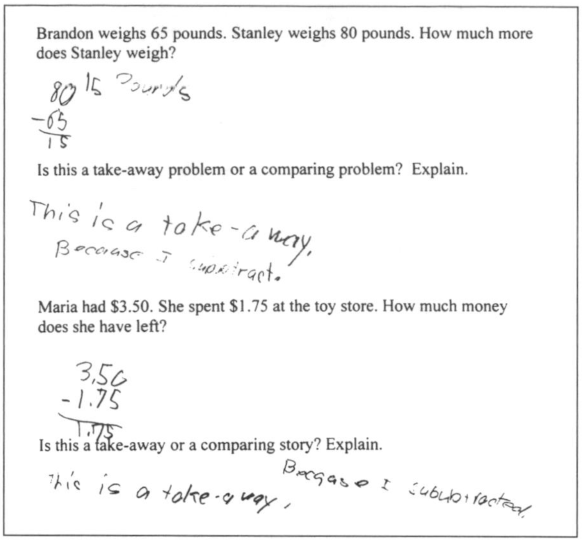

Brandon weighs 65 pounds. Stanley weighs 80 pounds. How much more does Stanley weigh?

80 15 Pounds
-65
15

Is this a take-away problem or a comparing problem? Explain.

This is a take-a way. Because I subtract.

Maria had $3.50. She spent $1.75 at the toy store. How much money does she have left?

3,50
-1.75
1.75

Is this a take-away or a comparing story? Explain.

This is a take-away, Because I subtracted.

▲▲▲▲▲▲**Figure 15** *Dylan thought that subtraction means only "take away."*

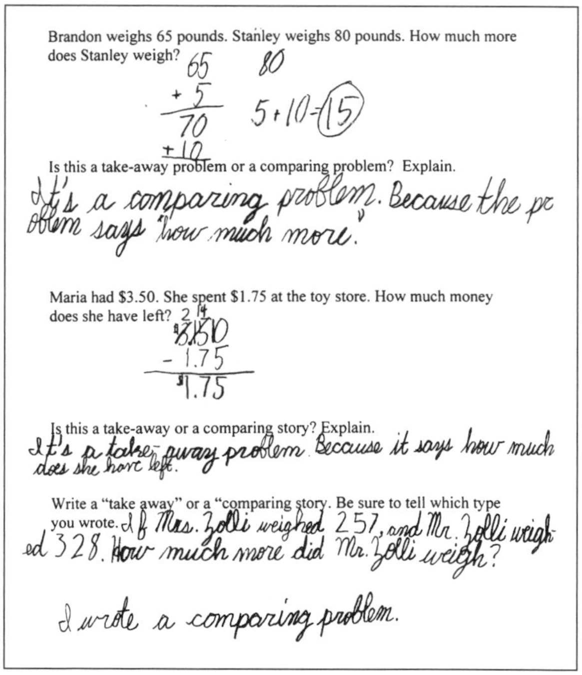

Brandon weighs 65 pounds. Stanley weighs 80 pounds. How much more does Stanley weigh? 65   80
+ 5   5 + 10 = ⑮
70
+ 10

Is this a take-away problem or a comparing problem? Explain.

It's a comparing problem. Because the problem says "how much more".

Maria had $3.50. She spent $1.75 at the toy store. How much money does she have left? 2 14
$3.50
- 1.75
1.75

Is this a take-away or a comparing story? Explain.

It's a take-away problem. Because it says how much does she have left.

Write a "take away" or a "comparing story." Be sure to tell which type you wrote. If Mrs. Zolli weighed 257, and Mr. Zolli weighed 328. How much more did Mr. Zolli weigh?

I wrote a comparing problem.

▲▲▲▲▲▲**Figure 16** *Jeffrey understood the models of subtraction and showed a sense of humor when he wrote his own story.*

The Penny Problem

PROMPT

Mary had 14 pennies. Billy had 17 pennies. Jane had 5 pennies. How many pennies would Mary and Billy have to give Jane so they would all have the same number of pennies? Show how you figure it out; use numbers, words, and, if you'd like, pictures.

Although this problem can be done by using a computational method for averaging, second- and third-grade students usually use addition and subtraction through trial and error to come to a solution. It's interesting to see how students keep track of their work and their various methods of organization.

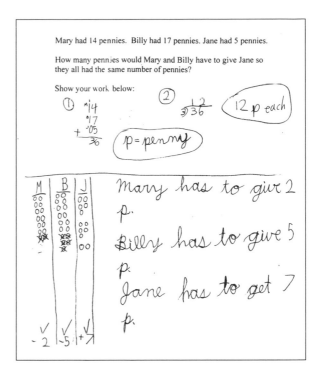

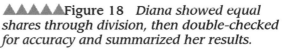

▲▲▲▲▲▲**Figure 18** *Diana showed equal shares through division, then double-checked for accuracy and summarized her results.*

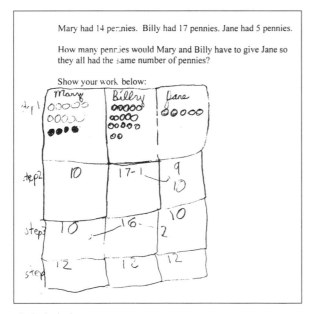

▲▲▲▲▲▲**Figure 17** *Gina made a chart to keep track of her work.*

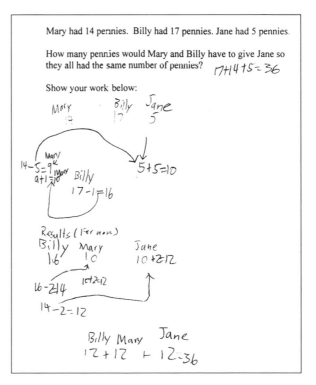

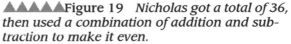

▲▲▲▲▲▲**Figure 19** *Nicholas got a total of 36, then used a combination of addition and subtraction to make it even.*

Is This an Addition or a Subtraction Problem?

PROMPT

Yesterday we counted 92 pockets in our class. Today we counted 68 pockets. Did we have more or fewer today? On your paper, find the difference and explain if this is an addition or a subtraction problem.

This assessment shows if students understand the inverse relationship between addition and subtraction. It can also reveal which computational strategies a student feels most comfortable using. The numbers in this particular problem came from real data collected in the classroom when comparing pockets. Generating problems from real situations is one way to bring meaning and context to computation and can show students how mathematics is used in the real world. You may choose to give the children this problem or use numbers from your classroom data.

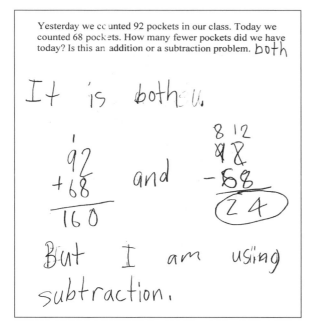

▲▲▲▲▲▲Figure 20 *Although Brendan said that the problem could be both addition and subtraction, he did not understand why.*

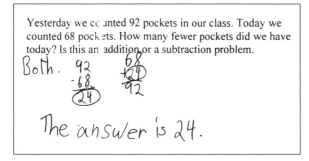

▲▲▲▲▲▲Figure 21 *Eric showed a clear understanding of the inverse relationship between addition and subtraction.*

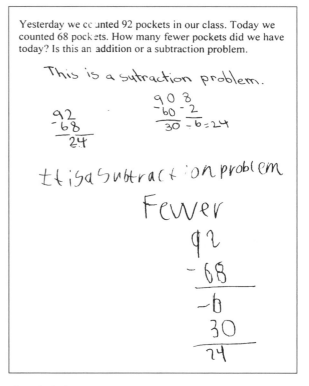

▲▲▲▲▲▲Figure 22 *Both of these students subtracted using negative numbers in the ones place to solve the problem.*

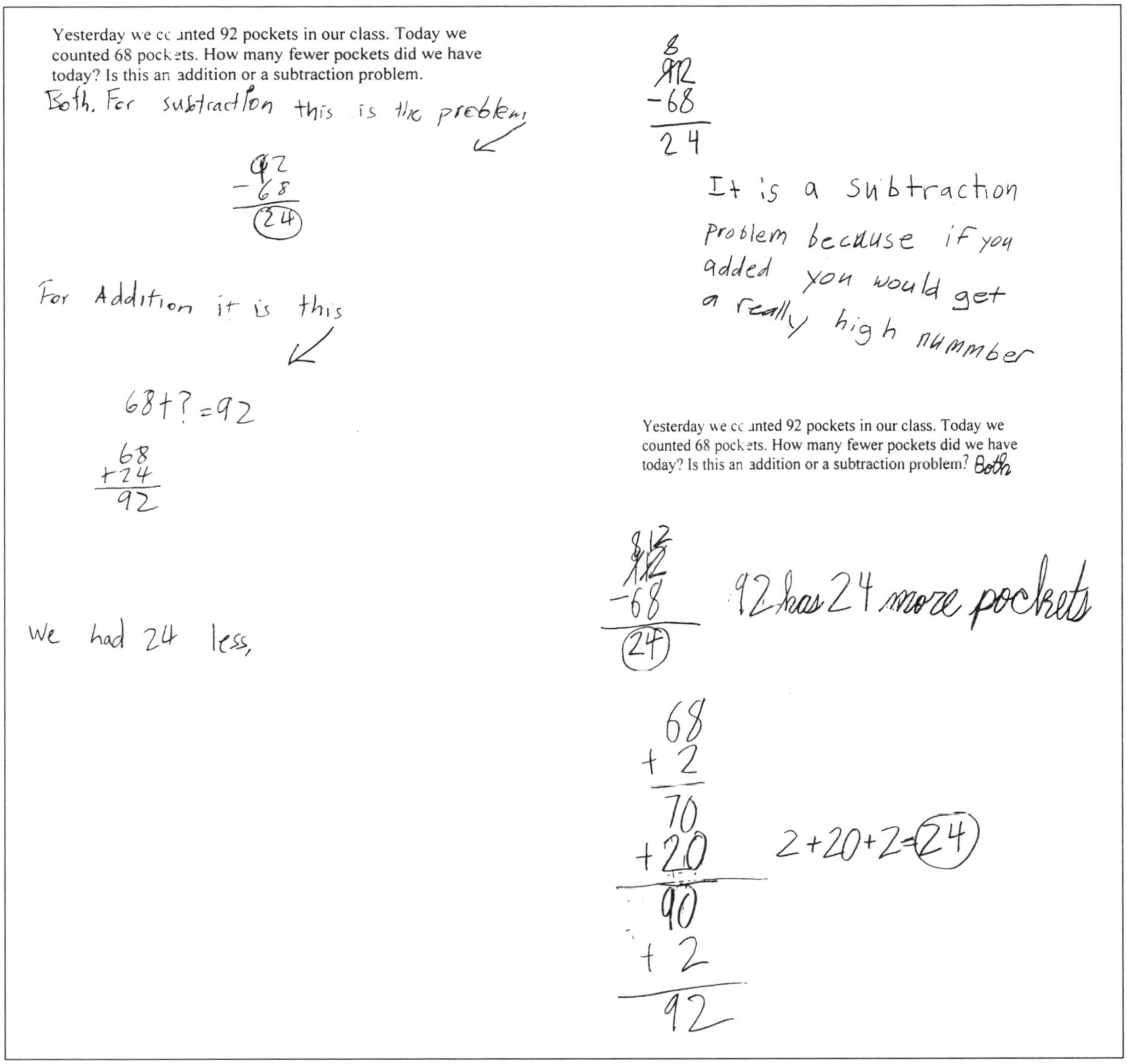

Yesterday we counted 92 pockets in our class. Today we counted 68 pockets. How many fewer pockets did we have today? Is this an addition or a subtraction problem.

Both. For subtraction this is the problem

$$\begin{array}{r} 92 \\ -68 \\ \hline \textcircled{24} \end{array}$$

For Addition it is this

$$68 + ? = 92$$

$$\begin{array}{r} 68 \\ +24 \\ \hline 92 \end{array}$$

We had 24 less,

$$\begin{array}{r} \cancel{9}^{8}\cancel{12} \\ -68 \\ \hline 24 \end{array}$$

It is a subtraction problem because if you added you would get a really high nummber

Yesterday we counted 92 pockets in our class. Today we counted 68 pockets. How many fewer pockets did we have today? Is this an addition or a subtraction problem? Both

$$\begin{array}{r} \cancel{9}^{8}\cancel{12} \\ -68 \\ \hline \textcircled{24} \end{array}$$ 92 has 24 more pockets

$$\begin{array}{r} 68 \\ +2 \\ \hline 70 \\ +20 \\ \hline 90 \\ +2 \\ \hline 92 \end{array}$$ $2 + 20 + 2 = \textcircled{24}$

▲▲▲▲▲▲**Figure 23** *These students showed multiple ways of finding the same answer to a problem.*

BLACKLINE MASTERS

More

Estimate and Measure

Estimate and Measure Record Sheet

Comparing Lengths

Billy Goes Shopping

Billy Goes Shopping Price List

Dollar Bills

One-Inch Squares

Letter Values

How Close to $100?

Directions for Making Little Boxes

Body Measurements

Measuring Ourselves in Inches

Measuring Ourselves in Centimeters

Teacher/Student Comparisons

In One Minute

How to Make a Book

X-Ray Vision

X-Ray Vision Record Sheet

Fifteen-Number Cross-Out

Roll Five Times

Roll Five Times Game Board

Addition Tic-Tac-Toe

Addition Tic-Tac-Toe Game Board

How Close to 0?

How Close to 0? Record Sheet

More

Name_____   Partner's Name_____

	Player 1	Player 2	Difference
Game 1			
Game 2			
Total			

Show how you found the differences and totals below:

More

Name_____   Partner's Name_____

	Player 1	Player 2	Difference
Game 1			
Game 2			
Total			

Show how you found the differences and totals below:

Estimate and Measure

You Need:
    interlocking cubes
    Estimate and Measure record sheet
    a partner (optional)

Measure the length of ten different things in the room using cubes. For each, do the following:

1. Make an estimate and record.

2. Measure the object with cubes.

3. Count and record.

4. Compare your estimate with the actual amount.

5. Record the difference.

Example:

Object Being Measured	Estimated # of Cubes	Actual Measurement	How Far Off?
Length of book	12	9	3
Width of computer	15	21	6

Estimate and Measure
Record Sheet

Name_____

Partner's Name_____

Object Being Measured	Estimated # of Cubes	Actual Measurement	How Far Off?

From *Lessons for Addition and Subtraction, Grades 2–3* by Bonnie Tank and Lynne Zolli. © 2001 Math Solutions Publications

Comparing Lengths

You Need:
    a partner
    a paper bag with 10 measurement strips inside

Height of backpack	28 cubes
Length of pencil	7 cubes
Width of picture frame	19 cubes

1. Pull out two strips from the bag.

2. Write the names of the objects and their measurements on your paper.

3. Find the difference. Record your strategy.

4. Repeat four more times until the bag is empty.

5. Put the strips back in the bag and repeat, or use a different bag.

From *Lessons for Addition and Subtraction, Grades 2–3* by Bonnie Tank and Lynne Zolli. © 2001 Math Solutions Publications

Billy Goes Shopping

You Need:
  a partner
  a price list
  a bag of dimes and pennies and a dollar bill
  paper to make receipt forms

Billy has $1.00 to spend. He wants to buy some new school supplies. What can he buy? How much change will he get back?

1. Take turns being the shopkeeper and Billy.

2. Billy chooses some things to buy. He can buy different things or more than one of the same thing. Reminder: Only two of each to a customer.

3. The shopkeeper uses the receipt form to write down the items purchased, the price of each item, and the total cost.

4. Billy gives the shopkeeper his dollar and gets back change if needed. The shopkeeper records this transaction.

5. Change jobs. Each person should go shopping two times.

 From *Lessons for Addition and Subtraction, Grades 2–3* by Bonnie Tank and Lynne Zolli. © 2001 Math Solutions Publications

Billy Goes Shopping
Price List

Eraser	$.10
Ruler	$.29
Pencil	$.25
Pen	$.39
Book cover	$.20
Key chain	$.32
Marking pen	$.28
Glue stick	$.30

(Limit: 2 each per customer)

One-Inch Squares

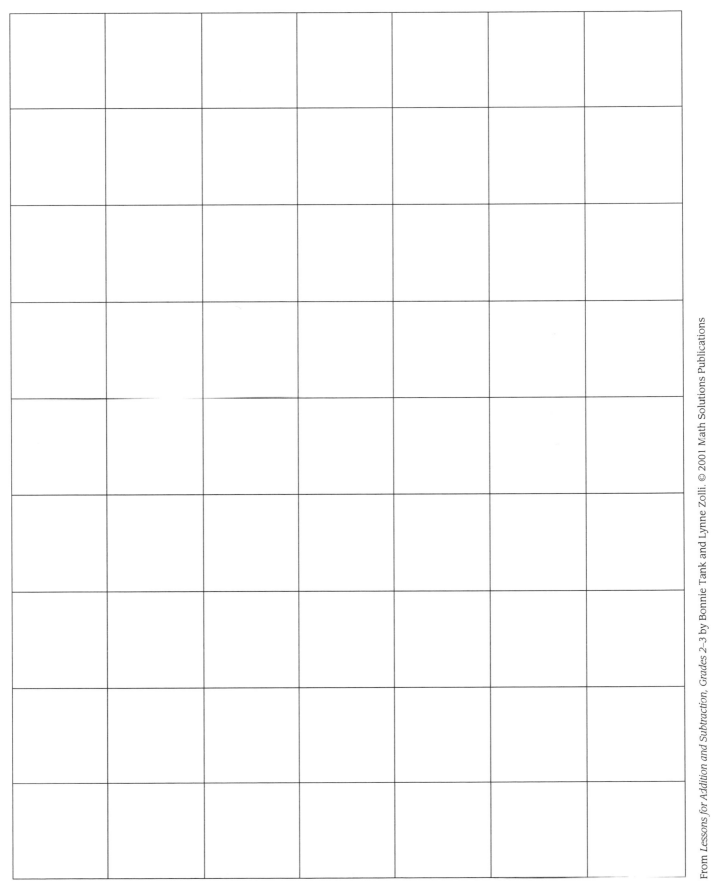

Letter Values

A	=	$1	N	=	$14
B	=	$2	O	=	$15
C	=	$3	P	=	$16
D	=	$4	Q	=	$17
E	=	$5	R	=	$18
F	=	$6	S	=	$19
G	=	$7	T	=	$20
H	=	$8	U	=	$21
I	=	$9	V	=	$22
J	=	$10	W	=	$23
K	=	$11	X	=	$24
L	=	$12	Y	=	$25
M	=	$13	Z	=	$26

 From *Lessons for Addition and Subtraction, Grades 2–3* by Bonnie Tank and Lynne Zolli. © 2001 Math Solutions Publications

How Close to $100?

Name of Student	Name Value	How Close to $100?

Directions for Making Little Boxes

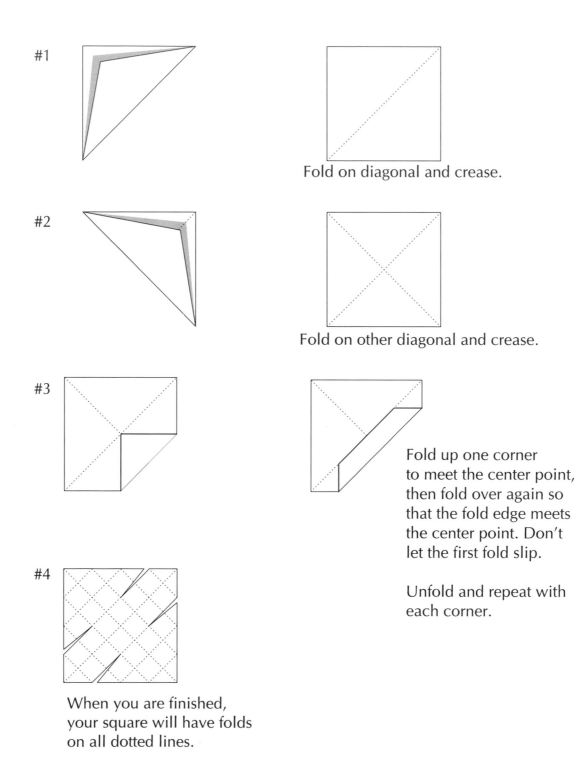

#1

Fold on diagonal and crease.

#2

Fold on other diagonal and crease.

#3

Fold up one corner
to meet the center point,
then fold over again so
that the fold edge meets
the center point. Don't
let the first fold slip.

Unfold and repeat with
each corner.

#4

When you are finished,
your square will have folds
on all dotted lines.

Cut as shown.

 From *Lessons for Addition and Subtraction, Grades 2–3* by Bonnie Tank and Lynne Zolli. © 2001 Math Solutions Publications

Directions for Making Little Boxes, *continued*

#5

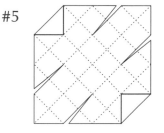

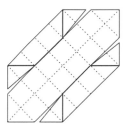

Fold in two opposite
corners on the first fold line.

Fold in each of these edges.

#6

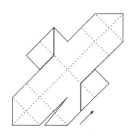

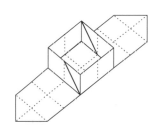

Fold up each of the four
flaps as shown.

The flaps you have just folded
are the sides. Stand them up.

#7

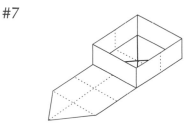

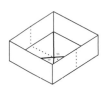

Fold each of the long flaps
over and inside the box.

If you like, put a drop of glue
under each point for added strength.

Body Measurements

You Need:
    a partner
    a tape measure
    a *Measuring Ourselves in Inches* record sheet for
        each partner
    a *Measuring Ourselves in Centimeters* record
        sheet for each partner
    a *Teacher/Student Comparisons* record sheet for
        each partner

1. Measure each other's height in inches.

2. Record both measurements on your own record sheet.

3. Compare your measurements and record the differences.

4. Repeat these directions, but measure in centimeters.

Example:

	Me	My Partner	Difference
Length of head	7 inches	8 inches	1 inch
Height	48 inches	55 inches	7 inches

5. Copy your measurements on the *Teacher/Student Comparisons* record sheet.

6. Find your teacher's measurements, record, and compare.

 From *Lessons for Addition and Subtraction, Grades 2–3* by Bonnie Tank and Lynne Zolli. © 2001 Math Solutions Publications

Measuring Ourselves in Inches

Name_____   Partner's Name_____

	Me	My Partner	Difference
Length of head			
Around neck			
Around waist			
Waist to floor			
Height			
Length of foot			
Around ankle			
Length of arm			
Length of hand			
Around knee			
Length of thumb			

What do you notice about your and your partner's measurements?

_____

_____

Measuring Ourselves
in Centimeters

Name_____   Partner's Name_____

	Me	My Partner	Difference
Length of head			
Around neck			
Around waist			
Waist to floor			
Height			
Length of foot			
Around ankle			
Length of arm			
Length of hand			
Around knee			
Length of thumb			

What do you notice about your and your partner's measurements?

_____

_____

 From *Lessons for Addition and Subtraction, Grades 2–3* by Bonnie Tank and Lynne Zolli. © 2001 Math Solutions Publications

Teacher/Student Comparisons

Name_____   Partner's Name_____

Inches

	Me	My Teacher	Difference
Length of head			
Around neck			
Around waist			
Waist to floor			
Height			
Length of foot			
Around ankle			
Length of arm			
Length of hand			
Around knee			
Length of thumb			

Centimeters

	Me	My Teacher	Difference
Length of head			
Around neck			
Around waist			
Waist to floor			
Height			
Length of foot			
Around ankle			
Length of arm			
Length of hand			
Around knee			
Length of thumb			

From *Lessons for Addition and Subtraction, Grades 2–3* by Bonnie Tank and Lynne Zolli. © 2001 Math Solutions Publications

In One Minute

You Need:
  a partner
  a way to time one minute

1. While your partner times one minute, write the letters of the alphabet. If you get to Z before time is up, start over with A.

2. Repeat, this time writing the numerals 0–9, continuing until the time is called.

3. Switch so your partner writes letters and numerals while you keep time.

4. Count the number of letters and numerals that you wrote. See if you wrote more letters or more numerals, and figure out how many more. Record your results.

5. Make comparisons with your partner. Write about what you notice.

 From *Lessons for Addition and Subtraction, Grades 2–3* by Bonnie Tank and Lynne Zolli. © 2001 Math Solutions Publications

How to Make a Book

You Need: 1 sheet of white construction paper
scissors

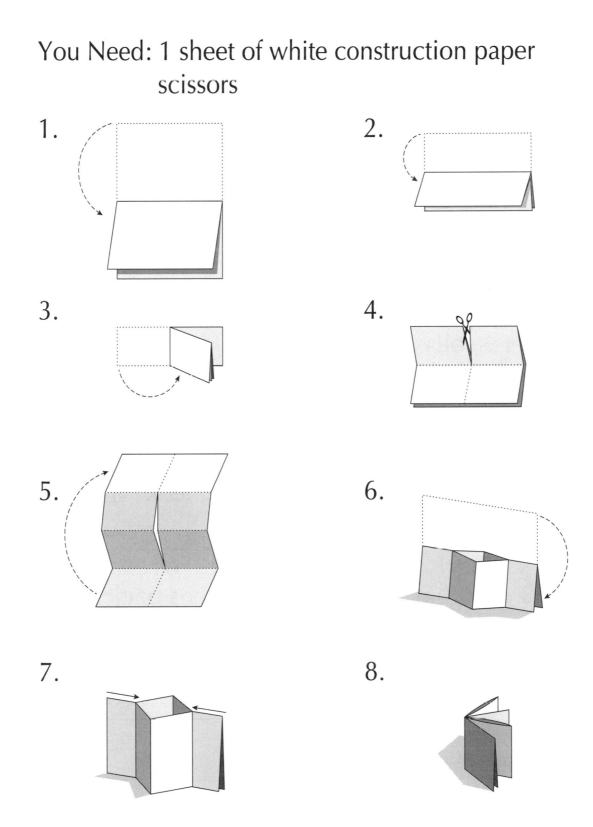

1.

2.

3.

4.

5.

6.

7.

8.

From *Lessons for Addition and Subtraction, Grades 2–3* by Bonnie Tank and Lynne Zolli. © 2001 Math Solutions Publications

X-Ray Vision

You Need:
   a partner
   a paper bag
   12 cubes
   2 dice
   X-Ray Vision record sheet

Rules

1. Player 1 rolls the dice, adds the numbers that come up, and takes that many cubes out of the paper bag.

2. Player 1 uses "x-ray vision" to see what's left in the bag.

3. Both players look in the bag to check.

4. Player 2 records the results in a number sentence under Game 1 on the record sheet. For example, 12 − 3 = 9. Player 1 places the cubes back in the bag.

5. Players switch roles and repeat. Continue switching roles until you have recorded ten number sentences.

 From *Lessons for Addition and Subtraction, Grades 2–3* by Bonnie Tank and Lynne Zolli. © 2001 Math Solutions Publications

X-Ray Vision Record Sheet

Name _____   Partner's Name _____

Game 1   Game 2

1. ___ − ___ = ___   1. ___ − ___ = ___

2. ___ − ___ = ___   2. ___ − ___ = ___

3. ___ − ___ = ___   3. ___ − ___ = ___

4. ___ − ___ = ___   4. ___ − ___ = ___

5. ___ − ___ = ___   5. ___ − ___ = ___

6. ___ − ___ = ___   6. ___ − ___ = ___

7. ___ − ___ = ___   7. ___ − ___ = ___

8. ___ − ___ = ___   8. ___ − ___ = ___

9. ___ − ___ = ___   9. ___ − ___ = ___

10. ___ − ___ = ___   10. ___ − ___ = ___

Fifteen-Number Cross-Out

You Need:
>   a partner
>   2 dice

Rules

1. Each player makes a list of fifteen numbers. Five numbers must be 5s; the other ten numbers can be any numbers from 1 to 9. You may repeat any of these numbers as many times as you like, and you don't have to include every number from 1 to 9.

2. Player 1 rolls the two dice; both players add the numbers and agree on the sum.

3. On his or her list, each player crosses out either the sum or a combination of numbers that makes that sum. For example, if the sum of the dice is seven, a player might cross out a 7, or a 3 and a 4, or a 5 and a 2, or a 3 and two 2s. For each roll of the dice, a player can make the sum only one way.

4. Player 2 rolls the dice and, again, both players add the numbers, agree on the sum, and cross out numbers from their lists.

5. If a player cannot make the sum that comes up with any numbers on his or her list, that player waits for the next roll of the dice to try again.

6. The game continues as long as one player is able to cross out numbers for the roll of the dice.

7. The game ends in one of two ways. If one player crosses out all of the numbers on his or list, the game is over and that player is the winner. Or, if both players are unable to make a play, the game is over and the winner is the player with the fewest numbers left on his or her list.

 From *Lessons for Addition and Subtraction, Grades 2–3* by Bonnie Tank and Lynne Zolli. © 2001 Math Solutions Publications

Roll Five Times

You Need:

    a partner

    a number die with two 10s, two 5s, and two 1s

    50 Unifix cubes

    a *Roll Five Times* game board and record sheet

Rules

1. Player 1 rolls the number die and places that many cubes on the game board, starting at the upper left corner and covering the squares in order. You must complete a row before starting at the beginning of the next row.

2. Player 2 records the number rolled in the first blank on the *Roll Five Times* record sheet.

3. Player 2 rolls and places cubes on the game board, continuing in the next available space.

4. Player 1 records the number in the second blank on the record sheet.

5. Play continues for five rolls with players alternating jobs. After five rolls, record how many squares are covered and how many are uncovered.

	Covered	Uncovered
1 +10+ 5 + 1 + 1 = 18	18	32

From *Lessons for Addition and Subtraction, Grades 2–3* by Bonnie Tank and Lynne Zolli. © 2001 Math Solutions Publications

Roll Five Times
Game Board

Name _____

Name _____

Name _____

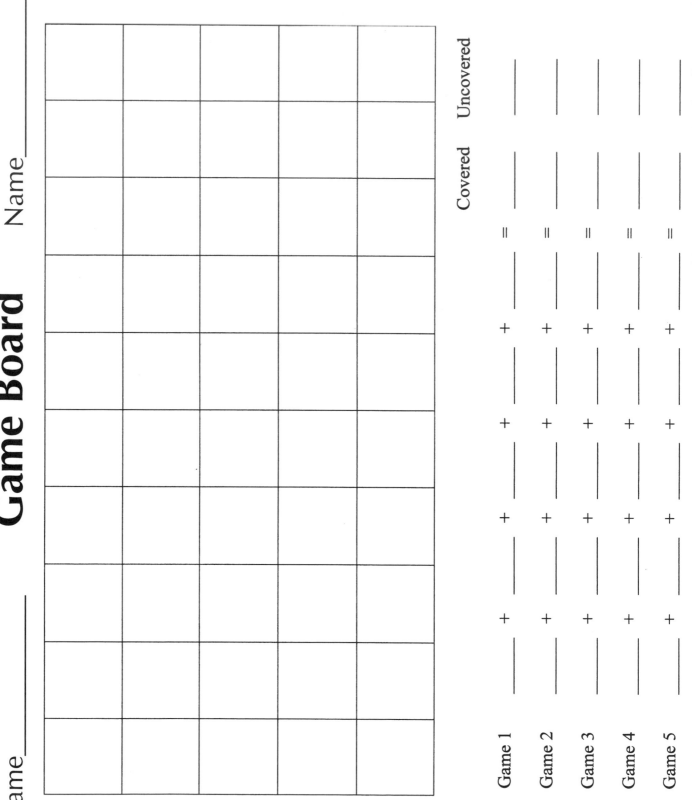

Covered   Uncovered

						Covered	Uncovered
Game 1	___ + ___	+ ___	+ ___	+ ___	= ___	___	___
Game 2	___ + ___	+ ___	+ ___	+ ___	= ___	___	___
Game 3	___ + ___	+ ___	+ ___	+ ___	= ___	___	___
Game 4	___ + ___	+ ___	+ ___	+ ___	= ___	___	___
Game 5	___ + ___	+ ___	+ ___	+ ___	= ___	___	___

Addition Tic-Tac-Toe

You Need:
   a partner
   2 paper clips
   cubes or other game markers in two colors, 12 of
   each color
   an *Addition Tic-Tac-Toe* game board

Rules

1. Each player uses a different color of cubes or game markers.

2. Player 1 chooses two numbers from those listed at the bottom of the game board, places a paper clip on each, and marks the sum of the numbers on the game board with a cube of his or her color.

3. Player 2 moves just one of the paper clips to another number, adds, and marks the sum with a different color cube. **Note:** It is legal to start the game with both paper clips on the same number and to move a paper clip to the same addend as the other paper clip. This allows for adding doubles, such as 6 + 6.

4. Play continues.

5. The winner is the player who places four cubes of his or her color on numbers in a row vertically, horizontally, or diagonally. If neither player has four in a row, and there are no more numbers on the board or it's impossible for a player to make any of the numbers left on the game board by moving just one paper clip, the game is a tie.

From *Lessons for Addition and Subtraction, Grades 2–3* by Bonnie Tank and Lynne Zolli. © 2001 Math Solutions Publications

Addition Tic-Tac-Toe

Players use cubes in two different colors. The first player chooses two addends (from 1–13 underneath the game board), places a paper clip on each, and marks the sum on the game board with a cube. The second player moves one of the paper clips to a new addend, finds the sum, and marks the sum with a different color cube. Play continues until one player has marked four sums in a row, a column, or a diagonal. Note: It is legal to move a paper clip to the same addend of the other paper clip to allow for doubles such as 6 + 6.

2	3	4	5	6
7	8	9	10	11
12	13	14	15	16
17	18	19	20	21
22	23	24	25	26

1 2 3 4 5 6 7 8 9 10 11 12 13

How Close to 0?

You Need:
   a partner
   a die
   How Close to 0? record sheet

Rules

1. Player 1 rolls the die, decides whether to use the number as a ten or as a one, and subtracts the number from 100. (Example: a 5 can be 50 or 5.) Player 1 records his or her calculation on the record sheet.

2. Player 2 does the same—rolls the die, decides whether to use the number as a ten or as a one, subtracts the number from 100, and records the play.

3. Play continues until each player has rolled seven times.

4. The player closer to zero after seven rounds is the winner and receives a score of whatever number is left for the opposing player.

5. If a player reaches zero before the seventh round, the game is over. The other player wins and scores the points left over from the opponent's previous round.

How Close to 0? Record Sheet

	Player 1	Player 2
ROUND 1	100 – ___	100 – ___
ROUND 2	___ – ___	___ – ___
ROUND 3	___ – ___	___ – ___
ROUND 4	___ – ___	___ – ___
ROUND 5	___ – ___	___ – ___
ROUND 6	___ – ___	___ – ___
ROUND 7	___ – ___	___ – ___

	Player 1	Player 2
ROUND 1	100 – ___	100 – ___
ROUND 2	___ – ___	___ – ___
ROUND 3	___ – ___	___ – ___
ROUND 4	___ – ___	___ – ___
ROUND 5	___ – ___	___ – ___
ROUND 6	___ – ___	___ – ___
ROUND 7	___ – ___	___ – ___

INDEX